Citizenship and Crisis in Contemporary Brazilian Literature

CITIZENSHIP AND CRISIS IN CONTEMPORARY BRAZILIAN LITERATURE

Leila Lehnen

palgrave
macmillan

First published in 2013 by PALGRAVE MACMILLAN® in the
United States—a division of St. Martin's Press LLC, 175 Fifth
Avenue, New York, NY 10010.

Where this book is distributed in the UK, Europe and the rest of
the world, this is by Palgrave Macmillan, a division of Macmillan
Publishers Limited, registered in England, company number 785998,
of Houndmills, Basingstoke, Hampshire RG21 6XS.

Palgrave Macmillan is the global academic imprint of the above
companies and has companies and representatives throughout the
world.

Palgrave® and Macmillan® are registered trademarks in the United
States, the United Kingdom, Europe and other countries.

ISBN: 978-1-137-27755-8

Library of Congress Cataloging-in-Publication Data is available from
the Library of Congress.

Lehnen, Leila Maria.
    Citizenship and crisis in contemporary Brazilian literature / Leila
Lehnen.
     pages cm
   Includes bibliographical references.
    ISBN 978-1-137-27755-8 (alk. paper)
    1. Brazilian literature—20th century—History and criticism. 2.
Brazilian literature—21st century—History and criticism. 3. Politics
and literature—Brazil—History—20th century. 4. Politics and
literature—Brazil—History—21st century. 5. Citizenship in literature.
6. Politics in literature. I. Title.

PQ9555.L34 2013
869.09'3588106—dc23   2012042271

A catalogue record of the book is available from the British Library.

Design by Scribe Inc.

First edition: April 2013

10 9 8 7 6 5 4 3 2 1

CONTENTS

Acknowledgments

I would like to dedicate this book to the women in my life. They have cheered me on, questioned me, argued with me, and inspired me at various stages of writing this book. Their help has reminded me of the importance of having a community and being able to rely on it. I would especially like to thank Cathy L. Jrade, who has been a mentor and an inspiration since I was a graduate student and who continues to guide and encourage me. A special thank you is in order to Anke Biendarra, whose friendship gave me strength, grounded me, prodded me, and gave me courage in moments of crisis. Her sharp readings of this text made it stronger. I also would like to thank Rebecca Atencio and Emanuelle Oliveira, who have been sounding boards, editors, and friends before, during, and after the writing of the book. Thanks are also in order to my colleagues Kathy McKnight and Tey Diana Rebolledo who have supported me since my arrival at the University of New Mexico. I also would like to thank Kathryn Sánchez, who read a version of the book's proposal, and Marguerite Harrison and Regina Dalcastagnè, whose work on Luiz Ruffato has stirred my thoughts. Finally, I would like to thank Anna Nogar for the writing sessions in the library that kept me on track and for the Saturday morning spin classes that kept me sane.

Of course this book would also not have come about without some men. I would like to thank them as well: Idelber Avelar for his inspirational ideas; David W. Foster, whose NEH workshop on contemporary urban fiction was the first spark for this book; Severino Albuquerque and Luis Madureira for the intellectual exchanges they made possible by inviting me to Madison, WI; Anthony Pereira, for letting me see that political science does indeed have a place in literary analysis; Rich Wood, whose conversations about publishing and social sciences encouraged me and gave me a different perspective; Camillo Penna, who led me down the path of academia and whose stimulating intellectual conversations have refined the scope of the book; Nelson Vieira and Luiz Fernando Valente for their work on contemporary

Brazilian fiction; and Alyosha Goldstein, who read and gave valuable feedback on one of the many versions of this book's proposal.

I would also like to thank Luiz Ruffato, Fernando Bonassi, Ferréz, Marcelino Freire, Marçal Aquino, Flávio Carneiro, and Nelson de Oliveira for our conversations about Brazilian literature and Brazil's social issues and for their works. Thanks also to Claudiney Ferreira for the invitations to the events sponsored by the Itaú Cultural.

Finally, I would like to thank my parents. Both have helped me through my journey and have instilled in me a desire to learn. Last but not least, I would like to thank the love of my life, my husband, Jeremy Lehnen. Without his patience, companionship, questions, readings of the book, wonderful cooking skills, and love I would not have been able to do what I have done.

INTRODUCTION

VOICES OF CONTESTATION
OBSTACLES AND PATHS TO CITIZENSHIP IN CONTEMPORARY BRAZILIAN LITERATURE

In 2005 I became an American citizen. My path to citizenship was a conscious choice. For me the decisive factor was that, as a citizen, I would have the right to vote, to engage in this country's public sphere in a full-fledged manner. In my route to citizenship, I passed various signposts, which culminated in the oath-taking ceremony—and, for me, in voter registration. Registering to vote was my first act as a newly minted American citizen, and this deed felt more momentous than the oath-taking ceremony.

But before I was an American citizen, I was (and still am) a Brazilian citizen. Unlike my American citizenship, my Brazilian one was inherited from my Brazilian father. Though I was not born on Brazilian soil, there was no decision making involved in becoming an integral subject of the Brazilian nation—at least from a legal standpoint. All my life, I used my (until recently) dark-green Brazilian passport to travel to other countries, including the United States. This document gave me rights in my home country and also certain responsibilities.

As a Brazilian citizen, I partook in the expected rituals that come with this role, including voting.[1] In 1984, I participated in the "Diretas Já"[2] campaign that made many Brazilians heady with the prospect of casting a direct vote for president, a promise that was delayed for four years. And in 1989 when I voted for the first time in my life, I was able to cast my ballot in Brazil's first direct elections in over two decades. More than ten years later, I cast another "first" vote, this time in the 2008 US presidential elections.

Though most of us are nominally citizens of one or more nations, this can have different meanings depending on national and historical contexts and, often, on variables such as socioeconomic status. Citizenship has symbolic and material gradations. Even when equal rights are apportioned to all subjects of a nation in writing, as they are in the 1988 Brazilian "citizens'" constitution, citizenship is crisscrossed by cracks that extend into the nation's physical and imagined body politic. The concept of citizenship, which implies both duties and rights and entails participation in the civic, political, and social spheres can be allotted, enacted, or denied at multiple levels. Social capital especially is often distributed unevenly, leading to disenfranchisement in other domains of citizenship, particularly in the civil arena.

Brazil's redemocratization, the drafting of a new constitution in 1988 and the country's recently improved social indicators (such as the emergence of 28 million people from poverty) have brought the issue of citizenship to the forefront of political, civil, social, and cultural discussions. Citizenship has become an increasingly important word in Brazil's public ambit in recent years, first because of the 1988 "Citizen's Constitution" and second because of the term's valorization since the 1985 democratic transition (Holston, *Insurgent*; Carvalho). Being a citizen (*cidadão, cidadã*) no longer has a derogatory signification (DaMatta). Rather, it is synonymous with rights and can mean access to them. The prominence of the issue of citizenship and social disparity in Brazil since 1985 is reflected in the country's recent literary production.

Citizenship and Crisis in Contemporary Brazilian Literature considers how recent literary texts address the socioeconomic and political changes that Brazil has undergone since its 1985 democratic transition and what these alterations have meant for the understanding and performance of citizenship in the literary realm. The manuscript discusses a total of nine literary texts that thematize differentiated and insurgent citizenship in Brazilian cities by four contemporary Brazilian writers: Luiz Ruffato's *Inferno provisório* (*Mamma, son tanto felice* [Mamma, they are so happy, 2005], *O mundo inimigo* [The enemy world, 2005], *Vista parcial da noite* [Partial view of the night, 2006], and *O livro das impossibilidades* [The book of impossibilities, 2008]); Fernando Bonassi's *Subúrbio* (Suburb, 1990) and *O menino que se trancou na geladeira* (The boy who locked himself in the fridge, 2004); Reginaldo Ferreira da Silva's, better known as Ferréz, *Capão Pecado* (Capão sin, 2000) and *Manual prático do ódio* (Practical handbook of hate, 2003); and Marcus Vinícius Faustini's *Guia afetivo da periferia* (Affective guide of the periphery, 2009). These literary texts both depict a lack of citizenship and propose symbolic means of counteracting this deficiency. My argument is that the nexus between insufficient socioeconomic, civil, and cultural rights and the reclaiming of citizenship via cultural expression is increasingly prominent in Brazilian artistic expression, notably in contemporary fictional output, where citizenship and crisis have become prevalent themes. Questions of citizenship, including its conceptualization, have become recurrent issues in Brazilian literature nowadays in part because citizenship—both in its theoretical and material personifications—has changed significantly since 1985. The development of citizenship—and its literary treatment—interfaces with the country's changing socioeconomic and cultural makeup.

Citizenship in Brazil has habitually been characterized by a discrepancy between its formulation and its praxis, what James Holston terms "differentiated citizenship" (*Insurgent*). While theoretically most Brazilians possess the same constitutional rights, their implementation is frequently far from egalitarian. Paradoxically, differentiated citizenship serves as a platform around which disenfranchised groups rally in an effort to obtain civic, social, and political rights through the dispute of legalized discrimination or insurgent citizenship.

This manuscript dialogues with Brazil's recent socioeconomic and cultural transformations and considers novels that antecede Luiz Ignácio Lula da Silva's election and literary texts that were published during his administration. *Citizenship and Crisis* contemplates two moments of Brazil's recent history: the overtly neoliberal period of the 1990s and the contemporary context in which neoliberalism has been combined with socially oriented policies. My analysis shows how in their novels, Luiz Ruffato and Fernando Bonassi portray the country's neoliberal entrenchment in the 1990s,[3] its attendant socioeconomic crisis, and consequently a marked increase in differentiated citizenship. As we progress into the twenty-first century, crisis and accompanying rituals of violence continue to be staples of literary narratives that deal with citizenship (Ferréz). This thematic persistence reflects the endurance of neoliberal policies in Brazil after Lula's ascension to the presidency (Rollenberg-Mollo and Saad-Filho). Nonetheless, increasingly, pessimistic storylines dialogue with instances of insurgent citizenship, pointing to examples of agency, particularly within the cultural realm (Faustini).

I use "citizenship" as the key concept around which I ground my analysis instead of other terms that also suggest social, civil, political, and cultural enfranchisement, such as "human rights," because the former term takes a more expansive view of what rights are. Indeed, as Hannah Arendt proposes, without citizenship—that is, without the right to belong to a political community, other rights lose their significance.

The notion of citizenship has experienced several incarnations since its original appearance in the classical Greco-Roman tradition. It is not the objective of this book to provide a comprehensive conceptualization of the term. Rather, I limit my discussions to the ideas about citizenship that are pertinent to Brazil's contemporary social, civil, and political makeup. In particular, I focus on what James Holston denominates "differentiated citizenship," and demonstrate how it appears, is problematized, and is contested in present-day Brazilian literature.

In its most basic understanding, citizenship entails a set of rights and obligations of a national community. Following this definition, a citizen participates in the political, social (socioeconomic), and civic realms of the nation while respecting its laws, paying taxes, and in some cases (including in Brazil) completing compulsory military service.

Who has the privilege of citizenship varies according to country. Citizenship has four basic templates: the Aristotelian model (inclusion of "adequate" members, who will conform to the general will of the population), *jus sanguinis* (right of blood), *jus soli* (right of soil) and universal citizenship (Yashar). With the emergence of the nation-state in the nineteenth century, citizenship also became a badge of national identification.

Citizenship has two principal dimensions: formal citizenship, which is the formulation of the privileges and obligations of the citizen; and substantive citizenship, the enactment of said privileges and obligations. The concept, therefore, is not limited to a subject's legal position within a (nation) state, but includes the performance of social, political, and civil rights and duties. Frequently, formal citizenship does not entirely correspond to substantive citizenship.

In terms of its politico-philosophical underpinnings, nowadays the two prevailing understandings of citizenship are the civic republican and the liberal traditions (Heater). The civic-republican conception dates back to Aristotle and was taken up by Jean Jacques Rousseau in his *Social Contract* (1762) (Heater; Avelar and Dunn). What defines the civic-republican model are its inherent communitarian impetus and the freedom of its members from arbitrary rule. Civic virtue prevents both internal and external oppression by a tyrannical power (Machiavelli). Civic-republican citizenship is composed of a community of "virtuous men" that are governed by a constitutional power, which expresses the community's best interest, what Rousseau called the "General Will" (Heater 69). In this context, "the people are consequently in turn citizens and subjects: citizens while formulating the General Will; subjects when obeying the implications of those decisions" (69). Whereas the republican model favors the community over the individual, the liberal paradigm of citizenship favors the individual over the community.

The liberal tradition evolved mainly from John Locke's *Second Treatise of Civil Government* (1690) and envisions the state as the provider of social, political, and civil goods for its citizens. In this structure, citizenship is synonymous with certain privileges that the individual attains from the state in exchange for her/his obedience and loyalty toward it (Oliver and Heater). According to the liberal formula, each citizen is not only born free, but also has the right to pursue the goods of citizenship. In the *Second Treatise of Civil Government*, Locke states that

> Man being born, as has been proved, with a title to perfect freedom, and an uncontrolled enjoyment of all the rights and privileges of the law of nature, equally with any other man, or number of men in the world, hath by nature a power, not only to preserve his property, that is, his life, liberty and estate, against the injuries and attempts of other men; but to judge of, and punish the breaches of that law in others, as he is persuaded the offence deserves, even with death itself, in crimes where the heinousness of the fact, in his opinion, requires it. (section 87 of Chapter 7)

The rights of man, according to Locke, encompass not only innate freedom, but also the right to life, property, and justice. Though a combination of the civic-republican and liberal models is possible (Goirand), the liberal principal has become dominant in Western democracies since the nineteenth century (Heater). However, with the emergence of the "New Right" in the 1980s and the accompanying neoliberal turn, the "entitlements" associated with the liberal model have come under attack (Oliver and Heater). After years of eliminating or diminishing social rights in favor of market-oriented policies, recently some Latin American countries, including Brazil, have moved to reinstate social rights.

In his influential *Citizenship and Social Class*, T. H. Marshall delimits three dimensions of citizenship: the civil (legal equality and protection), the political (voting rights and the right to participate in a nation's politics in general), and the social (social benefits such as health care and education). Marshall based his analysis on the development of these rights in England under capitalism. He describes the evolution of British citizenship as a progression from civil to political and finally social rights. Though Marshall's classification has been criticized for its limited scope (it is restricted to English men), the three categories are still the main parameters by which citizenship is judged. Accordingly, most discussions of citizenship nowadays reflect on these three facets.

Increasingly, cultural rights are also becoming a part of the debate about the formulation and implementation of citizenship at both the national and global level (Holston and Caldeira; Yúdice; Dagnino, "Citizenship in Latin America"; Armony). It is the cultural component of citizenship that is the main topic of this book. Cultural citizenship comprises the rights to identity and the material manifestations surrounding it and therefore includes the right to produce, communicate, and access the many forms of cultural expression, such as literature, music, and religious ceremonies, among others. Moreover, cultural citizenship also means the right to (self) representation and to information (Isin and Wood). This is to say, nowadays "[c]ultural citizenship is about becoming active producers of meaning and representation and knowledgeable consumers under advanced capitalism" (152). Cultural production and performance (i.e., cultural citizenship) play an increasingly prominent role in the reclaiming of citizenship within Brazil. Culture—principally literature and music—are privileged domains where social problems are addressed and through which solutions for these troubles are sought. Not coincidentally, the Lula administration augmented investments in both primary and higher education as a means to break intergenerational poverty. Culture—in the guise of education—is seen as one of the tools to counteract differentiated citizenship.

Brazilian citizenship is, in its current articulation, clearly influenced by the liberal thought that took root in the country at the end of the nineteenth century, although liberalism in Brazil has largely remained what Roberto Schwarz has called a "misplaced idea."[4] Brazil's latest constitution also has a substratum of the populist legislation implemented by Getúlio Vargas,[5] who significantly developed the working class's social citizenship. Thus, unlike in England, in Brazil the tripartite development of citizenship theorized by Marshall began not with the expansion of civil rights, but with the implementation of social rights during Vargas's presidencies (1930–45; 1951–54).

More recently, Brazilians saw political gains, especially after 1985.[6] Specifically, the 1988 charter, the "Citizen's Constitution," strongly emphasizes social rights—as suggested by its very name. The 1988 constitution reinstated and, in some cases, expanded civil rights that were curtailed during the military regime (1964–85), such as *habeas corpus*.[7] Notwithstanding these improvements at the constitutional level, substantive citizenship increased primarily in the political arena ("Brasil tem democracia forte"). In comparison, both civil and social rights still lag behind, perpetuating the differentiated citizenship model that has become commonplace in Brazil.

Differentiated citizenship is characterized by an egalitarian constitutional ideology accompanied by the legalization of differences (Holston, *Insurgent*). Differentiated citizenship also contains a discrepancy between formal and substantive citizenship. This means that though most Brazilian subjects possess the same constitutional rights, the implementation of such rights is frequently far from egalitarian because of legal clauses that validate distinctions between one citizen and another. In differentiated citizenship, civil and/or political rights are commonly associated to social criterions. Indeed, as Holston points out, in many instances the Brazilian constitution legalizes social differences and thereby perpetuates them. In this sense, Brazil is no different than any other nation-state. Differentiated citizenship is widespread because it manages differences by legitimizing them (7). Differentiated citizenship can occur both as positive and as negative discrimination. In its harmful variant, it uses distinctions as a means to deny rights or to apportion them only to privileged sectors. For example, according to Brazilian penal law, people with a university degree have the right to an individual prison cell before their trial, whereas people without a university degree must share a cell with other detainees. Anyone who is familiar with Brazil's overcrowded jails knows what this difference means. Difference, however, can also be used to bolster equal rights. As paradoxical as this might seem, in order to create commensurate rights, special entitlements must at times be conferred onto historically disempowered groups, such as members of gender and ethnic minorities (Young). In Brazil, an example of "positive differentiation" is found at the constitutional provisions that allow for preferential assistance to elderly people (above 60 years), pregnant women, and people with disabilities.[8]

Holston traces the origins of differentiated citizenship in Brazil to the colonial period, specifically to the Philippine Ordinances (*Ordenações Filipinas*) of 1603. This set of laws created the parameters that influenced political citizenship for centuries in Brazil: "the use of requisites of social and economic standing to exclude most Brazilians and a bureaucratic qualification of voters" (*Insurgent* 83). Since gaining its independence in 1822, Brazil has had eight constitutions,[9] not including a constitutional amendment to the 1967 charter (Emenda

Constitucional 01–69). Each document contains different provisions of inclusion and exclusion based on socioeconomic and/or bureaucratic criterions (*Insurgent*).

Following the indirect elections of 1985 that brought a civilian to power after 21 years of military dictatorship,[10] Brazilians set about to write a new constitution. In 1986 a constitutional assembly (Assembléia Nacional Constituinte) was formed with the mission of drafting a new national statute. Assembly members garnered feedback from various social sectors and organizations (Carvalho; Goirand; Paoli and Telles). The resulting document, the 1988 Brazilian constitution, has as its central premise the promise to safeguard the rights of the entire citizenry, without exceptions (Carvalho).

The 1988 charter opens with a preamble that articulates social rights and justice, in addition to liberty, fraternity, security (social) well-being, development, equality, and justice as the guiding forces of Brazil's social, political, and civil organization. The Constitution's opening paragraph posits social rights as the medium that will diminish and—ideally—suppress social inequalities.

This rationale reappears in Article 3, which declares the eradication of various social and other forms of differentiation (such as race and gender) to be one of the hallmarks of the Brazilian nation. According to it, the "fundamental objectives" of the Brazilian state are to "I—construir uma sociedade livre, justa e solidária; II—garantir o desenvolvimento nacional; III—erradicar a pobreza e a marginalização e reduzir as desigualdades sociais e regionais; IV—promover o bem de todos, sem preconceitos de origem, raça, sexo, cor, idade e quaisquer outras formas de discriminação" (*Constituição da República Federativa do Brasil de 1988*).[11] Several provisions guarantee the social rights of Brazilians. Examples include the payment of the minimum wage to disabled individuals, as well as elderly people without sources of income (Article 203), and five days of paternity leave at the time of a child's birth (Article 226).

Amendments incorporated into the constitution after 1988 also seek to eliminate biases that foment and/or create social differences. In 1989, for example, Lei No. 7.716 (Law 7.716) criminalized discrimination due to race or color. Additionally, social programs implemented during Fernando Henrique Cardoso's administration (1995–2003) and boosted during Lula's presidency (2003–11), such as *Bolsa Família*, and other plans put into practice during Lula's tenure (as for example *Minha Casa, Minha Vida* [My house, my life]) have also helped diminish the social inequities that have characterized Brazilian society throughout its history.

This is not to say that disparities, and for that matter, differentiated citizenship no longer exist. In 2010, the United Nations Development Program ranked Brazil as the third most unequal society in the world, despite its strides in social investment. Differentiated citizenship in the social and civil realms signals the continuation and, in some instances, the exacerbation of social stratification that has been present in Brazil since colonial times.

Social differentiation persists not only because of the commodification of social goods and unjust distribution of economic resources, but paradoxically also because of the equalizing impetus of the 1988 charter. Holston attributes this to "misrule of law, illegality as a norm of residence, restriction of political citizenship and education, state violence, servility and so forth," which "remained potent under every kind of political regime" (*Insurgent* 303). These markers of social inequity characterize the "disjunctive" democratic model that substituted military rule in Brazil. "Civilly disjunctive democracies" are political systems that are democratic electorally but have shortcomings in other realms of citizenship, especially in the civil and the social realms (Holston, "Citizenship in Disjunctive Democracies" 81). Because the three (social, political, and civil)—or four (cultural)—spheres of citizenship are intertwined, uneven access to either one of these ambits affects the other components of citizenship. Consequently, unequal political, civil, material, and/or symbolic rights, trademarks of civilly disjunctive democracies, result in and promote weakened citizenship.

After Brazil's redemocratization, a series of structural adjustment measures, imposed by international donor institutions such as the International Monetary Fund and the World Bank in response to Brazil's foreign debt (that grew significantly during the dictatorship), chipped away at social programs that serviced lower-income segments. Among the policies were reduction of government investment in the public sector, continued wage depression, increased flexibility in labor laws, and trade liberalization.

In 1990, with the election of Fernando Collor de Mello (1990–92) and, subsequently, of Fernando Henrique Cardoso to the country's presidency, Brazil officially entered the neoliberal era. Neoliberalism, with its emphasis on the state as a facilitator of the market, not only continued and intensified the privatization of the economic and social sector, but also deepened differentiated citizenship. In this framework, the meaning of citizenship changed from one defining the relation between the state and the subject—or, even between private citizens—into one describing a relation between the market and the individual.

One can argue that differentiated citizenship in Brazil has traditionally constructed rights as commodities, but within the neoliberal context, citizenship loses its communitarian ethos and instead becomes increasingly mediated by mass-media and market-oriented discourses (Baudrillard, *Consumer Society*; Canclini, *Consumers*; Bauman, *Liquid Times*). To be a citizen is to be a consumer. To be a citizen means you have the right—and the ability—to partake in the market. In this framework, rights such as access to health care, education, and even security are no longer provided primarily by the state, but become commodities that can (or must) be purchased by the individual.

Neoliberalism—and the accompanying increment of differentiated citizenship—also prevailed after Lula was elected Brazil's thirty-fifth president. For Alfredo Saad-Filho, Lula's adoption of neoliberal polices was the result of both national and international pressure to maintain the course set by Fernando Henrique Cardoso. Though Lula ran on an antineoliberal platform during his 2002 presidential campaign, jittery national markets, international banks, and investors and the International Monetary Fund compelled the 2002 presidential candidates to articulate a clear economic policy (Rollemberg Mollo and Saad-Filho). As a result, Lula offered assurances that he would honor Brazil's contracts while also calling for a change to the country's economic model in his "Carta Ao Povo Brasileiro" (Letter to the Brazilian people). Saad-Filho maintains that this "letter" prompted Lula's recovery in the polls, and gave him the "opportunity to move his coalition further to the right" (Rollemberg Mollo and Saad-Filho 113). Not only was the promise to respect Brazil's financial agreements maintained during Lula's presidency but also, as indicated by Saad-Filho, Lula chose a pro-neoliberal economic team and continued the policies implemented during the Cardoso presidency.

Nonetheless, under Lula's administration ongoing market-friendly policies were paired with renewed social investments, of which *Bolsa Família* is the flagship. As a result, social inequities, though still significant, have diminished in recent years. Between 2003 and 2009, poverty fell by 43 percent in Brazil. And if growth rates continue steadily, by 2014 the country will be able to slash the number of its poor people by half (Canzian). Since 2003, the new middle class, the Classe C,[12] has increased exponentially. During Lula's administration, 30 million Brazilians acceded to this new middle class. Now, of the 190 million Brazilians, 105.5 million belong to the "C" class—the lower-middle class ("Boom brasileiro"). In this configuration, traditionally disempowered groups—such as inhabitants of the urban periphery, ethnic minorities, and economically underprivileged segments of the citizenry—have begun to demand their right to substantive citizenship, often through "insurgent practices" that occur not only in the social and civil sphere, but also in the cultural arena.

Lula's election to the country's presidency represented a sociopolitical as well as symbolic watershed. All of a sudden, the son of poor rural migrants, a man with little formal education, held the nation's highest political office. Despite his humble origins, Lula was able to enter the inner sanctum of political, social, and civil citizenship. Lula's election crystallized the demand for across-the-board inclusion of Brazil's socioeconomically disenfranchised populace. And, for many Brazilians, his election symbolized a possible trajectory from marginalization to material, social, and cultural agency.

As Holston points out, Lula's personal and political path embodies the very process by which lower-income Brazilians have gained social and civil rights since the democratic transition (*Insurgent* 6). Similar to Lula, many other poor laborers had become empowered by challenging the sociopolitical structures that oppressed them. In Lula's case, it was Brazil's political system that by and large has excluded nonelite people from the nation's decision-making process. By becoming president, Lula defied this structure. In the case of urban workers, strategies of resistance vary from autoconstruction (*Insurgent*) to the resignification of peripheral culture (see Chapters 3 and 4). This modus operandi is what Holston denominates "insurgent citizenship," an "acting counter, a counterpolitics, that destabilizes the present and renders it fragile, defamiliarizing the coherence with which it usually presents itself" (*Insurgent* 34). Hence for example, the reinterpretation of the "periphery" as an incubator of cultural production contests the entrenched notion that this space engenders primarily violence and not art.

In Brazil, insurgent citizenship arises often at the very sites in which unequal allocation of civil rights is the most prevalent: the peripheries of urban agglomerations. It is in these arenas that civic rights are often denied or ignored, and yet it is also here that the (at time conflict-ridden) mediations over such rights take place.[13] Holston asserts that in the working class peripheries of metropolitan centers such as São Paulo, the elements that serve to create differentiated citizenship ("political rights, access to land, illegality, servility" [*Insurgent* 9]) are also the ones from which sociopolitical segregation is destabilized,[14] fueling the democratizing process itself. In contemporary Brazil, citizenship has expanded to also include the sociocultural dimension. Citizenship in this framework is not just an expression of general democratic rights (such as voting and freedom of speech). It also implies the demand for specific social goods such as health care and education on behalf of marginalized social sectors (Dagnino, "Citizenship in Latin America"). Sociologist Evelina Dagnino calls this a "citizenship from below" ("Citizenship in Latin America"). This type of citizenship calls for a new model of sociability in which otherness is recognized and respected. Citizenship signifies "the right to have rights" ("Citizenship in Latin America"), including the right to difference (gender, ethnic, religious). It is through demands for political, property, labor, and cultural rights that disenfranchised citizens change their social, and at times, economic positions.

Nonetheless, insurgent citizenship is not necessarily entirely counterhegemonic. Instead, insurgent citizenship can originate from hegemonic citizenship and can, therefore, continue its inequitable practices (Holston, *Insurgent* 13). Insurgent citizenship destabilizes entrenched inequalities instead of abolishing them entirely. In the cultural realm, an example of insurgent citizenship is how oppressed groups appropriate denigrating terms and transform them into markers of identity or pride, or into a code word used by the community in question. Even though insurgent citizenship has an emancipating potential, it can also spawn new forms of prejudice and disenfranchisement. Therefore, once formerly marginalized ethnic groups become hegemonic, they can create new patterns of discrimination toward other social and/or ethnic minorities.[15] The preoccupation with how citizenship is denied and, conversely, how it is attained has seeped into Brazilian cultural production (Avelar and Dunn; Yúdice) and therefore into its literary output.

The texts examined in this manuscript reflect the continuation of differentiated citizenship in a civilly—and one might add—socially disjunctive democracy in the last twenty-some years. Concurrently, they manifest, in different forms, insurgent practices. Brazilian literature has long been preoccupied with the codification of Brazilian social, historical, and cultural reality. Part of this endeavor has focused on the exposure of the nation's predicaments, especially its political and social shortcomings. Citizenship and, especially, inadequate citizenship are frequently subjacent themes in the depiction of a conflictive and hierarchical society.

I do not attempt to provide a comprehensive survey of how Brazilian fictional narrative has represented citizenship. Rather, I concentrate on how recent socioeconomic transformations have been absorbed by select literary texts. Citizenship's political dimension is not overtly discussed in the manuscript, though it inevitably underlies the literary texts at hand, and my analysis of them. And since culture interfaces with social, civil, and political rights, my analysis also includes these latter aspects of citizenship in posttransition Brazil.

Citizenship and Crisis in Contemporary Brazilian Literature combines Brazilian cultural studies with new historicism in order to delineate how literary texts dialogue with their respective social, economic, and political contexts. This is to say, due to the matrix of social and cultural forces that permeates the literary texts analyzed in *Citizenship and Crisis in Contemporary Brazilian Literature*, I approach the literary texts from an interdisciplinary perspective that combines literary and social analysis.

The literary texts this book discusses thematize both disjunctive and insurgent citizenship, and in the case of Luiz Ruffato's and Fernando Bonassi's novels, the narrative structure reflects the disjointedness that characterizes differentiated citizenship. Accordingly, I examine each of the nine texts from a literary standpoint, paying attention not only to their content, but also to how their narrative idiosyncrasies (language, syntax, and in Ruffato's case, formatting) interrelate with their subject matter and the sociohistorical context they allude to. The two approximations—literary and social—are superimposed upon a historical background that takes into account political (e.g., specific legislature), economic (particularly neoliberalization), and social developments (increment in socioeconomic disparities, autoconstruction, and erosion of public education, among others) that will transpire in the narratives that I contemplate in this book. That is to say, the texts this book examines emerge from and comment—directly and indirectly—on a specific social, political, economic, and historical conjecture.

The manuscript's hybrid approximation highlights not only how social and cultural discourses are linked in contemporary Brazilian fiction, but also how culture is an important element in confronting differentiated citizenship and articulating insurgent practices. The literary texts that *Citizenship and Crisis* analyzes reflect how citizenship is represented and how it is challenged and reconfigured. Ultimately, *Citizenship and Crisis* investigates the sociopolitical role of culture—more specifically of literary culture—in contemporary Brazil.

I choose the specific texts by Ruffato, Bonassi, Ferréz, and Faustini because they represent a broad spectrum of social inequalities that are paradigmatic of Brazil's varying modes of differentiated citizenship. In the literary texts discussed in this manuscript, citizenship has the immediacy of everyday interactions. Citizenship means being able to feed a family, having adequate employment and housing, possessing access to proper health care (or access to health care at all), and being protected from legal abuse. The denial of these prerogatives demonstrates how differentiated citizenship is commonplace within certain social segments, especially low-income sectors. Three of the authors examined in the manuscript (Ruffato, Bonassi, and Ferréz) focus on the deficiency and/or absence of the quotidian rights cited earlier. The fourth author, Marcus Vinícius Faustini, gives us a different vision of citizenship. In his book, *Guia afetivo da periferia*, we catch glimpses of the social transformation Brazil has undergone since 2003 as an increasing number of Brazilians access citizenship more fully.

By examining the formulation of differentiated and insurgent citizenship in contemporary Brazilian literature, I inquire into how cultural citizenship has become an integral part of the discourse around disenfranchisement and empowerment in Brazil. The texts discussed here bring excluded communities/subjects into the realm of hegemonic culture—literature. This visibility communicates the demand for augmented inclusion into all spheres of citizenship.

In the end, *Citizenship and Crisis in Contemporary Brazilian Literature* shows that if social inequity can silence marginal cultural expressions, it can also engender artistic practices (literary texts, visual and cinematographic productions, musical and theatrical performances) that contest social injustice and produce an "insurgent culture." Similarly, while socioeconomic disenfranchisement impedes access to cultural goods, it also has recently spawned social and cultural activism that has led to the establishment of alternative cultural networks. Community libraries, literary soirées in urban peripheries, independent and alternative literary presses that cater to both authors and readers who have little or no access to the mainstream printing venues or their products, and the literary texts discussed in this book are all examples of this development.

Contemporary Brazilian literature, limited here to texts that have been published since the 1990s, has a broad thematic spectrum (Resende; Schøllhammer, *Ficção brasileira contemporânea*). However, within this heterogeneity one can discern a strong social concern in many texts, especially in narratives that deal with the urban space. In this frame of reference, lack of citizenship, as well as demands for equal rights, are depicted primarily within urban settings.[16] Literary critic Tânia Pellegrini observes that contemporary Brazilian literature focuses on the city in crisis. It translates the city as a locus of social, political, ideological, and linguistic oppression (*Despropósitos* 34).

The city in crisis or the city as the locus of crisis reinforces the idea of the "divided city" (Ventura) that has become a staple of Brazil's literary, cinematic, social, and political imaginary and discourse. Consequently, all the narratives examined in this book occur in and revolve around metropolitan centers. The socioeconomically divided metropolis epitomizes differentiated citizenship at the territorial level. But the divided city is also the site that allows for different types of insurgent practices to emerge precisely in the socioeconomic borderlands of the metropolis. Accordingly, all the literary texts studied in the manuscript not only use the *urbe* as a narrative backdrop, but also deploy it as a trope of differentiated and/or insurgent citizenship.

All nine books reflect on the possibility of transforming literature into an *agora* (*Agorá*) (Resende), a forum of public discussion. By making the literary text an instrument of information and a space for public discussion, the authors seek both to reveal the erosion of the polis and to reclaim the (fictional) city as a space of political participation through culture.

The texts dealt with in my study approximate citizenship from different angles, contemplate the social and/or personal crises and conflicts that ensue from differentiated citizenship, and indicate potential spaces/forms of obtaining rights via insurgent citizenship. While Luiz Ruffato's novels address primarily differentiated citizenship, Fernando Bonassi's and Ferréz's novels demonstrate the clash between differentiated and insurgent practices. As a result, these books portray the "inherently unstable and dangerous spaces of citizenship in contemporary Brazil" (Holston, *Insurgent* 14). As suggested by Elizabeth Jelin, under conditions of extreme disenfranchisement, violence can become the discourse that allows disempowered groups to participate in the public arena. However, these same spaces—low-income urban peripheries—are also terrains where a positive articulation of insurgency occurs that can spread into the "hegemonic" city. Even though each literary text I study questions the hegemonic formulation of Brazil's social composition in its own way, Faustini's text proposes the most positive formulation of insurgent citizenship. *Guia afetivo da periferia* creates an urban cartography that destabilizes and, from this point, reconfigures the city as a space of cultural agency.

My manuscript is divided into four chapters. In the first two chapters, I consider how literary discourse depicts citizenship in the years prior to Lula's election. I focus on the literary output of Luiz Ruffato and Fernando Bonassi, two middle-class authors who represent differentiated citizenship within the urban working classes. Their works are paradigmatic of the seemingly paradoxical movement between social engagement and pessimism that transpires in what I call a "literature of disenchantment." Communicating the shattered hopes of Brazil's proletarian and *Lumpenproletarian* classes in the posttransitional years, their novels show the effects that the degradation of social citizenship due to neoliberal policies (such as labor deregularization, cutbacks in public spending, and privatization of social services) have on everyday life. In Ruffato's and Bonassi's novels, differentiated citizenship becomes the condition sina qua non for Brazil's working classes around the turn of the millennium. Their narratives elucidate how disjunctive citizenship transformed the members of Brazil's working classes into *de facto homenes sacers* (the sacred or accursed men) (Agamben, *Homo Sacer*): individuals who are subject to the law but who have no recourse to it. Ruffato's and Bonassi's narratives inextricably link citizenship to social and individual crises. Crisis (interpersonal violence, criminality, social disengagement) in this context does not possess an emancipating potential, this is to say, does not translate into productive insurgent practices, but rather is synonymous with anomie and anomic violence (i.e., lawlessness in which social norms and moral codes break down) that create negative insurgency. Differentiated citizenship in the social and civil ambits invalidates a communitarian ethos and opens the door to manifold types of contravention.

Chapters 3 and 4 contemplate the production of two authors who have emerged from São Paulo and Rio de Janeiro's urban periphery and have become eminent in Brazil's literary and critical circles. Reginaldo Ferreira da Silva, better known as Ferréz, and Marcus Vinícius Faustini communicate the realities of Brazil's socially disenfranchised populace, individuals who are perched on the border of citizenship and live in the spaces that emblematize this condition: the urban periphery. Ferréz and Faustini consider how culture, including literature, buttresses citizenship within these terrains. Their works are axiomatic of a burgeoning interest in the metropolitan socioeconomic edges as spaces not only of conflict, but also of creativity and cultural agency.

Ferréz and Faustini's works recover, or rather uncover, the spaces of marginality as perimeters of social action and transformation. Consequently, their texts take the reader beyond differentiated citizenship into insurgent cultural practices. Both Ferréz and Faustini employ the literary representation of inequality to denounce the prevalence of differentiated citizenship in the urban periphery. Tracing the inverse trajectory of the characters that populate the pages of Ruffato's and Bonassi's novels, Ferréz and Faustini describe the transformation of the peripheral subject from *homo sacer* into citizen. Their novels echo Brazil's recent socioeconomic and symbolic shift, as marginal groups increasingly demand and gain access to not only social, but also symbolic citizenship through insurgent practices and community initiatives. These programs foment the artistic talent of the *periferia* and as a result generate positive modalities of sociocultural identification.

The book's four chapters are representative of different socioeconomic backgrounds and of two historical moments. Because of this, I offer two distinctive perspectives on both differentiated citizenship and insurgent practices. Whereas the first two chapters indicate the expansion of differentiated citizenship, the second two portray insurgent practices that allow marginalized groups to regain agency through culture. All four of the manuscript's chapters communicate differing perceptions of culture as a tool of insurgent citizenship: The works investigated here are emblematic of not only Brazilian culture's present-day preoccupation with socioeconomic difference as a cipher of both identification and estrangement, but also the growing investment in culture as a means of social praxis.

Chapter 1 reflects on how Luiz Ruffato's novelistic cycle, *Inferno provisório*, hones in on the differential construction of citizenship in Brazil. *Inferno provisório* expresses, from different angles, socioeconomic and civil inequalities that result from and perpetuate differentiated citizenship. I focus my analysis on *Inferno provisório*'s first four volumes, *Mamma, son tanto felice*, *O mundo inimigo*, *Vista parcial da noite*, and finally, *O livro das impossibilidades*. These four tomes span approximately five decades (1950s–2000s), illustrating the diachronic development of differentiated citizenship in Brazil as the country transitioned from a rural to an urban nation. All four novels focus on working-class men and women who struggle with an adverse social environment. Their impoverishment and desire to ameliorate their social conditions leads them to migrate from the rural to the urban contexts and ultimately brings them to Brazil's large conurbations. Migration implies not only a physical dislocation, but also social and personal destabilization. *Inferno provisório* indirectly prefigures some of the expressions and consequences of the unequal distribution of—principally social and civil—rights that we will see in the following two chapters.

Taken together, *Inferno provisório*'s four volumes hint that socioeconomic empowerment can be achieved through insurgent practices. However in none of the volumes does this empowerment come to full fruition. Social and material development is foiled by the underpinnings that create and perpetuate inequalities, such as inadequate access to education and housing. In this, Ruffato's books resemble both Fernando Bonassi's two novels (discussed in Chapter 2) and, to a degree, Ferréz's rendering of Capão Redondo (analyzed in Chapter 3).

Chapter 1 addresses five different elements that influence how citizenship is perceived and enacted. The chapter begins by examining the formulation of rural and urban spaces in *Mamma, son tanto felice*. I analyze how Ruffato compares and contrasts different modes of socioeconomic disenfranchisement and personal isolation in the rural and the urban ambits. *Mamma, son tanto felice* links the "country" and the "city" (Williams) through differentiated citizenship. Segment two of the first chapter deals with *Vista parcial da noite* and focuses on how differentiated citizenship spawns various modes of violence. These violent manifestations peak in *O livro das impossibilidades*. Among the types of violence that I discuss is political violence (i.e., repression during Brazil's military dictatorship). Political violence feeds (on) socioeconomic inequality and exacerbates differentiated citizenship. The third segment of Chapter 1 centers on the impact that differentiated citizenship has on the experience of childhood. I examine how *Vista parcial da noite* portrays children as the primary victims of socioeconomic inequity. Their victimization impedes their transformation into "citizens of the future" and raises questions about the continuance of a public sphere and of sociability. The chapter's fourth segment discusses insurgent citizenship gone awry, examining how insurgent practices meant to change differentiated citizenship can result in violence. Violence, in its turn, accentuates social disjunctures. Finally, in the fifth segment, I consider three stories, two from *O mundo inimigo*—"Amigos" (Friends) and "A demolição" (The demolition) —and one from *O livro das impossibildades*, "Era uma vez" (Once upon a time). The three narratives propose urban to urban migration (from small or midsize towns to larger conurbations) as a possible mode of insurgency. All three stories do contain modes of insurgency (mainly through autoconstruction). But the price the characters pay for their new agency is the weakening and/or destruction of social bonds. Though they attain a measure of socioeconomic empowerment, the individuals who migrate from Cataguases to cities such as São Paulo and Rio de Janeiro are confronted with the breakdown of traditional social networks. They are solitary beings that are at home neither in Cataguases nor in their new settings.

Taken together, *Inferno provisório*'s books suggest the possibility of empowerment through insurgent citizenship, without, however, fulfilling this promise. I contend that this failure reflects a specific time frame during which Brazilian society saw an erosion of social rights and, as a result, the intensification of differentiated citizenship.

Chapter 2 examines Fernando Bonassi's two novels, *Subúrbio* and *O menino que se trancou na geladeira*. The chapter considers the novels' portrayal of a weakened social state and the subsequent increase of differentiated citizenship (i.e., the legalization of social inequality). Differentiated citizenship, in turn, foments variegated expressions of violence that preempt productive modes of insurgent citizenship.

Chapter 2 is divided into two segments, each dealing with one of Bonassi's novels. In the first segment of Chapter 2, I examine how Fernando Bonassi's *romance reportagem* (report novel) *O menino que se trancou na geladeira*, dialogues with Brazil's socioeconomic transformation in the wake of neoliberal measures. The novel is set in a fictional—yet uncannily familiar—country and depicts a dystopian immediate future that bears a striking resemblance to Brazilian society since its 1985 transition to democratic rule. Resorting to bizarre imagery and an inventive language, Bonassi highlights the fractures of social, civil, and political citizenship in an allegorical manner. I explore how *O menino que se trancou na geladeira* approaches the link between material infrastructure, differentiated citizenship, and the configuration of individual identity. Infrastructure is a significant gauge of citizenship because access to social and public infrastructure or lack thereof denotes full, partial, or inexistent citizenship. In the novel, restricted access to public infrastructure leads to the creation of private infrastructure that is meant to supplement/supplant public services and goods. Only citizens that have certain financial means can enjoy the advantages of functioning infrastructure. In light of this, insurgency against differentiated citizenship occurs on the individual, nonpublic stage.

In the chapter's second segment I concentrate on Bonassi's novel *Subúrbio*. I detail how *Subúrbio* locates disjunctive citizenship in the working-class perimeters of the outskirts of São Paulo. The periphery[17] is an anomic realm where social inequality manifests itself in everyday miseries. Abjection permeates both the novel's public and personal orbits. Specifically, *Subúrbio*'s rendering of the individual and communitarian bodies as inscribed by deterioration and contravention remits the reader to the increasing hostility and fragmentation of the sociospatial sphere the metropolitan subject occupies. *Subúrbio* hence establishes a continuum between individual and social crisis in the context of differentiated citizenship.

Social crises due to disjunctive citizenship is also a theme in Chapter 3, which discusses Ferréz's two novels: *Capão Pecado* and *Manual prático do ódio*. Both texts relay the violent quotidian existence of Brazil's favela dwellers. The two novels are set in São Paulo's marginal community of Capão Redondo, where Ferréz resides, a space that emblematizes the denial of citizenship as defined in terms of fundamental human rights (access to adequate housing, nutrition, security, and education, among other basic necessities). *Capão Pecado* and *Manual prático do ódio* endeavor to give voice to São Paulo's socio-economically disenfranchised residents. In this chapter, I investigate how Ferréz's narratives use an "insider" perspective to document the quotidian existences within the locales of differentiated or de facto noncitizenship and to promote cultural expression as a form of insurgent citizenship.

In *Manual prático do ódio* and *Capão Pecado*, Ferréz constructs interrelated snapshots of life in the *periferia* in order to portray how socioeconomic and cultural marginalization generate both the assimilation of subalternity as an identity and how discrimination based on socioeconomic status and/or race can nevertheless produce strategies of resistance and alternate forms of agency. Specifically, creative endeavors contest a *status quo* that promotes the continuance of marginalities (physical, psychological, economic, and cultural). According to this viewpoint, literature/literary voice can translate into social action.

In the two novels that this chapter examines, the characters feel trapped in their circumstances and, ironically, engage in behaviors that further marginalization (i.e., drug consumption and trafficking, domestic abuse, etc.). Not surprisingly, Ferréz's two novels concentrate on transgression (criminality, individual debasement) within Capão Redondo. As such, *Capão Pecado* and *Manual prático do ódio* seem to reinforce negative stereotypes of low-income communities.

Nevertheless, when read in the larger context of Ferréz's multiple sociocultural endeavors, including his clothing line *1dasul, Capão Pecado* and *Manual prático do ódio* transform (literary) discourse on socioeconomic and racial discrimination into a strategy of resistance. The interplay between Ferréz's rather pessimistic literary texts and his other cultural enterprises indicates how cultural production can empower disenfranchised groups. In this sense, Ferréz's literary production is emblematic of a new culture of citizenship that is emerging in Brazil's peripheries. In communities such as Capão Redondo, local artists are promoting culture as a means to counteract the socioeconomic and discursive marginalization that the residents of these areas experience. Their initiatives range from constructing community centers that sponsor cultural activities, to holding workshops on music, dance, painting, photography, and creative writing. Often, literature is the privileged medium to achieve social and, to a degree, economic empowerment. Literary texts that represent the reality of the *periferia*, such as *Capão Pecado* and *Manual prático do ódio*, are both indictments of differentiated citizenship and guidebooks to counteract these differences. In this chapter, I interpret *Capão Pecado* and

Manual prático do ódio against the blueprint of Ferréz's communitarian engagement. In particular, I examine the photographs included in *Capão Pecado*'s first edition, reading them as both a complement to the novel's plot and an example of community activism.

Lastly, in Chapter 4, I discuss how Marcus Vinícius Faustini's charting of Rio de Janeiro creates territories of agency for the narrator-protagonist of *Guia afetivo da periferia* and, by proxy, for the economically disadvantaged residents of the urban periphery. *Guia afetivo da periferia*'s narrator's journeys in/through Rio de Janeiro are not only a geosymbolic reconnaissance of sorts, but also a mode of claiming social and cultural empowerment by asserting presence—this is to say, the presence of a lower-income citizen—within Rio's official symbolic and material cartography. Through his urban excursions, *Guia afetivo da periferia*'s narrator establishes himself as a citizen of the entire metropolis, not as a subject relegated to its geographic and figurative borders. Because *Guia afetivo da periferia* demonstrates how sociocultural agency can be claimed through the (re)appropriation of the city, this book differs from the novels discussed in previous chapters. Whereas Chapters 1–3 focus primarily on differentiated citizenship in the metropolitan context, *Guia afetivo da periferia* concentrates on empowerment. Faustini's text thus shows a new perception of citizenship—the "right to have rights"—that is an expression of changed socioeconomic conditions in post-2003 Brazil.

The epilogue relates the topic analyzed in these with Brazil's current sociopolitical panorama. The chapter briefly inquires into how citizenship has been faring in Brazil since January of 2011. Specifically, I look into the status of social policies under Brazil's current president, Dilma Rousseff. In order to do this, I examine Rousseff's recent social policies and proposals and inquire into how global "cultural" events such as the 2014 World Cup and the 2016 Summer Olympics are impacting Brazil's urban spaces and its citizens.

CHAPTER 1

LUIZ RUFFATO

LANDSCAPES OF DISREPAIR AND
DESPAIR IN *INFERNO PROVISÓRIO*

> *Não quero ser cúmplice da miséria nem da violência, produto*
> *da absurda concentração de renda do país. Por isso, proponho, no*
> *Inferno provisório, uma reflexão sobre os últimos 50 anos do Brasil,*
> *quando acompanhamos a instalação de um projeto de perpetuação*
> *no poder da elite econômica brasileira, iniciado logo após a Segunda*
> *Guerra Mundial com o processo de industrialização brutal do país,*
> *com o deslocamento impositivo de milhões de pessoas para os bairros*
> *periféricos e favelas de São Paulo e Rio de Janeiro.*
>
> —*Ruffato, "Até aqui, tudo bem"*[1]

In this chapter I discuss how Luiz Ruffato's novelistic cycle, *Inferno provisório*, hones in on the differential construction of citizenship in Brazil through his portrayal of the nation's working class. *Inferno provisório*'s five tomes[2] express, from different angles, socioeconomic and civil inequalities that result from and perpetuate differentiated citizenship. The books that make up *Inferno provisório* span approximately five decades (1950s–2000) and concentrate on the history of the Brazilian working classes from the 1950s into the present. *Inferno provisório* encompasses five volumes: *Mamma, son tanto felice* (Mamma, they are so happy, 2005), *O mundo inimigo* (The enemy world, 2005), *Vista parcial da noite* (Partial view of the night, 2006), *O livro das impossibilidades* (The book of impossibilities, 2008), and *Domingos sem Deus* (Godless Sundays, 2012).

    Inferno provisório's initial volumes detail the transformation of Brazil from an agrarian to an industrialized and finally a globalized (in the neoliberal sense) nation, illustrating the diachronic development of differentiated citizenship in Brazil. In this way, *Inferno provisório* indirectly prefigures some of the expressions and consequences of the unequal distribution of rights—principally social and civil—that we will see in the following two chapters.

The working-class women and men that appear in the books are subject to the disparities in rights that make up differentiated citizenship. Though most of the characters struggle to counteract the inequities that they confront, *Inferno provisório* concentrates mainly on the failure of insurgent citizenship. The socioeconomic conditions depicted in the novels hinder productive expressions of agency. In this, Ruffato's books resemble both Fernando Bonassi's two novels (discussed in Chapter 2) and, to a degree, Ferréz's rendering of Capão Redondo (analyzed in Chapter 3).

This chapter contains five analytic segments that follow a general discussion of *Inferno provisório*. Each section examines a different manifestation of differentiated citizenship. In the first segment, I contemplate how *Mamma, son tanto felice* compares and contrasts rural and urban spaces. The stories in this volume revolve around the transformation of social bonds within the familial sphere resulting from Brazil's development from a rural to an urban nation.

The second segment considers the depiction of different modalities of violence in *Vista parcial da noite*. In this book, aggression occurs primarily in the domestic ambit. Nonetheless, domestic violence interfaces with the public context, specifically the oppressive conditions of Brazil's latest military dictatorship. The private aggressions that appear in *Vista parcial da noite* prefigure public forms of violence that are showcased mainly in *O livro das impossibilidades*. As in *O livro das impossibilidades*, *Vista parcial da noite* establishes a connection between socioeconomic disenfranchisement and violence.

In the chapter's third segment, I probe into the effects of differentiated citizenship upon Ruffato's child characters, looking into how children are represented in *Vista parcial da noite*. In this book, children are not the "citizens of the future." Their possibilities of entering the realm of citizenship are foiled by the legacy of differentiated citizenship. Through *Inferno provisório*'s child characters, Ruffato emphasizes the difficulty of insurgent citizenship, a theme that is taken up again in the discussion of Fernando Bonassi's novels.

The chapter's fourth segment continues to examine the problematization of insurgent citizenship in *Inferno provisório*. I concentrate on the story "Zezé e Dinim" (Zezé and Dinim) from *O livro das impossibilidades*. "Zezé e Dinim" reveals the at times violent intersection between differentiated and insurgent modes of citizenship. The story's biographical structure, as opposed to the mostly fragmentary and/or incomplete accounts of *Inferno provisório*, serves as a genealogy of both social and personal failure that condenses many of the other story lines contained in *Inferno provisório*'s tomes.

Finally, the fifth segment discusses three narratives: "Era uma vez" (*O livro das impossibilidades*), "Amigos," and "A demolição" (both from *O mundo inimigo*). All three stories suggest urban to urban migration (from Cataguases to larger metropolitan centers) as a potential way to counteract differentiated citizenship. The three narratives propose that it is possible to attain a measure of socioeconomic empowerment by becoming a consumer-citizen. But the material agency afforded by the mingling of social and consumer rights has a price—the erosion of sociability. Taken together, *Inferno provisório*'s books promise empowerment through insurgent citizenship but do not fulfill the promise. I contend that this failure reflects a specific time frame during which Brazilian society saw an erosion of social rights and, as a result, the intensification of differentiated citizenship.

Inferno provisório's almost epic focus on the country's working classes is somewhat idiosyncratic in Brazilian literature.[3] Brazil's literary tradition has not concentrated extensively on the country's working classes. Rather, it tends to favor middle-class dramas and, more recently, has gravitated toward narratives dealing with the country's most impoverished populace: its subaltern classes (and, more specifically, the criminal violence associated with these strata).[4] For Ruffato, the literary silence that surrounds the country's working classes indicates Brazil's hierarchical social configuration, in which the middle-class perspective predominates. This point of view tends to favor either self-representation or the depiction of the destitute social sectors as alternately violent and/or exotic others (Ruffato, Interview by Eliane Brum).

Questioning the at times violent mechanisms of exclusion that permeate the Brazilian social fabric specifically in its urban centers, *Inferno provisório* broaches the issue of contingency within the lower social strata without, however, falling into the aesthetization of misery and social violence that is commonly observed in some of Brazil's present-day cultural productions. For Ruffato, literature's function is to denaturalize violence by both cloaking and heightening its representation. In *Inferno provisório*, poverty and the modalities of violence associated with it are not turned into a commodity to be consumed by a privileged reading public. Rather, the illustration of manifold expressions of need that composes *Inferno provisório*'s narrative kernel fuel a sense of melancholic unease as the reader is confronted with many characters' lack of perspective.

Ruffato proposes literature as a means to denounce the country's imbalanced socioeconomic makeup. For him, literary creation transcends the aesthetic dimension and is imbued with a political impetus that should challenge institutionalized power(s) while also having a utopian potential (Sanglard). This viewpoint is also shared by Fernando Bonassi and other writers of Brazil's recent literary boom,[5] as well as by marginal and/or peripheral authors such as Ferréz and Marcus Vinícius Faustini.

Inferno provisório is innovative not only in regard to its narrative focus on Brazil's blue-collar and informal workers but also because it eschews the realist violence associated with narratives that deal with Brazil's poorer social segments. Instead, *Inferno provisório*'s violence, though pervasive, is mostly implicit. It goes beyond the material realm and seeps into the sphere of interpersonal relations and subjectivity.

Similar to *Histórias de remorsos e rancores* (Stories of remorse and resentment, 1998) and *(os sobreviventes)* ([the survivors], 2000), most of *Inferno provisório*'s stories are set in Ruffato's hometown of Cataguases, in the southeast of Minas Gerais. The books concentrate on the lives and travails of the working-class women and men that inhabit spaces where differentiated citizenship is prevalent. Many of the novels' characters congregate around the low-income tenement of Beco do Zé Pinto (Zé Pinto's Alley), which becomes the emblematic locus of differentiated citizenship.

The Beco do Zé Pinto resembles the *cortiço* (slum dwelling) portrayed in Aluísio de Azevedo's homonymous naturalist novel *O cortiço* (1890). In *Inferno provisório*, the Beco do Zé Pinto serves as a microcosm of low-income Cataguases and, more generally, of proletarian[6] and *Lumpenproletarian*[7] Brazil. The Beco's inhabitants are mostly low-level factory employees. But many are also occupied in the informal sector. They work as laundresses, popcorn vendors, or part-time laborers. Their existences, although generally not entirely outside the limits of citizenship, occur at its borders, its abject perimeters: low-income housing, low-level jobs, inadequate public education, and public health care. Due to their socioeconomic condition, their lives are circumscribed by the task of making ends meet. Only sporadically do the characters experience small pleasures, such as birthday celebrations or an occasional outing to the town square or the beach. There is no sense of futurity for the majority of the characters. When they attempt to transcend their constrained social and, consequently, existential milieu, or when they dream of overcoming it, they are generally disappointed. As a result, a sense of futility permeates *Inferno provisório*'s volumes, suggesting the ongoing lack of socioeconomic and civil agency that has affected Brazil's lower-income bracket.

Inferno provisório continues and expands Ruffato's project of documenting the lives of Brazil's working class, which the author began with *Histórias de remorsos e rancores*. Indeed, both *Histórias de remorsos e rancores* and *(os sobreviventes)* are blueprints for *Inferno provisório*. Samantha Braga observes that some of the stories featured in the latter are rewritings of texts that appear in both books 122). Ruffato concedes and plays with this self-referential intertextuality. In the epilogue to *Mamma, son tanto felice*, he admits that he has reworked some of the stories of *(os sobreviventes)* and of *Histórias de remorsos e rancores* into some of the narratives of *Inferno provisório* (173).[8]

The reinsertion of previously published stories into *Inferno provisório* occurs in all but two of the volumes: *Vista parcial da noite* and *Domingos sem Deus*, which contain all new texts. For Ruffato, intertextuality and narrative fragmentation communicate the fractured present. The books' structure is a sort of a "hypertext" (Interview by Eliane Brum). Hypertextuality, a signpost of our globalized, mediated sociohistorical moment, is juxtaposed not only to the present but also to a premodern and modern reality. In this sense, language and narrative structure allude to the books' changing temporal contexts while also highlighting the increased splintering of both personal and public spheres. Fracture peaks in the cycle's fourth volume, *O livro das impossibilidades*. The book's last story's ("Zezé e Dinim") layout bifurcates in certain passages, dividing into either alternating or parallel columns. Each column tells the story of one of the title characters. The narrative splitting evokes two different subjectivities as well as the idea of coming apart. Fracture occurs here as a separation between the two childhood friends and finally as a rupture in their life cycles. It also indicates a coming-apart of traditional social networks that leads to existential fissures in the two main characters.

Bricolage also emphasizes the books' polyphonic nature and its impetus to give voice to various faces/facets of working-class Brazil. Rewriting transforms the volumes of *Inferno provisório* into a palimpsest of sorts that endows the text with multiple meanings—social, historical, and cultural—that are intertwined. The reinsertion or rewriting of stories such as "A expiação" or "O segredo" (*Mamma, son tanto felice*) establishes a narrative genealogy[9] between various stories in *Inferno provisório*, as well as between the cycle's books and other of Ruffato's texts.[10] And yet, as suggested by Marisa Lajolo, all volumes can also be read independently as self-contained units.

Due to their analogous cyclical and fragmentary nature, the texts that compose *Inferno provisório* can be read in varying order. Intertextual elements string the books together without, however, necessarily creating a sequential order (neither temporal nor narrative). Although *Inferno provisório*'s volumes broach Brazil's development since the 1950s, the books do not follow a linear chronology. Instead, the volumes intersperse different narratives with diverse historical time frames. *Mamma, son tanto felice*'s first story, "Uma fábula" (A fable), takes place around the mid-1950s. However, the volume's second and third stories, "Sulfato de Morfina" and "Aquário," occur in the present. Their contemporaneousness is indicated by present-day slang expressions such as *galera* (clique, posse). All three stories are connected by the shared themes of difficult familial relations and abandonment. In line with the novels' fragmented, often elliptical structure, few narratives contain concrete dates. Rather, historical moments are mostly inferred from references to cultural icons (popular singers, hit songs, and soap operas and their stars) or from consumer goods (that also situate the volumes' characters within specific socioeconomic contexts). Commenting on *Mamma, son tanto felice*'s first story—or chapter— Lajolo maintains that the seemingly haphazard events that mingle in the narrative resemble the mnemonic flow (100). Certain episodes reappear seemingly at random, often affording us a different viewpoint of a given episode. Thus, for example, "A expiação" (*Mamma, son tanto felice*) combines three different stories[11] that, in nonchronological order, provide three different angles of one incident.

Inferno provisório's occasional sense of déjà vu recreates and underscores the monotonous rhythms of everyday life and the grinding routines of industrial labor and its impact on the workers' existences. But neither the narratives nor their characters are interchangeable. Rather, the individual tragedies, while remitting to a larger framework (both of working-class Cataguases and, by association, of working-class Brazil), personalize the social drama at hand, preempting the objectification of the characters into sociological "case-studies."

With *Inferno provisório*, Ruffato creates a literary expression that mixes aesthetic innovation and social awareness. Its volumes mingle the short story and novel formats without being constrained by either genre.[12] The amalgamation of different genres is combined with a predominately realist language that reproduces the oral register from southern Minas Gerais. Stories contain local idiomatic variations such as *trabesseiro* (*travesseiro*: pillow) or catchall terms such as *trem* (train, but also means "thing/s"). Often the narratives are written in the first person. The personal pronoun transmits an immediacy of experience and makes the protagonists both unique and paradigmatic of a specific geographic and socioeconomic *Lebenswelt*.[13] Many characters use "incorrect" variations of words such as *rádia*, *arrodeio*, or *quentando* (instead of *radio* [radio], *rodeio* [circumlocution], and *esquentando*, [heating/warming up] respectively), which connote deficient or lacking formal education and posit the speakers within the fringes of the socioeconomic strata.[14] Márcio Renato dos Santos indicates that the inclusion of regional or "incorrect" vocabulary inserts *Inferno provisório*'s speakers (even if fictitious) into the very sociocultural orbit from which they generally have been excluded. In this sense, linguistic and, more specifically, literary expression create a measure of sociocultural visibility for the subjects of differentiated citizenship that inhabit the pages of *Inferno provisório*.

Inferno provisório's linguistic experimentation and fragmented narrative structure prompt an alternative look at the other side of Brazil's "Order and Progress."[15] For Ruffato, the splintered account is a conscious choice. The fragmented narrative structure veers away from the traditional nineteenth-century novel that, for the author, represents a bourgeois worldview.[16] In contrast, *Inferno provisório* communicates the underbelly of this viewpoint and of the project of modernity proposed by said bourgeoisie.

Like the narrative scaffolding of his books, the language Ruffato uses extrapolates specific definitions. Though apparently "realist," Ruffato gives this narrative mode a twist. Marguerite Itamar Harrison points out that for the author, realist language becomes the springboard for linguistic and narratological innovation (155). Nonlinear temporality, abrupt spatial shifts, unorthodox syntax (that replicates spoken communication), and different fonts and typefaces disrupt *Inferno provisório*'s realist skeleton. Incomplete speech acts further disturb mimesis and offer fractional glimpses of quotidian existences. In a sense, *Inferno provisório*'s disjointed narratives gainsay the epic impetus of its books, signaling the complexity of life in the urban and socioeconomic peripheries. Finally, narrative fragmentation also mirrors the characters' differentiated citizenship and the brittleness of social relations that result in part from the socioeconomic exigency that said mode of citizenship generates.

Ruffato repeatedly employs ellipses to convey the often deficient and random nature of everyday communication and of interpersonal relations. Paradigmatic is "Sulfato de Morfina" (*Mamma, son tanto felice*), where the chatter of guests is reassembled as a random thematic mosaic: "*Lembra comadre, aquela vez que, Parece que esse ano não vai ser de chu, O cachorro da dona América, é. . . .*" (33).[17] The reproduction of seemingly haphazard conversations inserts the reader firmly within the narrative action—in this case, the consciousness of a dying woman who overhears her visitors' talk. Yet the fractured conversation also unmoors the reader. She is unable to construct a finite account from the scraps of dialogue. In this way, the shattered conversation reflects the broken consciousness and physique of the sick protagonist, Dona Paula, as she oscillates between life and death, past and present, awareness and unconsciousness.[18] In her final moments, Dona Paula retraces the family's slow disintegration. Disunity, in large part a consequence of her children's search for work in various parts of Brazil, wrecks the familial unit. This dissolution parallels Dona Paula's own bodily decay and is mirrored in her decrepit surroundings and her solitary agony and, coming full circle, in the disjointed conversation that she overhears.

Foreshadowing the migration highlighted in *Inferno provisório*'s last two volumes, Dona Paula's children went to São Paulo searching for better income opportunities. In tandem with the theme of socioeconomic dearth and migration, "Sulfato de Morfina" prefigures the interpersonal disconnect that reoccurs in *Inferno provisório*'s volumes. "Sulfato de Morfina" indirectly links the impoverishment of interpersonal relations to the socioeconomic disenfranchisement faced by Brazil's lower-income (elderly) citizens.[19]

Ruffato has indicated that *Inferno provisório* depicts Brazil's transformation from an agrarian economy to a (post)industrialized one and, concomitantly, from a rural to an urban society (Personal communication with the author). For the author, Cataguases is paradigmatic of Brazil's uneven industrialization and modernization,[20] its accompanying social inequalities, and the progressive atomization of social life. Accordingly, the cycle's novels touch upon the relationship between the city and the country and upon the alterations of the urban landscape, specifically in its public sphere and in the social relations that take place in the urban ambits. Ampler social modifications impact and are mirrored in the books' individual characters. These personages function like the glass shards in a kaleidoscope. Each reader rearranges them through her/his readings.

Similar to *Eles eram muitos cavalos* (They were many horses, 2000), the amalgamating element of *Inferno provisório*'s volumes is the axis of urban landscape and socioeconomic class. And, analogous to São Paulo in *Eles eram muitos cavalos*, in *Inferno provisório* Cataguases is the urban scenario where the character's existential tragedy is caught in the paradox between hope and the inexorable daily routine in which death is never far away (Resende 31). Similar to Fernando

Bonassi's depiction of São Paulo's outskirts, Ruffato's Cataguases is a microcosm of the differentiated modes of citizenship experienced by Brazil's working class. Both Ruffato and Bonassi portray the *urbe* as a wounded body, the site of multiple traumas (Dias 30).

Since the 1920s, Cataguases's economy has been concentrated in the industrial sector (principally textile manufacture and metallurgy). Several of *Inferno provisório*'s characters are employed in the manufacturing plants that are the backbone of Cataguases's economy. The weaving factories and other industrial loci symbolize the ambiguous process of industrialization that transformed Brazilian urban centers, including Cataguases. For an extended period of time the manufacturing industry was the city's main provider of stable jobs, generating economic circles that, in the novels, spread to the local brothel.[21] At the same time, Ruffato's books, similar to Bonassi's *Subúrbio*, suggest that industrial production promotes the disruption of public and private lives occasioned by mechanization of labor. As such *Inferno provisório* depicts the industrial plants and the lives of their workers as both physically and psychologically oppressive and deprived.

Discussing the relation between technology and labor in Marx, David Harvey maintains that the introduction of machinery in the production process means that the worker becomes "a slave of the machine" (*Limits to Capital* 108). Karl Marx and Friedrich Engels profess that the mechanization of labor erases the individualized characters of production. As a result, the worker "becomes an appendage of the machine" (87). *Inferno provisório*'s characters' existences are determined by the rhythm of the factories in which they toil. Leisure and pleasure are precariously inserted within the breaks between work schedules. Paradigmatic is Vanim, the protagonist of "A decisão" (The decision, *O mundo inimigo*). A self-fashioned "musician," he leads a suffocating life restricted by his work and by his (prospective) family. Vanim is an anonymous (and easily replaceable) part in the mechanism of production. He embodies capitalist production's effects upon the individual psyche. According to Marx, the mechanization of capitalist production represents, in effect, the laborer's enslavement. This occurs, first, because of augmented control over production that capitalist use of machinery provides. Second, mechanization also creates disengagement between the laborer's mind and body during the production process (Marx, *Results*). For Vanim, singing is the only outlet from his perfunctory life pattern. Artistic expression allows him the temporary illusion of regaining his individuality. However, he cannot reconcile creativity and labor. After arriving late for work several times—because of his artistic obsession—he loses his job: "*Perdeu hora de novo, tchau e bença! Lá fora está assim de gente querendo serviço! Uma fila!"* (Ruffato, *O mundo* 163).[22] Formulaic language (*tchau e bença*) and the pointer toward a supernumerary workforce detail Vanim's position as a mere "appendage to the machine" (87).

In the 1970s and 1980s, Cataguases experienced a downturn after several decades of economic prosperity that coincided, in part, with a national developmentalist project.[23] In part, Cataguases's economic decline reflects Brazil's socioeconomic crisis as the military dictatorship's much-touted economic miracle went bust in the wake of the 1973 oil crisis.[24] Cataguases's depressed landscape is a synecdoche for the country's 1981–83 recession and for Brazil's progressive economic liberalization after the 1985 transition to political democracy. Liberalization culminated in the adoption of neoliberal measures, such as the privatization of energy, telecom, transportation, and banking sectors after 1996.

Neoliberalization in Brazil aimed to curb inflation, reduce state inference in the economic sector, and therefore phase out the import substitution model that was in place since Getúlio Vargas's presidency.[25] However, contrary to expectations, the implementation of neoliberal measures brought only periodic bouts of economic growth. As the country's economy shifted from an import-substitution model it became increasingly dependent on foreign markets and investment. Fluctuations in these elements directly affected Brazil's growth rate and, as a result, also affected employment and income patterns. From the mid-1990s to 2001, unemployment rose in several metropolitan centers, including Rio de Janeiro and São Paulo. At the same time the informal sector grew and the average income declined between 1985 (21.6 percent) and 2001 (15.5 percent) (Rollemberg Mollo and Saad-Filho).

Lúcia Sá observes that the financial crisis that affected many Latin American countries, including Brazil, in the 1980s, 1990s, and early 2000s transformed not only the national employment landscape but also its urban topographies. Cities suffered the negative impact of mechanization: outsourcing and hence the loss of manufacturing jobs (5). Urban landscapes became or were perceived to be more violent as income disparities grew.

Inferno provisório's figurative cartography contrasts and juxtaposes different urban terrains, and highlights through geography Brazil's socioeconomic disparities. An impoverished working class links these different territories. Taken together, the books draw an intricate map of Cataguases that includes its central areas and its rural and metropolitan outskirts and extends to distant places such as Rio de Janeiro, São Paulo, and Santos. Different spaces are connected by the physical movements of the books' characters and by the symbolic traffic of dreams and disappointments that circulate between these various places. On the one hand, the urban perimeter represents socioeconomic progress while also revealing how these aspirations go bust. On the other hand, the countryside emblematizes both socioeconomic stagnation and, simultaneously, an idealized past.

Contradictory geographic locales are foregrounded in the cycle's first volume, *Mamma, son tanto felice*. This volume narrates the migration from rural areas in Minas Gerais's *Zona da Mata* into smaller conurbations such Rodeiro, Ubá, and Muriaré that surround Cataguases proper. The migrations transform social and personal relations. In the second tome, *O mundo inimigo*, the characters have moved from the small towns around Cataguases into the bigger conurbation (Cataguases). They inhabit the city's despondent central terrains, symbolized by the Beco do Zé Pinto. *Vista parcial da noite*, the fourth book of *Inferno provisório*, traces the trajectory from the poor urban center into the metropolitan periphery as the working classes seek social ascension through homeownership. They move into the low-income housing projects that emerge on the city's outskirts. *Vista parcial da noite* typifies Brazil's crescent urbanization during the 1960s and 1970s and the country's relative prosperity during this time period. Nonetheless, the move from city center to periphery ultimately does not represent social ascension. Like the "economic miracle" that justified the authoritarian regime, the petite bourgeoisie aspirations are quickly deflated as working-class salaries become depressed during the 1968–75 period. Labor, once perceived as a means of social ascension, loses this connotation. In this framework, the working classes are pushed into the ranks of the "excluded" (Souza Martins 34).[26] The cycle of socioeconomic marginalization culminates in *O livro das impossibilidades*. Here the characters leave Cataguases and its periphery looking for better socioeconomic opportunities in metropolitan centers such as Rio de Janeiro and Santos. They settle in impoverished and/or industrial neighborhoods in the urban periphery, reproducing the pattern of marginalization that led them to abandon their hometown. The socioeconomic and geographic alterations detailed in *Inferno provisório* characterize Brazil's uneven modernization (Caldeira 43)[27] and subsequently its insertion into the globalized economy.

Brazil's uneven modernization and its ensuing socioeconomic disparities are signaled in Cataguases's dichotomous layout that reflects its social divisions. Mirroring the configuration of many Brazilian cities, Cataguases has two separate and yet contingent dominions: the destitute sectors inhabited by the proletarian and *Lumpenproletarian* subjects and the (for the aforementioned social sectors) inaccessible exclaves of the city's upper and middle classes. While the Beco do Zé Pinto represents the former, the local Clube do Remo (Rowing Club) symbolizes the latter. Sitting on the margins of the Pombas River, which splits the city both materially and metaphorically, the club's expanse is visible and yet unapproachable to the working-class inhabitants of the Beco do Zé Pinto, who dwell on the opposite bank. The two realms are implicitly connected through the mechanisms of production that define the city's economy. While the Clube do Remo represents the sphere of consumption and of capital, the Beco do Zé Pinto signifies the domain of production and of labor. In the middle are the areas inhabited by small entrepreneurs, such as Zé Pinto and the owner of the Mercearia Brasil (Brasil Market), seu Antônio Português. Whereas the latter two spheres coincide in everyday interactions and business transactions, the elites are conspicuously absent from the common urban spaces and, to a large degree, also from the narrative itself. By mostly effacing the middle- and upper-income social segments, Ruffato reverts the direction of the hegemonic gaze and points it to Brazil's less visible social sectors.

"A solução" (The solution), from *O mundo inimigo*, is axiomatic of the book's sociogeographic divisions. The story refracts the divided city from a working-class perspective. Its main character, Hélia, works at one of Cataguases's textile factories. On her way home, she dejectedly turns away from the vision of the well-off "moças e rapazes queimando nas piscinas do Clube do Remo" (Ruffato, *O mundo* 72).[28] The juxtaposition of sunlight (*queimando*) and water creates a radiant tableaux vivant that associates luminosity to prosperity. In contrast, Hélia's existence is circumscribed by her family's stultifying living quarters, where every object suggests poverty and where she will find her "mãe esfregando roupas no tanque, olhos sem cor, pele queimada de muitos sóis" (69).[29]

Hélia's home stands in direct opposition to the scene she witnesses at the club. Brightness is contrasted with the home's dark and asphyxiating atmosphere. The indicators that portray Hélia's social condition, such as cheap plates and worn pots, coalesce in her mother's figure. She launders clothes for a wage and her eyes and skin register this hard-earned existence: both are burned by the family's continual struggle for subsistence. The subject's body maintains a mimetic relation to its environment: it serves as a canvas on which the rips of social citizenship become apparent. While the sun-kissed bodies of the Rowing Club's members suggest affluent leisure, Hélia's mother's tan connotes arduous labor.

Caught in a dreary quotidian, which rotates between her job at the textile factory, the suffocating family home, and the dull leisure activities she can afford, Hélia dreams of escaping by marrying "um homem . . . assim . . . bem rico . . . alguém que me tire . . . que me leve embora daqui . . . desse buraco. . . . Vou conquistar um homem rico, bem rico" (Ruffato, *O mundo* 65).[30] The young woman repeats the adjective "rich" in the manner of a mantra, as if the mere mention of the word could will into existence her prince charming. Like most other of *Inferno provisório*'s characters, Hélia's expectations also come to naught. Ultimately, she is a prisoner both of her dreams and of her disappointments.

FAILED MIGRATIONS: *MAMMA, SON TANTO FELICE* AND THE DYSTOPIA OF THE COUNTRY AND THE CITY

As indicated previously, *Inferno provisório* retraces Brazil's historical development from the 1950s to the present period. In particular, the volumes portray Brazil's shift from a predominantly rural to a mostly urban society. This transformation is at the center of *Inferno provisório*'s first text, *Mamma, son tanto felice*. The book's title quotes a Neapolitan song from the 1940s by Cesare Andrea Bixio.[31] Similar to the song, *Mamma, son tanto felice* deals with familial disjuncture occasioned by forced and/or voluntary migrations, and several of the stories are impregnated by a nostalgia for an idealized past.

Mamma, son tanto felice portrays two types of migrations. First, the novel alludes to the Italian migration to Brazil that spanned the second half of the nineteenth century to the early decades of the twentieth century. During this period, Italians came to Brazil, fulfilling the country's increased demand for agricultural labor.[32] Second, *Mamma, son tanto felice* thematizes the rural emigration that occurred in the course of the twentieth century, especially in the latter half of the century. Lured by industrialization, agricultural labor moved to metropolitan centers and fed the ranks of both the urban proletariat and the *Lumpenproletariat*. For many migrants the rural exodus signified not only an alteration of labor practices but also a modification of their social life.

The first dislocation, from one country to another, prefigures the multiple internal migrations that punctuate this and *Inferno provisório*'s other volumes. In the novels, geographic displacement implies a transformation in the characters' *Lebenswelt*. For Ruffato, *Mamma, son tanto felice* reproduces the sense of identitary unmooring

that characterized the descendants of Italian immigrants in his community (Ruffato, Interview by Heloísa Buarque de Hollanda and Ana
Ligia Matos).

Transition and loss of identity are at the heart of the book's opening story, "Uma fábula" (A fable). The text begins in the rural space
of the Zona da Mata and alludes to the period after the initial wave
of Italian migration to the interior of Minas Gerais, when the settlers
constructed their social identities around agricultural labor. Due to its
time frame, which antecedes most of *Inferno provisório*'s other narratives, and because of its focus on the rural terrain, "Uma fábula"
seems somewhat dislodged not only from *Mamma, son tanto felice* but
also from the cycle's other books. Nevertheless, according to Ruffato, this text encapsulates both the project's beginning and its end:
Genesis and Apocalypse (Ruffato, Interview by Heloísa Buarque de
Hollanda and Ana Ligia Matos).

"Uma fábula" echoes the biblical story of Genesis and focuses on
the dominion of nature by the Velho Micheletto (Old Micheletto).
Similar to a pioneering demiurge, he fashions a semicontrolled environment from the chaos of the natural world. In another biblical
reference, his endeavor lasts seven months, after which he seeks "a eva
que iria povoar aquele mundo virgem de vozes" (Ruffato, *Mamma*
17).[33] But unlike the biblical paradise before the fall, Micheletto's
compound is not a peaceful oasis. Nature constantly threatens to
retake the cultivated domains of the farm. In addition to the ferocious
natural world, the human world is disorderly. Madness and discord
undermine the order that Micheletto seeks to impose.

"Uma fábula" links familial friction to the conflict between rural
and urban terrains. While the patriarch Micheletto epitomizes the former, his son, André personifies the latter. One represents an archaic
social configuration based on a violent law, and the other signifies a
new order that breaks away from the father's primal rule. Micheletto
is a character from the Old Testament and André represents the New
Testament.

Italian immigrants to Brazil came either to work on coffee plantations or to settle the rural areas in Southern Brazil. The ultimate goal
of both groups was to save enough money to buy a plot of land—or,
in the latter instance, to own the land that on which they were toiling.
In the case of immigrants who worked on coffee plantations, landowners saw them first and foremost as substitutes for slaves and often
exploited them.

In his discussion of the Italian migration to Brazil, Angelo Trento
elucidates that beyond the lack of pecuniary and social assistance, the

new arrivals also had limited freedom, a heritage of slavery (Trento 37). Trento explains that the abuses were aggravated during periods in which the coffee economy was in crisis. Low profitability justified social and civil abuses, including the de facto detention of the Italian workforce on the plantations and the withholding or delay in pay for services rendered (38). For Trento, the curtailing of rights signals the schism between an incipient technological modernization that was taking place in São Paulo's coffee plantations and the premodern labor and social relations that were still largely in place in the rural economy.

Nonetheless, despite the variegated difficulties that many immigrants faced upon arriving in Brazil, some thrived and went on to own a small amount of land (Murari). Micheletto partly exemplifies the experience of material success and in part negates it. Following the pattern of social mobility pursued by many of his compatriots, he gains ownership of the land after arduously working on a coffee plantation and amassing enough funds to buy his own property.

However, "Uma fábula," ultimately challenges the stereotypical notion of the "American Dream" that underlies several of the chronicles of European migration to Brazil. María del Pilar Tobar Acosta avers that Ruffato's migrant characters leave one impoverished context for another, without achieving the goals that set them in motion. They are eternal nomads who lose their sense of belonging (5).

The story of settlement and domestication of the land and succeeding economic progress—that is, the ascension of the migrants into the middle-class echelons, which has become a staple of immigration and of migration accounts—is deconstructed as a futile endeavor. "Uma fábula" does not maintain the promise of social progress that is sketched at its beginning. The land arduously conquered from nature slowly reverts back to its original state as Micheletto himself becomes part of an overwhelming natural world. He becomes isolated in his authoritarian/archaic violence and his frenetic productive energy reverts to inertia. At the end of his life, he merges with the environment that he sought to control, becoming part of the natural world (Ruffato, *Mamma* 23). Nature here stands in opposition to the utopian promise subjacent in many Brazilian narratives about the natural environment.[34] Though powerful, nature is an ominous force, destructive instead of creative. Micheletto blends into this telluric timelessness, becoming disengaged from human community and memory.

As the veiled reference to the book of Genesis suggests, Micheletto embodies the reminiscence of an archaic social structure within a modernizing country. He emblematizes a precapitalist logic in which labor and its fruits remain under the control of the worker. As such, Micheletto's identity is attached to the land he settles and to its fruits. He feels at the same time protective of these elements and regards them as possessions. Micheletto has a similar relationship with his family; they are expected to be productive like the land. Social relations, including familial ones, are subordinated to the rationale of production. Micheletto repeats the exploitative relations of labor that the immigrants experienced on the Brazilian plantations within his own home and transforms his family into working animals, inured to the *pater familia*.

As indicated, several undercurrents of violence—latent and manifest—run through "Uma fábula." Hostility permeates the land itself and seeps into the various characters. Dangerous creatures such as ocelots, scorpions, and snakes roam the story and threaten humans and farm animals. Nonetheless, the most dangerous creatures are the humans. Periodically the undercurrent of violence explodes in acts of brutality such as domestic abuse and murder. Hence, for example, Micheletto dehumanizes and abuses his wife, Chiara Bicio, also known as *a Micheletta velha* (the old Micheletta). Tobar Acosta suggests that the transformation of Chiara's name into a feminine form of her spouse's indicates her erasure as a social, and also civil, subject. She is restricted to her reproductive functions, which allow her husband to control her entirely: "algemando-a nos cordões umbilicais de gravidezes sem-fim, largando-a desamparada, minguando num quarto de portas e janelas trameladas por fora, de onde saiu, trinta e cinco anos, rija, enrolada numa toalha-de-mesa, tão pássara que até o vento insistia em carinhá-la em sua derradeira viagem" (Ruffato, *Mamma* 31).[35] Confined to the bedroom, the locus of reproduction, the woman's humanity wears away in tandem with her body, as if every birth were carved out of her flesh. Chiara simultaneously loses her mind and her physical contours. Here, motherhood is not synonymous with fertility and the creation of a new life that will reinforce familial sociability. Rather, it signifies death, the wastage of human life that is subjugated by patriarchal violence. Familial relations come to represent the obverse of sociability.

Domestic violence, especially the type directed against women and children, is a continual subject in *Inferno provisório*. Beyond imprisoning his wife, Micheletto kills one of his daughters when she attempts to flee with a traveling salesman. Like her mother, the young woman does not resist her father's violence. What is more, the legal system—represented by the chief of police—overlooks Micheletto's actions. As the *pater familia*, he yields absolute authority over the members of his family.

Familial abuse highlights multifarious forms of aggression that are either condoned or made invisible by a patriarchal social structure that continues to infuse quotidian relations.[36] Luiz Eduardo Soares links what he terms "criminal violence" (*violência criminal*) to the negation of citizenship. He identifies three modalities of said violence: transgressions that are performed by the national elites (white-collar crimes), violence that happens principally within the subaltern classes and has as its objective profit making (drug trafficking, armed robberies, etc.), and finally, domestic violence (*Uma interpretação*, 40–41). In Soares's opinion, gender domination provides one of the matrixes of socialization in Brazil (42). According to this template, both social and individual identities are constructed within an exclusionary gender dynamic that justifies women's status as "second-class" citizens.

Strained relationships between husbands and wives, between fathers and daughters, and between fathers and sons link and separate the countryside and the city. In "Uma fábula," Micheletto's son, André, epitomizes the desire to immigrate to the city and thereby enter modernity. The son signals a generational shift and a transformation of the country's economic makeup. He rejects the attachment to the land and wishes instead to insert himself within the industrial modernity that began taking root in Cataguases in the 1920s. André represents the first wave of rural exodus that has consistently characterized Brazil's development and that gained added momentum after the 1940s.

Industrial modernity is allegorized by the quintessential modern transportation medium: the car, or rather, in an indication of the proletarian status of the characters, the bus. André is haunted by the sight of the bus that connects Cataguases to Ubá, which he imagines to be a big and modern metropolis (Ruffato, *Mamma* 24). The bus is a symbol of transit and the harbinger of the modern spaces that lie beyond Cataguases. It is also a metaphor of ephemerality, a provisional territory that provides the unstable bridge between two localities. Paradoxically, for André, the bus is a metaphor of his own immobility. Contrary to his aspirations, he remains tied to a locus of transition between country and city, between the father's archaic life world and his desire for "modernity."

"Aquário" (The fish tank), *Mamma, son tanto felice*'s fourth story, gives continuation to the theme of disjointed families and conjoins it with the topics of domestic abuse, migration, and solitude. The story is both a physical voyage (a road trip to the sea) and a journey down memory lane. Carlos, the narrator-protagonist, returns to Cataguases from São Paulo, where he lives, for his estranged father's burial. After the funeral, he and his ageing mother, Dona Nina, travel to the coastal city of Guarapari in Espírito Santo. The trip unearths Carlos's remembrances and underlines the family's malfunctioning: "uma família, eis tudo o que não fomos" (Ruffato, *Mamma* 62).[37]

"Aquário" emulates a travelogue and is organized around headings that list specific geographic signposts of the trip and the time that Carlos and his mother pass them. The markers function as narrative divisions and as mnemonic signboards. Each leg of the journey induces a new conversation topic between mother and son and, correspondingly, evokes a different epoch in Carlos's and his family's lives. Dialogue and individual remembrance are distinguished by parentheses that frame the latter. Furthermore, Carlos's childhood reminiscences are juxtaposed to the memories of his life in São Paulo. The varying time frames and modes of narration (remembrance versus dialogue) are unified by the overarching sense of loss and disenchantment that mother and son experience and are differentiated by font. Memories appear in italics and the mother-son conversation in normal font. When Carlos asks, "Mãe, a senhora . . . foi feliz . . . com meu pai?" (Ruffato, *Mamma* 50),[38] he receives a hesitant answer. Dona Nina's tentative affirmation contrasts with Carlos's own memories of a childhood dominated by domestic violence (50). His mother's connivance with his father's aggression reveals the perverse family dynamic in which the female body is reduced to the man's possession (Martin 256). As such, it can easily morph into a surface onto which to exert violence. "Aquário" deconstructs the configuration of the home as protective oasis in which "intimate and affectionate relationships among spouses, parents and children, and siblings become richer and deeper with each passing year" (Martin 253). Rather, it is a dystopian arena where interpersonal relations grow increasingly brittle.

Domestic abuse is a recurrent theme in *Inferno provisório*. This type of violence addresses and critiques the prevalence of a misogynist culture and, in the novel's framework, suggests the disjuncture of citizenship not only within the public but also in the private sphere, in a direct reference to Brazil's sociohistorical context.

In August of 2006, the Brazilian congress passed Lei No. 11.340 (Law 11.340), also known as Law Maria da Penha. This decree implemented new measures against domestic violence directed at women. Nonetheless, the low number of convictions in cases of domestic violence and the frequency of crimes against women[39] points to the gendered rift between formal and substantive citizenship.

Discrepancy between the formulation of women's rights and their implementation straddles the private and the public domains and permeates institutional practices. Angela Maria Pereira da Silva observes that in Brazil the recognition of rights, especially those of women, is still precarious.[40] This contributes to discrepancies in salaries, physical abuse, and cultural perceptions that claim men's supremacy. Male privilege is naturalized.

In this frame of reference, men possess material and symbolic power within the private sphere of their house. It is within the house that aggressive modes of male domination are generally perpetrated. Argentine sociologist Elizabeth Jelin maintains that the unconditional separation between the private and the public domains contributes to the incidence of domestic violence and, as such, to the erosion of women's citizenship (179). And though Brazilian law penalizes spousal or filial abuse, the intimate space of the house is often beyond the state's legal purview.[41]

"Aquário" highlights the separation between the public domain, subject to social management, and the private sphere, controlled solely by patriarchal law. Carlos's father and his older sibling, Fernando, are considered "model" citizens, though they flaunt their own moral standards openly. For both men there is no contradiction between these two behaviors. The veneer of respectability exerts leverage over the female body, especially if this is a relative's body. In a culture where male identity is based on the notion of being the provider of financial stability and where it is often constructed vis-à-vis female "honor," the passage of women from the confinement of private space into public terrains, such as the workplace, challenges traditional gender identifications. Aggression against women, especially female members of the household, constitutes an aberrant manner of identification for the male subject. Through the force he exerts on the female body and psyche, he can reassert a masculinity weakened by manifold frustrations (professional, social, personal) (Franco, *Decline and Fall* 211–12). Not surprisingly, Fernando attacks his sister, Norma, for her public performance (short dresses, amorous encounters) that purportedly tarnish the family's—that is, the father's—name.

Communities often deny the existence of domestic violence "fearing that an admission of its existence is an assault on the integrity of the family" (United Nations 2). Conscious omission is justified through patriarchal notions of honor and the autonomy of the nuclear family. Acceptance of violence against women exacerbates gender inequalities (Jelin 180) and, by extension, differential conceptualizations and enactments of citizenship. Civil citizenship, which includes the maintenance of privacy, is applied selectively to guarantee the primacy of masculine power. Meanwhile, women's civil and social rights, such as the right to physical and psychological integrity, fall within the cracks of differentiated citizenship in both the fictional and the nonfictional realms.

In *Mamma, son tanto felice*, different modalities of violence establish a symbolic bridge between the countryside and the metropolis. In both localities, violence is one of the defining features of individual and social relations. Often aggression becomes a perverse legacy and transfers from one place into another, pursuing the characters like a shadow. Paradigmatic is the narrative "A expiação" (The atonement).

"A expiação" is structured into three parts: "Ritual" (Ritual), "Fim" (The end), and "Tocaia" (The ambush), respectively. The three segments relate different moments of a tragedy: the supposed murder of Orlando Spinelli by his "adoptive son," Badeco, a young black boy. "Ritual" corresponds to the middle of the plot although it opens the story and is related from the point of view of one of the Spinelli sons, Zé. The story narrates the day of the dead man's funeral. Zé is a reluctant participant of his father's service and an unwilling witness to his cousins' chase of the fugitive Badeco. "Fim" is, as the title suggests, the end point of the story. Finally, "Tocaia," though located at the end, initiates the narrative. We can read the story in different ways—from end (i.e., beginning) to beginning or vice versa, or from the middle point onward. Although the three accounts are complementary, they can also be read separately. All three segments center on violence.

In "Ritual" Zé's conflicting feelings for his late father point to the latter's abusive nature. Orlando Spinelli oscillated between tenderness and a brutality fuelled by alcohol (another recurrent theme in *Inferno provisório*). During the wake, Zé contemplates Spinelli's lifeless eyes. The dead eyeballs carry the memory of Spinelli's mercurial disposition: "Aqueles olhos azuis que eram água anilada, represada no tanque, e que eram chispas de fogo. Aqueles olhos azuis que enleavam com carinho e esganavam com ódio" (Ruffato, *Mamma* 77).[42] His father's death inspires both relief and guilt in the child. The dichotomy of love and hatred, domesticity and brutality, unfurls through "Ritual" and reappears in "Tocaia."

The term "ritual" has a twofold meaning. Ritual connotes both mourning (i.e., Orlando Spinelli's wake and burial) and retribution. Retaliation signifies an archaic form of law that invalidates formal justice. In the story, vengeance occurs in a paralegal terrain where those lacking proper anchoring in the domain of citizenship can be punished. One of Zé's cousins suggests that when the police catch the suspect of the crime they request that he be handed over to them for punishment (Ruffato, *Mamma* 79).

Although race does not play a significant role in *Inferno provisório*, it is relevant in "A expiação." Race is a module in the structure of disenfranchisement that sets in motion the cycle of violence related in "A expiação." Not only is Badeco black, but he also comes from a lower socioeconomic stratum (and it is suggested that he might be orphaned). He is even poorer than the immigrant families and their descendants featured in *Mamma, son tanto felice*. Badeco's positioning within the Spinelli family reveals the complex structure of informal patronage and its intermingling with race that permeates Brazilian society.

Badeco is emblematic of the *enteado* (stepchild) who coalesces the role of godson/goddaughter, "adopted" child, and often informal servant. The *enteado* holds an ambivalent location within the familial affective and domestic economy. He is both inside and outside the formal bonds of parentage, and he is also within and beyond the labor relations that configure household services. Badeco calls Orlando Spinelli *padrim*, a variation of *padrinho* (godfather), while at times fulfilling the role of a menial servant in the Spinelli household. His body becomes the locus where the boundaries between servant and relative are trespassed. In like manner, his status within the networks of power that constitute civil and social citizenship are also uncertain.

Abuse pinnacles when Orlando, miffed by his *enteado*, ties him up in the manner of a horse, "riding" him around the town square. The scene discloses the convergence of social and racial disenfranchisement exacted upon Badeco's body. Orlando further dehumanizes the boy and conflates the discourse of animalization with that of racism. Parading the young boy, he calls him a "monkey" (*macaco*) (Ruffato, *Mamma* 104). During this scene, the townspeople remain at the margins, either passively or actively condoning the man's actions.

Badeco's dehumanization effectively removes him from the realm of civil and social citizenship. In order to reclaim his human dignity, Badeco must, in turn, execute a ritual of his own, staging violence, but not acting it. He wants to "ambush" his godfather, but only to scare him and, by extension, reclaim his humanity. Nonetheless, Badeco's representation of aggression turns deadly. Having, albeit accidentally, committed patricide, Badeco becomes *homo sacer*. Symbolically, he is banned from human and legal community and, as such, is both within its legal frontiers and outside them. According to Agamben, the ban implies that "what has been banned is delivered over to its own separateness and, at the same time, consigned to the mercy of the one who abandons it—at once included and excluded, removed and at the same time captured" (Agamben, *Homo Sacer* 110). Situated in an indefinite locale between the familial realm and the space of labor and banned from the legal sphere by virtue of this indeterminate position, Badeco's punishment straddles the domain of the public and the private.

Neither inside nor outside, Badeco can be killed without punishment, though he cannot be sacrificed within the realm of the law. He is an easy target for Orlando Spinelli's nephews, who want to exact vigilante justice on him. Recourse to vigilante justice reveals "a pervasive cultural pattern that associates order and authority with the use of violence and that, in turn, contributes to the delegitimation of the justice system and of the rule of law" (Holston and Caldeira 273). This is the case especially when law, or the absence thereof, pertains to lower-class citizens. For Badeco, the only manner to counteract banishment is to reposition himself into another geosocial terrain, seeking, so to speak, sanctuary in the *urbe*.

Badeco's movement from the familial and communitarian brutality of the countryside into the supposed security of the metropolitan terrain inverts the traditional perception of city versus rural areas in which the former is associated with social predicament and aggression and the latter is configured through a bucolic discourse. Nevertheless, neither space ultimately provides respite from crises.

As suggested by the title, the last segment of "A expiação," "Fim" (interleaved between "Ritual" and "Tocaia") presents Badeco many years after his escape from his involuntary murder. He flees to São Paulo, assumes a new identity, and becomes Jair. Similar to Dona Paula of "Sulfato de Morfina," Jair is presented to the reader on his deathbed. And, comparable to "Sulfato de Morfina," "Fim" has two parallel timelines: the story alternates between the protagonist's current death throes and his remembrances of his life after arriving in São Paulo. Analogous to other segments of *Inferno provisório*, different fonts indicate distinct temporalities. Once again, italics signal the past, and normal font indicates the present. Like in "Aquário," italics imbue remembrances with a fluidity that vanishes in the lived moment. The present is truncated by recent events and by imminent death.

Emotional bereavement also underlies "Fim." However, whereas in several of *Inferno provisório*'s narratives loss is interrelated with material deficit, in "Fim" it is, paradoxically, juxtaposed to a measure of social advancement attained by Badeco/Jair. His social mobility parallels the increment of spaces of working-class empowerment in the urban periphery, the locales that James Holston has identified as being the primary locales of insurgent citizenship.[43] Nonetheless, in "Fim" insurgent citizenship becomes a broken promise (*Insurgent* 167). Initially the city represents an escape from arbitrary violence for Badeco/Jair. São Paulo is a domain where a, perhaps, rudimentary performance of citizenship is possible for the fugitive boy. Repeating the trajectory of countless rural migrants, the protagonist of "Fim" gradually achieves the privileges of working-class status. Material and symbolic signposts such as a full-time job, marriage, and home-ownership divulge the piecemeal increment of social citizenship that parallels the development of the urban space and, more concretely, the insertion of its peripheral terrains into the geographic and social mapping of the official *urbe*.[44] Homeownership especially can signify not only social improvement but also advancement through both the performance and the enactment of values such as entrepreneurship and responsibility (Holston, *Insurgent* 173).

Landed property ownership is of fundamental importance in the execution and (self-) perception of citizenship (171). "Fim" affiliates the transformation of the family, whose very growth is an index of augmented financial stability, with the expansion of the home via autoconstruction and the transformation of the peripheral landscape in which the family resides: "*E os filhos e o progresso foram chegando: Josué, luz elétrica e rede de esgoto e água; Jairzinho, asfalto e um puxado com mais dois quartos; Orlando, supermercados e lojas e mais um andar com banheiro; Rute, posto médico e um quarto só para ela*" (Ruffato, *Mamma* 94).[45] Similar to *Guia afetivo da periferia*, in "Fim" domestic expansion is synonymous with not only private "advancement" but also with the "progress" of the public sphere through the periphery's gradual urbanization.

However, as Holston elucidates, centrifugal urban development does not necessarily correlate with the continual betterment of social and civil rights for the inhabitants of these exclaves. Following the mold of differentiated citizenship, peripheral expansion is often fraught with ongoing disparities. Referring to the period between 1940 and 1980, when many of the urban exclaves around São Paulo developed, Holston observes that differentiated citizenship follows the continuous move toward the metropolitan outskirts that has characterized São Paulo's development (*Insurgent* 185–6). This geo-social taxonomy has not changed substantially, even though insurgent expressions of citizenship have actualized in the metropolitan enclaves examined by Holston.

The dichotomy between spatial and social evolution and, by extension, familial involution is the drama that unfurls in "Fim." Exigency contaminates the working-class idyll, claiming two of Badeco's/Jair's sons, who get involved with drug-related criminality. The violence that bit by bit envelops the two young men literally penetrates the domestic heaven, tainting all its residents and transforming the house into a microcosm of the larger community.

The transformative potential epitomized by the security of landed property—which fertilizes social aspirations—is curtailed by the social violence of drug-related criminality that irrupts into the private sphere. Badeco's two younger sons, who are ominously named Jairzinho and Orlando, are executed by local drug lords. In the face of drug-related, urban violence, the space of autoconstruction, of potential citizenship, loses its valence.

Here again "Fim" destabilizes the dichotomy between city and rural areas. Fleeing from arbitrary violence in the countryside, Badeco/Jair nonetheless encounters other forms of exigency in the metropolis. "Fim" thus signals the ending of one story but portends the tales of rural exodus and social crises that constitute the kernel of *Inferno provisório*'s following books. Migration from one location to another does not preempt the repetition of violence and does not counteract social exclusion. Rather, the movement, motivated by hopes of social ascension and the accompanying insertion within social and civil citizenship, is an interchange between one space of disenfranchisement into another.

Conflict and failure also underlie the subsequent three volumes of *Inferno provisório*. In the books, crisis assumes different hues and reveals the various manifestations of differentiated citizenship. The fourth volume in the cycle, *O livro das impossibilidades*, brings the reader into the twenty-first century, ending in November of 2001. *O livro das impossibilidades* focuses on the aborted personal projects of its characters and the slow crystallization of an incomplete modernity that parallels differentiated forms of citizenship and highlights the difficulty in asserting more equitable modes of citizenship (especially in what it pertains socioeconomic rights) within certain social segments.

VIOLENCE AND TRAUMA IN *VISTA PARCIAL DA NOITE*

Among the modalities of violence that *Inferno provisório* broaches are historical violence. Paradigmatic are two texts included in *Inferno provisório*'s third volume, *Vista parcial da noite*. The first, "Inimigos no quintal" (Enemies in the backyard), references the trauma of World War II by replicating the distressed consciousness of one of its veterans. The second story, "O ataque" (The attack), also takes up the issue of military violence by hinting at Brazil's most recent military dictatorship (1964–85). In both stories, history irrupts brutally into the characters' lives in the form of psychological disturbance. If in the first narrative the character's life is split schizophrenically, torn between the reliving of his wartime experiences and his present existence, then in the second story the narrative slips between reality and fantasy.

"Inimigos no quintal" constantly shifts between the internal and the external frameworks, between the protagonist's imagination and his dilapidated material surroundings. The two contexts appear side by side, mimicking the main character's confusion: "A sirene! Os aviões! As bombas! Mais perto: os vagões, o apito. O pijama-de-flanela amarelo espanta-se, o mijo escorre pelas pernas. Uuuuuuuuuuuh! Braços esquizofrênicos apressam-se em refugiar-se sob as árvores. . . . A cabeça rompe em estilhaços. Leite de camela, Simão?" (Ruffato, *Vista* 18).[46] In this passage, the main character, Simão, continually relives his memories of war. These past experiences are juxtaposed to the images and sounds of Cataguases's daily routine, revealing the character's split consciousness. Mental dejection is underscored by physical wretchedness, symbolized by the soiled yellow flannel pajamas. In contrast to Simão's mental chaos, the question "Leite de canela, Simão?"—set in a different font, to indicate the clash between the protagonist's interior reality and quotidian materiality—is an irruption of a mundane reality into the character's interior mental chaos.

Schizophrenia, which in "Inimigos no quintal" and in "O ataque" is literal, also transverses other narratives. It represents a sentiment of social inadequacy that permeates the existences of various characters of *Inferno provisório*. At times, this social schizophrenia is the result of foiled ambitions, engendered and disappointed by the discourses of "modernity and progress" that underlies several stories in the books.

In "O ataque," the arduously achieved social ascendance of a working-class family—emblematized by the dual ownership of a home and a television—is also progressively dismantled as the family's youngest child manifests signs of mental instability. Paradoxically, it is the child who narrates the story from a lucid third-person viewpoint. Similar to "Inimigos no quintal," the antithesis between two conflicting narrative planes, in this case the narrator's rational depiction and his own psychological disintegration as a character, establishes a fissure in the narrative that reproduces the psychological tension the text illustrates. In this story, mental illness both brings about and parallels economic decline and social undesirability. "O ataque" is a parable of social bias.

The narrator-protagonist's mental illness creates a web of solitude around the other family members, who become progressively ostracized by their community. Neither they nor their neighbors understand the nature of the child's delusions. Under these circumstances, social bonds become brittle. The mother, for example, becomes isolated from the social ties that grounded and sustained her not only materially but also emotionally.

The erosion of sociability parallels a cartography of isolation. Following their dream of homeownership, the family moves away from their established milieu in Cataguases into Paraíso, a low-income development in the city's periphery. Paraíso is an in-between space that mingles the urban with the rural. It is also a space that represents a potential and fragile financial security emblematized by homeownership (Ruffato, *Vista* 56). In this setting, the dreams of surpassing material constraints and entering the realm of futurity[47] at first gain contours, only to dissipate with the irruption of the unexpected and unexplained affliction. Similar to "Fim," "O ataque" portrays insurgent citizenship (signified by homeownership and by autoconstruction) as an uncertain and ultimately fallible tool of citizenship.

In tandem with the child's mental degradation and the erosion of social bonds, the coveted and yet precarious indicators of lower middle-class existence gradually wear down. First the television, an emblem of the inception into proletarian comfort and into the modern nation, disappears. Then the recently bought house becomes neglected. And all the while the tight-knit family slowly comes apart. Whereas the mother falls into depression, the father turns to alcoholism. Finally, the protagonist's two siblings, who once wanted to transcend the family's socioeconomic status, end up adjusting their social and personal ambitions and conform to the limitations that their social standing dictates.

Both the vanishing of the television set and the dilapidation of the home are metaphors not only for the implosion of the family's social aspirations but also for its de facto banishment from the symbolic terrain of the modern nation with its conception of citizenship as a regulated construct. According to this formula, what exceeds the rationality and order imposed by modernizing discourse is expelled from (at least) the realm of social citizenship and restrained by the institutional mechanisms that regulate "deviant" behavior.

In this context, "O ataque" links personal tragedy to the country's public drama during the 1960s–70s. It is relevant that the time frame of *Vista parcial da noite* spans the early to mid-1970s,[48] the height of Brazil's military dictatorship.[49] Nonetheless, unlike Bonassi's *O menino que se trancou na geladeira*, *Vista parcial da noite* generally does not allude explicitly to the sociopolitical violence that was widespread during this time period. Rather, references to civil abuses transpire circuitously through some of the stories (principally "O ataque" and "O morto" ["The dead man"]).

"O ataque's" title alludes not only to the air strike imagined by the narrator-protagonist but also to the government's attack on civil liberties, epitomized by Cataguases's police chief. Brazil's two recent military dictatorships relied on a discourse of modernization and exclusion to justify various exploitive social and political measures. For the military, modernity implied a regimented order in which either social or individual deviance was punished by incarceration, torture, and often death. "O ataque" depicts the climate of paranoia instilled by the military dictatorship as a means of sociopolitical control. The town's chief of police warns the narrator-protagonist's father that the rumors his son inadvertently spreads about an impending attack on Brazilian soil by German military forces, a result of his schizophrenic hallucinations, pose a communist threat. Admonishing the father, the captain reproduces the negative clichés divulged by official propaganda during this period of lecherous, incestuous, antireligious, and lawless "communists" (Ruffato, *Vista* 66). The police chief's rambling rebuke implicitly duplicates the narrator-protagonist's delusions, creating a link between individual schizophrenia and the sociopolitical psychosis that frequently underlies authoritarian regimes.

Evading direct confrontation with authoritarian violence, Ruffato uses the individual—specifically the individual's body (in this case, the young boy's body)—to draw a map of the multiple locales of differentiated citizenship and its specific sites during the military dictatorship and beyond this time frame. Biopolitics, the exertion of power on all aspects of human life (Foucault), constitutes and erases the citizen vis-à-vis a state that is both omnipresent (in its authoritarian surveillance and control mechanisms)[50] and absent (in its perpetration of differentiated citizenship). As we will see in *O menino que se trancou na geladeira*, here too brutal biopolitics and, more covertly, private control of bodies is but a symptom of a larger structure of violence.

MELANCHOLY TERRITORIES:
THE PROLETARIAN GEOGRAPHY OF
CATAGUASES IN *VISTA PARCIAL DA NOITE*

If *Inferno provisório*'s first volume concentrated on the initial socio-geographic transformations occasioned by Brazil's industrialization and uneven modernization, portraying the migration from the country to the city and the tensions this movement implies, then the third volume of the cycle, *Vista parcial da noite*, narrates the quotidian existences of the working class and the *Lumpenproletariat* in Cataguases and its periphery. *Vista parcial da noite* has as its backdrop the lower-class *habitats* within and outside Cataguases. The book relates Cataguases's peripheralization, locating its narratives mainly within the suburban development of Paraíso.

In *Vista parcial da noite*, Ruffato symbolically maps the working class's and the *Lumpenproletariat*'s *Lebenswelt*[51] by entering the homes of the men and women who participate in the city's industrial production and in its informal economy. As in *Mamma, son tanto felice*, the author resorts to individual stories to piece together the social history of Brazil's working class. As we glance into the domestic spaces of the proletarian and *Lumpenproletarian* existences, their suffocating alcoves and dried-up vegetable gardens, we glean the pattern of differentiated citizenship that permeated the country's social fabric in the 1960s and the 1970s.

A significant portion of *Vista parcial da noite* takes place in Cataguases's periphery, as the city expanded in the wake of the nation's modernizing process and the poorer populace, seeking affordable homeownership opportunities, moved to the urban outskirts (see for example the stories "O ataque" and "Haveres" [Chores]). These locales, however, were situated outside the city's infrastructural grid. In *Vista parcial da noite*, lack of infrastructure emblematizes what Holston recognizes as the double process of geographic exclusion and differentiated citizenry that accompanied the nation's modernizing endeavor in the 1930s–70s.

As in *O menino que se trancou na geladeira*, deficient infrastructure perpetuates the diagram of differentiated citizenship that the newly minted residents of urban exclaves such as Paraíso are attempting to escape (by moving into the city's outskirts). This pattern of unequal citizenship is reproduced as their children leave the—albeit improved—peripheral territories and establish themselves in the metropolitan exurbs of larger conurbations such as Rio de Janeiro and São Paulo, becoming themselves incomplete citizens. Nonetheless, despite their socioeconomic and infrastructural shortcomings, *O livro das impossibilidades* suggests that it is only in conurbations such as Rio de Janeiro and São Paulo that tentative blueprints of a more inclusive citizenship become possible, even if plagued by brittle sociability.

By focusing on dystopian space in *Vista parcial da noite*, Ruffato suggests that the process of insurgent citizenship that has taken and continues taking place in larger urban centers has largely bypassed medium-size cities, such as Cataguases, that remain mired in decreased sociability.[52] Among the reasons for the continuation, or increment, of social crises in cities such as Cataguases in the context of *Inferno provisório* is their economic stagnation, which, in turn, impels the exodus of its younger residents to bigger urban enclaves. Compounding economic paralysis, Ruffato's Cataguases is plagued by exaggerated traditionalism, of which patriarchal violence is but an example. The Cataguases of *Inferno provisório* is a suffocating landscape of differentiated citizenship.

Continuing the template initiated in *Mamma, son tanto felice*, overt and implicit violence are *Vista parcial da noite*'s prevailing themes. Like in the cycle's first tome, domestic abuse is a focal point of almost all the stories of the volume. In *O mundo inimigo*, the home becomes a microcosm of the nation, with abusive—and even murderous—father figures—that mirror, at an intimate level, the brutality saturating the social realm.

Slavoj Žižek avers that subjective aggression is "violence produced by a clearly identifiable agent" (1). Subjective violence encompasses objective violence, which operates at the symbolic and ideological level (as for example through language) and systemic violence, which occurs in the institutional sphere. *Vista parcial da noite* portrays a world in crisis where the struggles occasioned by systemic and objective violence peak into private tragedies. The exigency that was announced in *Mamma, son tanto felice* finds in the third volume of *Inferno provisório* its most pungent expression.

"O profundo silêncio das manhãs de domingo" (The profound silence of Sunday mornings) coheres the book's themes of social disentitlement, which in the story culminate in a filicide. After his wife leaves him and their four young children, the story's protagonist, Baiano, takes his eldest son, Cláudio, to the river and drowns him. Baiano then commits suicide. The murder-suicide is a climax of a string of failures that compose Baiano's material and affective worlds.

Baiano and his family are poised at the very edge of the socioeconomic scale. They are the *Lumpen* that stand outside the formal realm of production but partake in and are dependent on this sphere,

often completing its most perilous or least rewarding tasks. Therefore, though Baiano maintains ties to the institutional economic
domain, performing its abject tasks, he is not an integral part of it
(Ruffato, *Vista* 82). The menial labors he carries out imprint on his
body, a cartography of exploitation: "No Rodoviário Mineiro, car-
regou e descarregou mercadorias das carretas que aportavam do Rio
de Janeiro, de São Paulo, de Belo Horizonte. 'Me descadeirou aquele
tempo . . .' . . . De barco, tirou areia do fundo do Rio Pomba. 'Estra-
gou minhas juntas, friagem'" (85).[53] The slow erosion of physical
strength is complemented by professional informality that transmog-
rifies into financial instability. This conjuncture obstructs the citizen's
participation in the network of social rights (M. Davis 181). In Brazil, without the *Carteira Assinada* (Employment contract), access to
unemployment benefits, paid vacations, health care, and retirement
are unattainable. In other words, outside the sphere of formal work,
social citizenship wanes to a large degree.

Nonetheless, parallel to the differentiated citizenship that characterizes Baiano's and his family's daily life, vestiges of insurgent citizenship
emerge in the form of laborious homeownership. Insurgent citizenship also appears in both actual and projected improvements within
the household: the installation of a water tank so that his wife need
not to go to the water hole and the hope of connecting the house to
the electric grid (Ruffato, *Vista* 88). As in Badeco/Jair, Baiano's autoconstruction projects manifest a futurity with a tenuous foothold in
the realm of social citizenship—symbolized here by two infrastructural
goods: running water and electricity. Access to urban infrastructure is
synonymous with admittance to the legal metropolitan terrain and
therefore an expression of social citizenship.

In "O profundo silêncio das manhãs de domingo," lack of equal
access to social rights, a consequence of informal labor and makeshift living conditions, extends to the children. Due to the family's
impoverishment, Baiano's son and daughters have but the most basic
access to education. Education—even if precarious—represents a possibility to change social conditions. Schooling is an effective tool in
the construction of both citizenship and its negation (Reiter 53–4).
Access to the formal labor market and to the social advantages associated with this sphere are inextricably tied to an individual's level and
quality of education. Brazil's public education system has traditionally served the middle-income sectors and neglected the poor social
echelons. Additionally, since the 1980s, public education in Brazil
has been in crisis, plagued by lack of funding and policy, personnel,
and infrastructure issues. The division between the private and public

schooling structure has served to perpetuate systemic inequality and social tensions.[54]

Most of Ruffato's characters are bogged down by their inability to enter the privileged spheres of education—that is, private schools. They must attend public schools and/or do professional training. None of the characters of *Inferno provisório* has a university degree and many interrupt their education at an early age to go work in Cataguases's factories. As a result, the characters' future is generally circumscribed to the narrow circle of industrial labor or to other forms of low-wage employment. Cláudio, Baiano's son, holds both the promise contained in education and its malfunction. He therefore represents both differentiated citizenship and the (ultimately failed) insurgent practices that flourish in the cracks of social inequality.

The boy, who evidences an unusual intellect and drive, assiduously spends his afternoons in the town's improvised school (Ruffato, *Vista* 81). Dedication to study signifies the possibility of transcending the social constraints that limit his father. Nonetheless, despite his acute intelligence and passion for learning, the boy's social options remain restricted to the narrow and stultifying milieu of the parochial school. These conditions are symbolized by the description of the school's dilapidated physical environment. In order to assist the family financially, Cláudio must also work and take care of his younger siblings,[55] further diminishing his educational possibilities.

The reader is left in the dark about the motivations for Baiano's wife's desertion. The text only hints in passing that unsatisfactory material conditions, specifically Baiano's lack of formal employment, might be at the root of her abandonment. Open-endedness multiplies the reasons for the private crisis (indirectly linking it to public crises) and preempts a single interpretation and, implicitly, a single motif for the woman's desertion. As a response to the marital collapse—that stands for and compounds Baiano's other failures—"O profundo silêncio das manhãs de domingo" weaves a web of violence that emanates from the kernel of disenfranchisement. "Silence" refers to the oppressive structures surrounding the characters and that culminate in Cláudio's murder. The boy's drowning is a metaphor for the suffocating conditions in which he and his family live. His death also signifies his inability to speak, literally, to cry for assistance as he goes under.

For Baiano, his son's murder constitutes both vengeance and a perverse agency in the face of social and existential disempowerment. Violence transforms the boy's body into an object onto which his father can project his anguish, both reiterating upon it the brutalization and disillusionment that suffuses him and exorcizing it through death. Ruffato plays with the arrangement of words on the page and emulates the act of sinking by writing the verb *submergiu* (he submerged) vertically down the page. The disposition of the word duplicates the water's pull on the body, the pull of the social disenfranchisement on the bodies of impoverished citizens, and lastly the pull of violence on the individual body. Ruffato's narrative and stylistic virtuosity transform the account's very structure into a duplication of the young boy's agonizing submersion while also pulling the reader into the text, into the very moment of catastrophe. Horizontal lines interrupt the downward draw as the boy temporarily reemerges and calls out to his father: "*Pai!*" (*Vista* 90).[56] Emphasized typeface and exclamation points underscore the child's desperation as he seeks help in the father's arms, which remain beyond the boy's reach. The sinking/emerging movement recurs two more times, but instead of the appeal, a lonely verb, *voltou* (he came back), indicates the mechanic upward motion and recreates the boy's creeping loss of consciousness. After the son is sacrificed in lieu of the absent mother, the father expiates his crime and his failures by committing suicide. Paradoxically, in this anomic act (Durkheim), he remains literally tied to his deceased son's body, in a perversion of the familial ties that have come apart with his wife's departure.

Social and existential anomie and its consequences are also the central themes of "Vicente Cambota." This story revolves around an outcast, the narrative's namesake, who, ironically, does not truly have this name ("Vicente não chamava Vicente" [Ruffato, *Vista* 119][57]). Officially naming an infant apportions it civil identity. Naming therefore formally inscribes a subject into the public archive, inserts the *zoe* (pure physical life) into the polis, and therefore transforms it (*zoe*) into *bios*.

The story contains a partial "copy" of Vicente's birth certificate that both underlines the importance of and erases the legal document's content. Inverting the naming process, "Vicente Cambota" outlines *zoe* (by reproducing the main character's birth certificate), only to transform it into *bios*. We learn that Vicente's official name, Ascelpíades, does not last. In the text, the replica of the recording is juxtaposed to the sentence: "Nada durou Asclepíades" [*Vista* 119]). The contrast between official document and de facto erasure of its contents multiplies the meanings of the name, simultaneously creating and dismissing the narrative's central character. In its ambiguity, the sentence "Nada durou Asclepíades" can refer to the insubstantiality of both the name and the person (in its legal sense) bearing the name. Not long after the boy's birth his given name is replaced by

"Vicente," a name that evidences his orphaned social condition. His second name derives from the charity where his mother begs for food (Ruffato, *Vista* 119). Vicente straddles a frontier territory between inclusion and exclusion and, ultimately, between humanity and nonhumanity. While he interacts with children his own age, he does not follow the practices that regulate childhood: regular hygiene, schooling, and a daily routine. Though this lack of rules represents freedom for the young boy, its flipside is that Vicente is also outside any social system that could afford him protection and enable him to effectively become a "citizen." Vicente's incomplete socialization hampers his integration into Cataguases's community, and his social existence erodes progressively as he moves from the city center to its periphery and finally beyond the urban limits. Geography replicates Vicente's psychological and emotional displacement.

After Vicente's mother suffers a nervous breakdown and is forcibly interned, Zé Pinto, the owner of the shacks inhabited by many of *Inferno provisório*'s working-class characters, allows the boy to move into the plot of land he owns in Paraíso. Initially the boy integrates into this environment, becoming a part of its slow development. He helps his neighbors in the autoconstruction of their homes. In this process he inserts himself in the manufacture of a fragile social citizenship (i.e., home ownership) and is therefore able to, at least superficially, partake in a social sphere of sorts. Nonetheless, his participation quickly disappears and is supplanted by his emotional solitude.

In the exurb, spatial liminality coincides with Vicente's social and personal marginality. For the title character the former highlights and reinforces the latter. Located at the juncture between the *urbe* and a state of nature that is the defining obverse of urbanity, Vicente comes full circle from the initial scene of naming that connotes both his inception and his attendant removal from the legal sphere. He retreats first into alcoholism and gambling and, gradually losing his connection with other people, draws back into nature. His progressive social estrangement ends in madness. In this condition he becomes *zoe*. Like Micheletto from "Uma fábula," Vincente merges into the natural world.

Using parenthesis and a smaller type, Ruffato ends the story with a postscript of sorts that both expels and negatively reinserts Vicente into the social realm. The formatting highlights Vicente's gradual erasure from Cataguases's social milieu. While the smaller font alludes to his disappearance, the parentheses transform his denouement into an afterthought, emphasizing the character's marginality. The story's finale, echoing its initial concentration of abject bodily matter, once again focuses on the protagonist's diseased corporality, linking it to both his physical and social environment. Vicente's body, like Baiano's, is a map of the desolation that has marked his life and that explodes into the physical manifestation of corruption: "então, a minúscula mancha rubra, arranhadura de unha-de-gato ou picada de pernilongo . . . transfigurou-se em chagas doloridas, que, semeadas à perna direita, provocavam espasmos à mínima agitação, boca contraída, franzida a testa, odor putrefato exalando dos poros" (Ruffato, *Vista* 126).[58] In an abject economy, the body pollutes the protagonist's living environment and vice versa (the shack were Vicente is living becomes impregnated by his pestilent odor) in a continuum of dereliction that exacerbates his isolation and aggravates his disease.

Outcast from the narrow *communitas* in which he partook—mainly the drinking and gambling circles of Cataguases's incipient suburbs—the protagonist metamorphoses into society's negative paragon and in this condition is, paradoxically, integrated into its imaginary of control and exclusion. Exiled into madness and nature, he unbeknownst to himself becomes the negative role model for Cataguases's disobedient children (Ruffato, *Vista* 126). "Vicente Cambota," comes full circle in the text's finale: the protagonist is partially sunk in a manhole, his body both inside and outside of the cavity, mirroring once again the inclusion/exclusion dichotomy that punctuates the narrative. As in "O profundo silêncio das manhãs de domingo," the open ending of the story points toward the ultimate lack of explanation for lives such as Vicente's.

In July of 1990, the Brazilian government approved Lei No. 8.069 (Law 8.069), the Estatuto da Criança e do Adolescente. Article 1 of the law, assures all Brazilian children of full human rights and theoretically guarantees them the means to access these rights and hence attain full physical, mental, moral, spiritual, and social development. According to Article 4 of this law, society as a whole is responsible for safeguarding children's rights to life, health, food, education, sports, leisure, professionalization, culture, dignity, respect, and community and family lives. Vicente has no family, and though under normal circumstances he would be considered a ward of the state, he in effect stands outside any social realm—indicated in the story by his truanting and later by the lack of medical assistance when he becomes ill. Without assistance from family, community, society, or the state, Vicente is not privy to the elements from which citizenship derives (education, professionalization, culture, dignity, respect, liberty, and both familial and social relations). "Vicente Cambota" and other stories of *Vista parcial da noite* mingle realism and allegory to convey a reality pervaded by systemic violence that reproduces *homenes sacres*, inscribing the bodies of these subjects with the brutality of institutionalized and subjective violence.

INTO THE TWENTY-FIRST CENTURY: *O LIVRO DAS IMPOSSIBILIDADES* AND THE IMPOSSIBILITY OF CITIZENSHIP

O livro das impossibilidades describes a pendular movement between various larger conurbations (Santos, Rio de Janeiro, and São Paulo) and Cataguases, which is both the point of departure and the locus of real or imagined returns. As such, this text harks back and completes the dislocation initiated in *Mamma, son tanto felice*. The fourth volume of *Inferno provisório* details the rift between the characters who remained in Cataguases's stultifying ambiance and those who decided to try their luck elsewhere—this elsewhere always being the larger metropolitan centers. Thus, *O livro das impossibilidades* constructs an apparent dichotomy between different urban spaces that translates into a duality of social ascendancy/agency and social immobility/differentiation. Nonetheless, while it is true that migration into the larger cities creates domains of insurgent citizenship whereas geographic immobility ascertains social stagnation, the binary between different urban spheres is only partial. Underlying both perimeters is the sentiment of affective estrangement and social splintering that is apparent throughout the novel's narrative structure.

As in other narratives of *Inferno provisório*, Ruffato employs polyphony to create a layered picture of Brazil's working class and to give its subjects a voice within the traditionally bourgeois realm of fiction. *O livro das impossibilidades* contains three longer narratives: "Era uma vez" (Once upon a time) "Cartas a uma jovem senhora" (Letters to a young lady) and "Zezé e Dinim (sombras do triunfo de ontem)" (Zezé and Dinim [shadows of yesterday's triumph]). The first story is the most hopeful of the three, indicating the possibility of access to social citizenship.[59] "Cartas a uma jovem senhora" and "Zezé e Dinim" take up the themes of disenchantment and anomie that are a *Leitmotif* in most stories of *Inferno provisório*. *O livro das impossibilidades* thus juxtaposes varying outcomes of the struggle to access socioeconomic enfranchisement. In this tome of *Inferno provisório*, we glimpse a tenuous light at the end of the tunnel, a promise that is fulfilled—in the frame of this manuscript—only in *Guia afetivo da periferia*.

In *O livro das impossibilidades*, polyphony communicates the divergent and yet similar routes taken by the book's various characters as they attempt to transcend their constricted material circumstances. Emblematic is the book's last story, "Zezé e Dinim," which relays the life of the two title characters from their birth, during the carnival celebrations of 1960, to their demise. "Zezé e Dinim" has a dual structure that echoes both the book's geographic dichotomy and the discrepancy between aspiration and reality, between possibility and impossibility, which confronts many of the volume's and of *Inferno provisório*'s characters.

Dichotomy is foreshadowed by the citation from Genesis 1:1–5 that opens "Zezé e Dinim." The passage, which describes how God created day and night, highlights the duality between light and darkness. This differentiation allegorizes the two paths traced by the story, namely the lives of the title characters, whose biographies coincide, bifurcate, and finally merge tragically. Zezé and Dinim represent two expressions of social and existential implosion. The metaphor of darkness and light evokes the options faced by the story's two central characters. But unlike the duality delineated in the biblical citation (sky and earth, day and night), "Zezé e Dinim" highlights the grey zones of sociability in which violence is pervasive. Nonetheless, as in most of *Inferno provisório*'s stories, violence is not overt. Instead, it simmers beneath the narrative surface, in constant tension until it explodes at the very end. According to Regina Dalcastagné, the insidious violence in this and other of *Inferno provisório*'s stories conveys the everyday tragedies faced by the books' characters ("A cidade e seus restos" 5).

Zezé and Dinim are born on the same day, under different and yet similar circumstances. Whereas the former's father ambles thoughtlessly about in an alcoholic stupor, barely conscious of the arrival of his firstborn, the latter's awaits in the hospital lobby, prognosticating for the newborn the hopes of a better life, one that will compensate his own mediocre and frustrated existence. Though Afonso, Dinim's father, is relegated to the ranks of the *pés-rapados* (literally "scrapped-foot," the expression translates into "dirt poor"), he wants his son to climb the social ladder.

Social rank is, like in other stories of *Inferno provisório*, delineated in the description of the characters' living quarters. While Dinim's surroundings portent a paucity that aspires to a lower-middle-class status, Zezé's environs indicate a functional but indelible poverty. Thus, in the first instance, the dilapidated sofa, a metaphor of the family's unsteady financial stability, coexists with the little comforts painstakingly afforded by Afonso's fixed but barely sufficient income, such as an Avon brochure. These small luxuries "esganavam o mês inda inconcluso" (Ruffato, *Livro* 96).[60] The impression of material comfort afforded by the small luxuries is contradicted by the verb *esganar* (to strangle), which anthropomorphizes the family's expenses, imbuing them with a menacing power. In the midst of this barely concealed lack, Dinim occupies center stage. Both parents project onto him their respective yearnings. Dinim, whose name, Antônio Dionísio, evokes an (im)possible *joie de vivre*, sublimates their petit bourgeois aspirations.

In contrast, Zezé, similar to the protagonist of *O menino que se trancou na geladeira*, grows up in the midst of corporeal and psychological neglect. His physical environs reveal inadequate access to the goods of social citizenship, such as health care and childcare. Whereas Dinim's father is a foreman at a local factory and hence part of Cataguases's formal economy, Zezé's mother, like many other female characters in the narrative, is part of the informal economy. She is a laundress. We never learn what the father does, but can assume that he too labors in the informal sector. Exacerbating the father's unstable figure is his alcoholism that renders him, similar to other male characters in *Inferno provisório*, violent. In sum, Zezé's family lacks the minimal economic security of salaried employment. Their living quarters mirror their financial contingency. The miniscule house is dark and damp, impregnated by the smell of stale cookies and urine-soaked diapers. As in previous stories, dirt and disarray signify not only personal abjection but also social despondence.

Though Zezé and Dinim live in the same sociogeographical space, the Beco do Zé Pinto, Dinim's circumstances reveal an uncertain attempt at social mobility. In contrast, Zezé's positioning suggests social paralysis. Dejection is stressed in the everyday subjective violence that surrounds him: the physical castigations that his parents inflict upon him. Corporeal punishment is a way to vent their frustrations. His mother, overburdened with household chores, a constant stream of infants, and an unvarying lack of money, castigates him for real and imaginary infringements. His father's aggression, on the other hand, is random and infuriates the young boy.

Everyday utensils such as a broomstick, a clothes iron, and a belt are transformed into tools of punishment, emphasizing the boy's tense domestic quotidian and the recurrence of violence within the house. The narrative relates the violence the boy suffers by enumerating these objects and the targeted body parts in a comma-less sentence. The lack of punctuation mimics the arbitrariness of the aggression, the father's blind and drunken blows. The description comes to an abrupt end in a ruptured sentence ("[d]aquele homem que, jurava um dia . . ." [*Livro* 97][61]), suggesting the transformation of physical into symbolic violence. Silence represents the unutterable, the act of patricide—the mirror image of child abuse (Cárdia).

In "Zezé e Dinim," Ruffato once again mines the text's visual dimension and transforms its composition into a polyphonic exercise. Formatting conveys the merging and the separation of the two protagonist's lives. In some parts, the story contains only one column, calling attention to a single perspective. A single narrative column juxtaposed to a blank space (where the other column should be) underscores one life story over the other, usually at different times. Finally, the text contains sections in which the page is split into two columns, each relating a different perspective.

The two columns narrate two texts, referencing the protagonists' parallel stories. Parallel texts describe the moments in which their lives take different routes. The split text can be read either contiguously or by first reading one and then the other. In contrast, a single text signifies the convergence of the characters' two life stories. "Zezé e Dinim" transforms reading into an exercise of arrangement. If we read the two columns together, the text blends the two stories and emphasizes the ties that link the two protagonists despite their disparities. The amalgamation between the character's similarities and differences is evidenced in the portion titled "O muro (novembro, 1979)" (the wall [November, 1979])

"O muro" is a fragment ripped out of secondary school notebook. The font emulates childish handwriting and the content reveals the universe of two 11-year-old boys who, in a ritual typical in Brazilian grade schools, answer their schoolmate's questionnaire. The responses reveal as much about the boys as about the time period: "Qual o seu ator preferido? 13. Tarcísio Meira *14. Tarcísio Meira* Qual a sua atriz preferida? 13. Regina Duarte *14. Renata Sorrah*" (*Livro* 132).[62] Number 13 and 14 correspond to Dinim and Zezé, respectively. Their replies allude to soap opera stars who were at the height of their popularity at the time.[63] Other answers reveal the boys' professional and social aspirations. In response to the question "What job will you have when you grow up?" Dinim replies "bank employee" and Zezé, "plumber" (*Livro* 132). While the first boy desires to enter the white-collar middle class, the second aims to have a blue-collar job in the formal sector. Indirectly, the boy's professional dreams echo their parents' job shortcomings and ambitions for their progeny. And whereas the two friends have different visions of their future, their responses also indicate a common childhood experience that transcends class. Asked what their favorite season is, both

Zezé and Dinim write "summer" (*Livro* 133), suggesting the joys of long vacations. However, in contrast to the brief moments of childish carelessness, the boys' biographies are increasingly connected by two sorts of childhood dystopias. Zezé undergoes the haphazard tyranny of his abusive father. Dinim experiences the opposite: the freedom of parental abandonment. Unifying the two paths is the dreary terrain of the school.

Insertion of precise dates at the beginning of each new section underscores the text's biographic configuration. Exact temporality, unusual in *Inferno provisório*, indicates the coming together of individual and collective histories. Zezé and Dinim's biographies intersect the country's historical development (1960–2001). Private and public spheres inform one another, and the vagaries of the individual lives are intimately connected with the transformation of the collective realm. Hence the story's subtitle *sombras do triunfo de ontem*" alludes to the development from the modernizing optimism of the 1960s and 1970s to the disenchantment at the beginning of the millennium in which the globalizing economy generates "obsolete citizens." At the end of the story—in a reference to the neoliberal globalized economy—subjects no longer fit into the models of production dictated by the global marketplace and consequently are also excluded from its patterns of consumption and, therefore, of social participation. What remains is the abject economy of criminality.

"Zezé e Dinim" focuses on how work and familial relations contribute to the subject's insertion into or exclusion from the social sphere. Whereas familial relations establish possible models of sociability, work provides or denies the individual access to social citizenship. In their article on impoverished urban juveniles, Ana Maria Q. Fausto Neto and Consuelo Quiroga identify a contradiction between the sociocultural preeminence of youth and youthfulness and the lack of opportunities for large segments of young metropolitan adults (221). Zezé and Dinim emblematize the restricted socioeconomic perspectives many lower-class young people confront, especially as jobs in industrial production wane.

Dinim's family's social ensconcing collapses after Afonso loses his job in the manufacturing plant. From this moment, lack is the keyword that organizes Dinim's life: "falta *tudo: empregocasaescolacolegasmãefamíliasossego: tudo*" (Ruffato, *Livro* 69).[64] Lack (of mother, employment, schooling, home, family, etc.) encumbers Dinim's inception into Cataguases "official" social economy. After inadequate schooling, the young boy gets involved in illicit dealings, first driving smuggled alcohol from Rio to Cataguases and then dealing drugs.

Similar to his father, whose dreams for his son turn sour, Dinim's life slowly submerges into despondency.

Zezé's trajectory is, at the same time, similar and divergent from that of his childhood friend. His path temporarily deviates from Dinim's when, fleeing his father's drinking and gambling debts, the family moves to Rio de Janeiro. It is 1972 and the Rio-Niterói Bridge is under construction. Matias, Zezé's father, finds employment at the site and the family experiences a frugal prosperity. This passage, titled "Oculto pelas nuvens" (Hidden by clouds), juxtaposes Zezé's story to radio announcements about the bridge offset by different fonts. The parallel texts suggest a connection between the modernity emblematized by the bridge and the family's own trajectory. Matias's stable employment introduces the family into the official national ambit.

Significantly, the next segment dealing with Zezé, "Queria que você estivesse aqui" (I wish you were here), set in 1975, follows the family to Brazil's Independence Day parade. Small indicators of a modest financial stability insinuate themselves into the picture: the father's polyester suit and the mother's new shoes. An obverse scenario follows this passage; when the bridge is concluded, Matias reenters the informal economy. Economic unsteadiness is accompanied by a return to drinking and gambling and by the subsequent familial crisis.

The family's dwellings tally the movement of ascension and descent: From the middle-class neighborhood of Cacuia, on the Ilha do Governador, Zezé's family must move into the Morro do Dendê, a favela also located on the Ilha do Governador. Their movement inverts the geographic impetus of social citizenship resulting from the insurgent practices that Holston describes. Instead of autoconstruction and expansion of infrastructure, Zezé and his relatives are relegated to a space of hubris.

In conjunction with lack of education, the liminal vicinity to which the family moves creates a social barrier and imbues its inhabitants with the stigma of transgression. Zezé observes that his address limits his employment prospects (Ruffato, *Livro* 145). The narrative voice demystifies the rationale of hard work as a tool of social betterment and inclusion. Indeed, employment is problematic for poor young individuals that have to cope not only with a lack of competitive resources but also with a restructured marketplace. Sociologist André Langer maintains that in the last quarter of the twentieth century, technological advancements and globalized capital require less human labor to be highly productive. In this context, the informal sector grows in detriment to formal employment. The primary victims of these changes are, according to Langer, women, minorities, workers over 45, and young people, especially impoverished youth. Poor young people are relegated to the most unstable positions. As a result these youth are haunted by insecurity and feelings of abandonment (Langer).

"Zezé e Dinim" relays the impact of these changes upon the two main characters. Like Naldinho, the young bandit in Bonassi's *Subúrbio*, Zezé and Dinim are unable to enter the formal economy. And like Naldinho, both men ultimately turn toward criminality to solve their economic woes. They are doubly banned from the realm of citizenship. On the one hand, they are barred from accessing social citizenship because of their socioeconomic standings and their status as "waste-products" of modernity (Bauman, *Wasted Lives* 12). On the other hand, their transgression, tied to the supernumerary position in which they find themselves, intensifies their social exclusion. Zezé and Dinim's physical localization on the metropolitan outskirts and the prison, respectively, translates this segregation into the material realm. In this framework, the liminal space of the penitentiary becomes an alternate terrain of socialization. It is here that Zezé and Dinim cross paths again, and it is here that they establish a community of sorts with other detainees.

Interactions within the penal territory create dubious webs of agency through illegal exchanges. Zezé becomes a mule for his friends and his companions. He transports illicit wares to and from the prison with the goal of saving money to buy a house for his mother. Zezé's dream of homeownership, a marker of budding insertion into social citizenship, is perversely attained. The real estate he purchases is a nondescript lot in the municipal cemetery. Anonymity—that is, social irrelevance—beyond death is underlined by the grave's arrangement: a mere heap of earth topped by a meager cross. The layout suggests the dead woman's invisibility within the public sphere while alive (and after her death).

The story's ending, titled "Ecos" (Echoes), is set in the new millennium (November of 2001), and is a précis of the chain of frustrations that punctuated the characters' lives. Incarcerated after a failed kidnapping, Dinim confronts his past actions, including his guilt over Zezé's death, a fallout of the ill-fated abduction. Dinim has no memory until after his friend's death. But this memory is his symbolic shackles. His memories disrupt his present, leaving him prostrate in the face of the past. He has agency over neither his memories nor his corporeality.

Within the prison, Dinim experiences systemic brutalization: "Doem as costas, murros socos pontapés chutes bicudas bofetões sopapos pescoções bordoadas pancadas pauladas cabeçadas pisões, o médico ficou de pedir uma chapa, até hoje" (Ruffato, *Livro* 153).[65] Once again the unbroken enumeration of physical aggression transmits both the recurrence and the arbitrariness of violence within the penal system. Different types of beatings emphasize brutal randomness. And while certain types of thrashing are particular to institutional agents (*bordoadas*), others can be perpetrated by either guards or fellow inmates, conjuring omnipresent violence. Indeed, state-endorsed and unofficial biopolitics of violence are used to control the hubristic subject and to strip him of his *bios* (Agamben, *Homo Sacer* 126). Situated between two forms of aggression and without recourse of civil or social protection, Dinim is effectively in a space beyond citizenship.

UNCERTAIN JOURNEYS: MIGRATION AND CITIZENSHIP IN *O MUNDO INIMIGO* AND *O LIVRO DAS IMPOSSIBILIDADES*

As indicated earlier, the transformation of the urban and social landscape is a recurring theme of *Inferno provisório*. The books describe the geographical movements of its working-class characters from rural to urban terrains and from one metropolitan area to another. Voluntary or involuntary relocation results from economic transformations and represents the search for better living conditions. *Inferno provisório*'s characters continually struggle to accede to a more inclusive form of social citizenship. They seek better employment in conurbations such as São Paulo and, consequently, must forcefully extract themselves from familiar networks of sociability.

O mundo inimigo specifically contrasts Cataguases to São Paulo. The two cities are linked by the aspirations and the disillusionments of the people that transit between them. Paradigmatic are the stories "Amigos" (Friends) and "A demolição" (The demolition). The two narratives center on individuals that left Cataguases to try their luck in the megalopolis and who, for various reasons, return to their hometown.

Speaking of Brazilian novels that thematize migration, Tânia Pellegrini ascertains that these texts touch upon the formation of the country's middle class, formed, in large part, by immigrant populations (*Despropósitos* 30). "Amigos" and "A demolição" underscore the nexus between migration, middle-class formation, and changing sociability. While internal migration creates new forms of identification, it also engenders new modes of estrangement. In the two stories, the pendular movement between departure and return home condenses the characters' sense of isolation (despite or because of their entrance into the petite bourgeoisie). The characters of "Amigos" and "A demolição" are at home neither in Cataguases nor in São Paulo.

Beyond oscillating between two geographic territories, "Amigos," which opens *O mundo inimigo*, also centers on the tension between the space of the past and the terrain of the present. The story depicts the reencounter of two childhood friends: Luzimar and Gildo. Luzimar lives in Cataguases and works in one of the local factories. Gildo has moved to São Paulo and is visiting his mother over Christmas. This narrative is complemented by the volume's second story, "A demolição," which concentrates on Gildo's brother, Gilmar. Gilmar, a former soccer prodigy, also resides in São Paulo. Both brothers repudiate Cataguases as a place of mediocrity and stagnation. In contrast, São Paulo epitomizes social advancement, access into the sphere of consumption, and as such, access into the ambit of citizenship. Both Gilmar and Gildo, who become part of the urban consuming public, symbolize the accomplishment of the urban working class (Holston, *Insurgent*).

Gilmar and Gildo lead a solid middle-class existence—emblematized by the latter's 1300 VW Beetle and by the former's status as a small business owner. Autoconstruction—Gilmar's establishment started out as a remodeled garage—enables him to enter an incipient middle class, and to aspire to the symbolic goods that define this class—in this case, a trip to Disney World.

Homeownership, having a car, and being able to travel signify a new mode of perceiving citizenship. Instead of being constructed in terms of social, civil, or even political rights (education, access to health care and social security, public security and adequate infrastructure, voting and association rights, to name but a few), citizenship is associated with the right to consume. Expediency allows for new modes of group identification and representation (Canclini, *Consumers*; Appadurai and Holston). Global culture—exemplified here by Disney World—exacerbates the disavowal of local ties and of local forms of citizenship (such as participation in neighborhood associations or general involvement with local and national politics). Instead, globalized culture establishes alternate forms of identification. Symbolic goods that connote a global consciousness assert middle-class status in Brazil (O'Dougherty 94). The desire to travel to Disney World, a symbol of North American mass culture that has spread internationally, represents a metaphoric entrance into a typical Brazilian middle-class imaginary in which this kind of excursion is perceived as both a rite of passage (from childhood into teenager) and a status symbol.

Similarly, the possession of a car, together with homeownership, suggests the integration into this same imaginary. Both car and home are private spaces in which the citizen finds refuge from a conflicted public sphere. Referring to the importance of homeownership within Brazilian working classes, sociologist Lúcio Kowarik maintains that owning (and building) a residence points to the change of citizenship from the public to the private sphere. Through homeownership the subject becomes what Kowarik terms a "private citizen." The private citizen represents the successful self-made man (94). If a home of one's own denotes a measure of financial stability and is a signifier of achievement (Banck), then the private vehicle serves equally as a means of distinction from those who depend on public transportation for their locomotion. The car reproduces the private space of the home, inferring consumer status on her/his proprietor.

In comparison to the two brothers, who have attained all the afore-mentioned indicators of middle-class status, their childhood friend Luzimar tethers in the brink of solvency. He does not even have enough money to buy a Christmas gift for his wife. Cataguases, which in *Mamma, son tanto felice* signified the possibility of partaking in Brazil's incipient modernity, now represents socioeconomic and personal stagnation. In "Amigos," each character's social condition parallels her/his respective geographic location. São Paulo is metonymic for progress and the potential of socioeconomic improvement. Cataguases signifies backwardness and socioeconomic immobility.

Beyond his car, Gildo flaunts the brand new television he bought for his mother. The disparity between this gift and Luzimar's inability to purchase a present for his wife highlights the differences between the two men and the two geoeconomic spaces they represent. Cataguases, which suffered an economic decline in the late 1970s, is paradigmatic of Brazil's transforming economic panorama. Though this trend has been changing recently, until the early 2000s industrial production had been concentrated around large metropolitan areas, such as São Paulo. Human and capital flight created a blighted urban landscape in midsize industrial towns such as Cataguases, impacting their inhabitants' *Lebenswelt*.

Luzimar feels trapped in Cataguases's stultifying reality, bogged down by the personal and material circumstances that inhibit change, let alone betterment. When Gildo suggests that he accompany him to São Paulo, Luzimar responds that it is too late for him to begin anew. Their dialogue interleaves Gildo's deprecation of Cataguases with the men's evocations of their childhood games. But these remembrances no longer provide Gildo with an anchor. His dislocation has erased the human bonds that linked him to the city. For him, Cataguases is a mirage from the past.

Disengagement becomes Luzimar's sine qua non condition. It is therefore significant that after his encounter with Gildo, he ends up in a bar. It is 11:30 pm on Christmas Eve. The return home to his wife and the holiday, a symbolic date of peace and unity, loses significance in light of a constrained futurity. Cataguases becomes the space of a living past, as is evidenced in both Gildo's and Gilmar's problematic relation to the city.

Though both brothers despise their hometown, they seek in it (vainly) a sentiment of belonging. Repudiation is tinged with nostalgia. In both "Amigos" and "A demolição," memory figures prominently. "A demolição" deals with the impending demolition of Gildo and Gilmar's childhood home after the neighbor's son, who had immigrated to the United States, buys it to expand his mother's home (which is located next door).

On the one hand, the house's sale and destruction allows the brothers to fulfill their social ambitions (i.e., the trip to Disney World). On the other hand, the demolition also connotes the ruins of childhood and of the attachments of this period. Significantly, "A demolição" ends with a symbolic return to the space of childhood, represented by an unfinished basement. The basement suggests the terrain of recollection, where experiences are lost in an in-between space. It is here that one of Gilmar's friends "vanishes" looking for a lost soccer ball. The boy's disappearance foreshadows the progressive dismantlement of the group of companions and, by extension, Gildo's and Luzimar's estrangement.

Notwithstanding the economic differentiation between the two men and the two conurbations, "Amigos" ultimately does not construct a dichotomy between São Paulo and Cataguases. Rather, the two cities are linked by the same fragmented sociability that prevails in both spaces. The community afforded by family and friends has eroded in the face of the necessity to either survive or advance materially.

Similar to "Amigos" and "A demolição," "Era uma vez" (Once upon a time, *O livro das impossibilidades*) concentrates on the small achievements of the urban working class in the wake of migration to large cities. In this manner, the book augurs the social shifts of the present that will be discussed more in depth in Chapter 4. First, like the two stories discussed in this segment, "Era uma vez" too signals the increment of population in metropolitan areas. Second, the account points toward the promise of socioeconomic ascension that will materialize in the twenty-first century. Since 2002, increasing numbers of people have climbed from poverty into the lower middle classes thanks, in part, to social programs such as the *Bolsa Família*.[66]

"Era uma vez" centers on how the working classes attain a measure of material agency within Brazil's structure of differentiated citizenship. Set in 1976 and in an undated present, "Era uma vez" gives continuation to the stories of migration and partial socioeconomic empowerment charted in *O mundo inimigo*.

"Era uma vez" opens with a chance encounter in a São Paulo department store. The first-person narrator recognizes an old acquaintance in the security guard at the Mappin store. As implied by the title, the meeting triggers a flood of memories that constitute the narrative body: "*Nílson, tapa no ombro, lembra de mim?* Lembraria? Uma semana que descarrilhou um até então assegurado destino, que, de estação em estação, tragava os dias sonolentos e galhardo rumava para a mesmice de pais, irmãos, amigos" (Ruffato, *Livro* 15).[67] How the narrator's destiny changed remains vague throughout the story, though the locale of the encounter (São Paulo), and the remembrances that ensue from this event suggest his displacement from the middling quotidian of industrial labor in Cataguases to a more promising future in the megalopolis.[68]

Journey is the keyword of "Era uma vez." The story is constructed around three voyages. Framing the narration is the protagonist's and his father's weeklong trip to São Paulo to visit family. Encapsulated in this account is Nelly's journey. Nelly, the daughter of Guto's godmother, abandoned Cataguases looking for better opportunities in São Paulo. Finally, the last journey of "Era uma vez" is the one alluded to in the story's opening: the narrator's own dislocation to São Paulo and the transformation of his destiny thanks to that long-ago trip.

Nelly embodies the possibility of social ascension yearned for by Cataguases's blue-collar migrants. After moving to São Paulo, she discovers that her husband, who she thought belonged to the ranks of the urban petit bourgeoisie, lives in a shack in the Saúde neighborhood. Her trajectory, nonetheless, affirms the notion of self-made success that characterizes the upward mobile social sectors in Brazil's urban centers.

Nowadays Saúde is a middle-class neighborhood located to the east of São Paulo's downtown. It has a large Japanese- and European-descendant population and was one of the first districts to be serviced by metro (since 1976). Thus, though initially Nelly's house suggests low-income status, the localization intimates the possibility of entering the ranks of what sociologist Jessé Souza calls *Os batalhadores* (the fighters). Unlike the traditional middle class that, according to Souza is defined as such due to their access to cultural capital, the *batalhadores* must generally enter the job market early and do not possess the cultural capital that characterizes the middle sectors. They tend to compensate for this lack with extraordinary personal effort, particularly in terms of labor (Souza, Interview by Uirá Machado).

The *batalhadores*, as suggested by the term, are partially motivated by the dissatisfaction caused by their positioning in the fissures of social citizenship. Their work ethic functions as a tool against their precarious socioeconomic condition. They employ strategies such as autoconstruction to chip away at the mechanisms of differentiated citizenship—to varying degrees of success.

Nelly, for example, transforms herself through an incessant cycle of production that allows her to attain the material indicators of financial stability. Her time is spent in constant labor. She is able to "erguer um puxadinho, adquirir uma geladeira, pôr tacos no chão, pintar as paredes, levantar um dois-cômodos para alugar, concretar uma laje, crescer, demarcar o mundo, preenchê-lo . . . dinheiro não falta" (Ruffato, *Livro* 18–19).[69] Nelly's incessant movement suggests both ambition and discipline.

For James Holston, the influx of working-class members into cities—specifically, into the peripheries—affected a transformation not only in their social status but also in their self-perception. Their access to the "modern urban economy" (*Insurgent* 8) prompted them to develop agency as inhabitants of the city and as modern consumers. As such, they became an integral part of Brazil's civil, social, and political realms. Both the autoconstructed working-class homes and working-class neighborhoods reflect this process (8). Of course, since insurgent citizenship can promote other types of differentiation, the urban boundaries are pushed further away from the metropolitan center. Insurgency promotes a constant redefinition of the city's frontiers.

"Era uma vez" highlights what Holston terms "unequal achievements" through the contrast between Nelly's success and the relative decrepitude of the house. The dwelling represents both the security of homeownership and the constraints faced by the family. Its atmosphere is dark and damp, echoing the description of Cataguases's poor homes. In fact, Nelly's residence appears more suffocating than the working-class homes in Cataguases. The adjectives that describe the house—constricted, dark, airless (Ruffato, *Livro* 28)—evoke dilapidation and disease and expose the cracks in the veneer of wellbeing that homeownership and access to modern consumption supposedly guarantee. It is significant that "Era uma vez" contains more detailed descriptions of the domestic interior and of the characters' clothing than any other story of *Inferno provisório*. These elements situate the characters within both a given social and cultural milieu. They are the markers of (albeit limited) economic progress and at the same time of the limits of this progress.

Juxtaposed to the signposts of modern consumption that express the working class' insertion into the realm of social citizenship (via expenditure) is Guto, the narrator, who is 15. At this age, he represents Cataguases's stagnation, the limited futurity outside the country's large metropolitan spheres. His clothes disclose the inherent inertia of his existence. Unlike his São Paulo cousins, who don the fashion emblems of teenage identity, Guto's attire expresses his middling social status and his discomfort with the new, supposedly urbane, reality surrounding him. His clothes are clean but modest and antiquated. Unlike Nelly and her two children, Nílson and Natalia, Guto does not have access to the realm of modern consumption, the result of the agency afforded by insurgent practices of citizenship, and the residence in Brazil's center of consumption: São Paulo.

Interestingly, the story ends with Guto and his father returning to Cataguases. Looking through the bus window, the boy observes a dejected scene: a vagrant with a putrid leg, surrounded by stray dogs. The picture does not encapsulate the metropolitan reality, but it does expose another of its facets. Contrasted to relative success stories of social empowerment are the manifold modes of disempowerment occasioned by differentiated citizenship. The vagrant condenses several of them that constitute differentiated citizenship: inadequate access to housing, health care, and employment. In his lack and desolation, he echoes many of the characters that compose *Inferno provisório*'s working-class fresco. In a way, the scene witnessed by Guto though the bus window prefigures and, at the same time, provides closure to Luiz Ruffato's *Eles eram muitos cavalos*. In this "novel," São Paulo and its manifold stages of differentiated citizenship take center stage.

CONCLUSION

In the context of *Inferno provisório*, differentiated citizenship is enacted at manifold levels, generating variegated forms of resistance and violence (as well as, at times, violent resistance). Notwithstanding, unlike the insurgent citizenships examined by Holston, in *Inferno provisório* the possibility of contestation and of reclaiming alternate forms of social and civil engagement are ultimately rather limited. The Cataguases of *Inferno provisório* is at the same time the prototype and the negation of the working-class peripheries that both deny and enable civil agency as analyzed by Holston.

While Ruffato's Cataguases contains many of the same conditions for generating insurgent manifestations of citizenship that, as Holston indicates, are present in the urban periphery of São Paulo, Cataguases is also a terminal site. If in the first volume of the series, the city represents modernity and signals the hope of social ascension through migration into the industrial urban terrain—noted initially in the book's title then, as the cycle develops, this expectation is slowly eroded by the continual failure of its many characters. By the fifth installment of *Inferno provisório*, the anticipation of socioeconomic advancement is largely foiled by the transformation in modes of production and the accompanying modification of the state's role vis-à-vis its citizens. This is to say, as *Inferno provisório* develops, we also see the development of a capitalist and, more recently, a neoliberal rationale.

The subjects of Ruffato's narratives are mostly trapped in existences that vary from mediocre to miserable, and several struggle to transcend not only their geographic space (by repeating the trajectory of countless rural, small, and midsize town migrants into the larger conurbations of southeastern Brazil) but also their social conditions. Most of the characters in the books are unsuccessful in this endeavor. And when they do not fail entirely, their relative success becomes a measure of their middling existences. This is particularly evident in *O livro das impossibilidades*, whose very title alludes to the paralysis that governs the characters' lives. Emblematic is Nelly of "Era uma vez." Though she struggles and attains a degree of socioeconomic success, this does not presuppose personal fulfillment: "Feliz talvez fosse. Pensasse nisso, talvez não. Mas não pensa" (Ruffato, *Livro* 19).[70] Underlying disenchantment permeates *Inferno provisório*'s other stories of—apparently—successful migration. Although economic success is achieved, there remains a residue of dissatisfaction that implies a continual struggle for admittance into the spaces of citizenship. In *Inferno provisório*, citizenship is thus not a guaranteed right, but rather the result of ongoing practices of (mostly symbolic) insurgency and parallel acceptance of the *status quo*.

CHAPTER 2

FRIDGES AND SUBURBS IN THE NEW WORLD ORDER
FERNANDO BONASSI'S SPACES OF ABJECTION

In this chapter, I examine how Fernando Bonassi's two novels, *Subúrbio* and *O menino que se trancou na geladeira*, portray the correlation between deficient social policies, the result of neoliberal measures and differentiated citizenship. In both of Bonassi's novels, differentiated citizenship leads to violent and sterile forms of insurgency that further weaken an already fragile public sphere.

After a general discussion about Brazil's infrastructural woes and about Bonassi's literary output with respect to its social commentary, the chapter is divided into two parts, each dealing with a different novel by Bonassi. In the first segment, I examine how Bonassi's *romance reportagem* (report novel), *O menino que se trancou na geladeira*, dialogues with Brazil's socioeconomic transformation in the wake of neoliberal measures. *O menino que se trancou na geladeira* is an allegory of posttransitional Brazil and of the country's adoption of a neoliberal agenda. In his novel, Bonassi communicates the sense of estrangement and disrepair that prevailed in Brazil during the 1980s and 1990s. The novel's innovative, peculiar, and disjointed language is a metaphor of the fissures in political, civil, and social citizenship during these two decades.

The metaphorical fissures become material in the text's representation of infrastructure. In *O menino que se trancou na geladeira*, infrastructure (hospitals, schools, public spaces) is the vortex around which social citizenship is constructed. Inadequate access to proper infrastructure denotes differentiated citizenship. In this context, insurgent citizenship aims to rectify the infrastructural deficit by constructing a parallel, private infrastructural grid. This recourse to the private sphere as a "remedy" for differentiated citizenship signals the decline of the public sphere due to differentiated citizenship.

In the chapter's second segment, I analyze how *Subúrbio* locates differentiated citizenship in the working-class neighborhoods of São Paulo's outskirts. In this manner, Bonassi's text continues and expands upon Ruffato's portrayal of the impact of differentiated citizenship upon Brazil's working classes. In the *paulista* periphery, social inequality manifests itself in everyday miseries and infuses the landscape, its residents, and their social relations with abjection. *Subúrbio* creates a link between individual and communitarian bodies—both are depicted as deteriorating organisms; both experience the effects of differentiated citizenship upon their own "flesh." The corrosion of social landscape, of physical bodies, and of interpersonal relations creates nets of violence that are both a reaction to and continuation of differentiated citizenship.

Citizenship is a byproduct of the modern state. Holston observes that modern states have used citizenship as a means of establishing social programs that structured the populations within geopolitical borders. Conversely, the idea of citizenship also fomented social cohesion among national populations (*Insurgent* 21). As part of the configuration of citizenship, the modern state ordered national spaces through the creation of an infrastructure that maintained a vigilant eye on its citizens (Foucault, *Discipline*) while, at least in theory, providing them with a measure of social assistance (through hospitals, schools, recreational areas, prisons, etc.). At the same time that the citizen had access to the nation's infrastructural goods, she or he also accepted the parameters the state established that regulated belonging and, by extension, entitlements. The sociopolitical subject thus was inextricably linked to the nation's symbolic and physical infrastructure, as citizenship became defined not only in terms of civil and political rights and responsibilities, but also in terms of access to public goods (Marshall). Citizenship therefore implied belonging to a certain sociocultural as well as political community.

In Brazil, the modernizing impetus of the Vargas era transformed the conception of citizenship while simultaneously preserving some of the nation's socioeconomic as well as political structures (Reis). Sociologist Eliza Reis observes that in Brazil, social citizenship actually developed *before* both political and civil rights—the opposite of the order conceptualized by T. H. Marshall. Specifically, during Getúlio Vargas's tenure, access to social citizenship grew while both civil and political rights remained circumscribed (Reis 174). In this context, access to social citizenship was tied to formal labor.[1]

Formal employment was linked to Vargas's national-developmentalist project in which the state became a provider of economic development and social goods. Nonetheless, at the same time that an emerging working class gained more social rights, a large segment of the populace continued to be excluded from social citizenship (not to mention, from civil and political rights). Informal laborers lacked—and to a degree still lack—the entitlements afforded by formal work (minimum wage, paid vacations, maternity leave). These are members of what sociologist Jessé Souza calls Brazil's *ralé* (riff-raff), alluding to their disenfranchised status.[2]

Industrial production not only defined the status of the individual, but it also represented/supported a unified project of nationhood. Theoretically each citizen's work contributed to the collective good by impelling the country's economic development. Reis maintains that this ideology, a "compound involving nationalism, statism, and developmentalism," created a sense of national belonging and helped people to obviate some of the country's social inequalities (190). This configuration has undergone significant changes in the last three decades, as Brazil's posttransition governments retreated from the national-developmentalist model and adopted—to varying degrees—a neoliberal paradigm.

Nowadays the profusion of consumer goods, peoples, images, and ideas destabilizes the notion of "national belonging" (Appadurai; Hannerz). This is particularly evident in global metropolises where the contact between the local and transnational becomes intensely manifest (Appadurai and Holston). Cities, especially large conurbations such as New York, Los Angeles, Paris, London, and São Paulo, alter the notion of citizenship (Appadurai and Holston; Holston, "Spaces"). For some of the denizens of these cities, citizenship is no longer bound to geopolitical boundaries. Rather, as Appadurai, Holston, and Sassen indicate, in metropolitan centers associations that transcend the nation-state are apparent in everyday life. Transnational influences and alliances become visible, for example, through the adoption of fashion and music styles and through the presence of diverse ethnic and business communities in a single, if sprawling, urban landscape.

It is also in big metropolitan centers that the differentials, especially in social and civil citizenship, are the most apparent. As a result of these disjunctions, the conception of citizenship as a communitarian experience becomes brittle (Appadurai and Holston). Differences in formal and substantive citizenship that are the product of past (colonialism and neocolonialism, slavery, etc.) and recent sociopolitical, historical, and cultural developments highlight the heterogeneity of the performance (if not always in the formulation) of citizenship.

The weakening of social citizenship no longer entirely runs down the lines that separate formal and informal labor; socioeconomic divisions continue to typify Brazilian society. With the Washington Consensus and the spread of neoliberal globalization, traditional conceptions of citizenship based on the liberal model have declined due to the transformed role of the state vis-à-vis its citizens. Since the late 1970s and early 1980s, the prevalence of a neoliberal rationale has decreased the role of the state as the provider of social goods. This, in turn, diluted national identifications. According to David Harvey, the main goal of the neoliberal state is to create favorable conditions for private investment and profitability (*History of Neoliberalism* 7). The idea of the "national good" that corresponds to a contract between the state and the community of its citizens becomes secondary to "economic viability" and "fiscal responsibility." In this frame of reference, citizenship no longer is defined in terms of the rights and responsibilities of the members of a given nation, but rather as rights to consume the goods traditionally associated with citizenship (Bauman *Liquid Times*; Giroux). The guiding principle of profitable capital accumulation implies that individual rights are constrained by the logic of capital and are analogous to the citizen's ability to contribute to this rationale, especially through her/his capability to consume. The subject becomes increasing cast into what Wendy Brown calls *homo œconomicus. Homo œconomicus* is determined by the rationale of investment, productivity, and profitability (40–41).

As suggested in Chapter 1, the impact of socioeconomic, civil, and (albeit to a lesser degree) political transformations on the formulation and enactment of citizenship has become a recurrent theme in the fictional output of writers that identify literature with social action. Texts such as Ruffato's *Inferno provisório* and Ferréz's *Capão Pecado* and *Manual prático do ódio* depict the pitfalls of differentiated citizenship (public and private violence, anomie, and manifold expressions of material need, such as hunger and the inability to access proper health care and education). At the same time, these books suggest modes to create agency via literary, or more generally, cultural production.

Like Ruffato and Ferréz, Fernando Bonassi is among the contemporary authors who view literature as a tool of social critique and action. And just like Ruffato, Bonassi sees in Brazil's working class and, until recently, vanishing middle class a barometer of the social changes that affected the country in recent years (M. Silva, "A narrativa"). His prose thus covers Brazil's recent military dictatorship and the transition to democracy (*O céu e o fundo do mar* [The sky and the bottom of the sea, 1999] and *Prova contrária* [Counter proof, 2003]), as well as the dilapidation of the country's working classes since the 1970s (*Subúrbio, Um céu de estrelas* [A sky full of stars, 1991]). Bonassi also has written about the everyday violence that devastates Brazil's metropolitan centers (*[Pânico—horror and morte]. O amor em chamas* [(Panic—horror and death): love in flames, 1989], *100 histórias colhidas na rua* [100 stories gathered from the streets, 1996], and *Entre a vida e a morte. Casos de polícia* [Between life and death: police cases, 2004]).

Beyond this, Bonassi has produced allegorical fictions that merge both present and past forms of sociopolitical violence in Brazil. Among these are *Diário da guerra de São Paulo* [Diary of the battle of São Paulo, 2007) and *O menino que se trancou na geladeira*. Both novels are set in an unspecified and dystopian future that resembles contemporary Brazilian society. Their protagonists are children who have precociously and violently lost their innocence. The texts' linguistic disruptions (neologisms, unfamiliar syntax and punctuation, among others) highlight the social dysfunction that they portray and, in a Brechtian move, also defamiliarize this reality by establishing a critical distance between reader and text.

Indeed, like Ruffato, Bonassi paradoxically resorts to realist language in order to subvert the realist narrative mode. Maurício Silva classifies Bonassi's narrative as "suburban realism" (M. Silva, *Imaginários suburbanos* 2). Many of Bonassi's texts, such as *Subúrbio*, employ everyday speech while at the same time severing the speech act. In *Subúrbio*, Bonassi reproduces the fractured coexistence between an elderly couple by mimicking its laconic communication:

—Você tá ouvindo esse barulho?
O braço de ferro. Ainda o velho:
—Esse . . .
A velha voltou e sentou encolhida num canto. No mesmo lugar. Ele olhou a têmpora dela. A velha não pôde mais evitar:
—Eu?
—É.
—Não.
E como o velho duvidasse do que ela estava falando, perguntou para se certificar:
—O quê? (60)[3]

Fragmented dialogue transmits the spouses' estrangement and the bitterness that contaminates their relationship. Their "communication" is sterile—indicated by the single words that dot the pages—and cannot produce mutual understanding.

Disjointed language also communicates the disrupted realities of Brazil's working-class citizens as they deal with the manifestations and consequences of differentiated citizenship. In *Subúrbio*, the narrative voice oscillates between first, second, and third persons, multiplying perspectives and truncating the mimetic mode. Multiple points of view suggest a quotidian marked by social and existential fragmentation and isolation.

Like in *Subúrbio*, in *O menino que se trancou na geladeira* Bonassi both remains within and departs from the realist mode. He destabilizes not only narrative language, but also the reality that this language purports to communicate. Specifically, *O menino que se trancou na geladeira* parodies the hyperrealist genre of the *romance reportagem* by subverting the genre's realist language and narrative framework. In the book's epilogue, titled "D.F. Depois do Fim (a pedido, ou imposição dos editores)" (A.E. After the end [upon the request or the imposition of the editors]) the third-person narrative voice disproves the mimetic mode of the *romance reportagem* by calling attention to the genre's imperative of verisimilitude that makes the text more marketable (Bonassi, *Menino* 215).[4]

In contrast to the realist prerequisite for narrative coherence, *O menino que se trancou na geladeira* offers us a splintered plotline that often meanders into the absurd. This structure repudiates precisely that which it purports to communicate: a reality that can be conveyed in an unproblematic fashion. Indeed, if *O menino que se trancou na geladeira* is an incongruous narrative, it is because the conditions that the book sets out to describe are absurd and escape the signifying powers of language.

Therein lies the "power" of *O menino que se trancou na geladeira*. The novel juxtaposes real-life events (the 1964–85 dictatorship, the country's neoliberal turn, the influence of global culture, etc.) to a highly fictionalized version of these occurrences. In the interstices between the two versions, the narrative creates a symbolic space of contestation, a terrain of insurgency that relies on the discourse it interrogates to undermine it and consequently establish a critique of differentiated citizenship.

CRUMBLING CITIES, CRUMBLING SUBJECTS: THE DISINTEGRATION OF PUBLIC AND PRIVATE INFRASTRUCTURE IN FERNANDO BONASSI'S *O MENINO QUE SE TRANCOU NA GELADEIRA*

Fernando Bonassi's (anti) *romance reportagem*, *O menino que se trancou na geladeira* approaches the link between the material and symbolic dimensions of public infrastructure, connecting these facets with the construction and deconstruction of citizenship, individual identity, and the public sphere in contemporary Brazil. Through the representation of the decadence of public and private (infra)structure (material and figurative), the novel allegorizes the transformation of the Brazilian nation and of citizenship in the globalized era, in which the state's task is downgraded to "prover todos de um pouco insuficiente, de forma que muitos se exasperassem coletivamente" (Bonassi, *Menino* 92).[5] Infrastructure, coupled in Bonassi's novel with a neoliberal agenda, becomes inextricably linked to expediency and to differentiated (or inexistent) citizenship.

Published in 2004, in the aftermath of Fernando Henrique Cardoso's term and one year into Lula's presidency, *O menino que se trancou na geladeira* unearths the legacy of the country's most recent authoritarian experience and critiques Brazil's increased neoliberalization during the 1990s. *O menino que se trancou na geladeira*, like *Subúrbio*, attempts to come to terms with the changes that this process has wrought on Brazilian society and on its sociopolitical and cultural imaginary.

Whereas *Subúrbio*, like Ruffato's *Inferno provisório*, deals with the erosion of citizenship within the ambit of the urban working classes, *O menino que se trancou na geladeira* focuses on how the weakening of social citizenship encroached on the country's middle class. In the decades following the bust of the Brazilian economic miracle in the 1970s and the ensuing economic crisis, the country's middle classes underwent a sociocultural identity crisis. The markers that hitherto had defined middle-class status—such as stable employment, access to education, homeownership, and the ability to save and consume (O'Dougherty 9)—unraveled in the face of the economic crisis that gripped the country. Maureen O'Dougherty asserts that the crisis that gripped Brazil and its middle classes during this period led to the very questioning of what she calls the middle class "project," characterized in large part by models of consumption.

Alluding to this sociohistorical context, *O menino que se trancou na geladeira* demonstrates how class definition is intimately tied to lifestyle, which the bourgeoisie takes for granted. This social standing, which is connoted not only by material but also by symbolic goods (Bourdieu), teeters on the brink of disaster. Instability creates tensions that affect social relationships within the domestic and the public ambits. The result is conflicted conviviality. The novel's protagonist rejects any human interaction (Bonassi, *Menino* 48).

O menino que se trancou na geladeira combines different narrative genres: science fiction, satire, and dystopian Bildungsroman. The novel illustrates the "socialization" of its protagonist while also tracing a panorama of Brazilian society in recent decades. Parodying Christian historiography, the text is divided in four segments: "Primeira parte: A.G. (Antes da Geladeira)" (First part: B.F. [(Before the fridge]), "Parte do meio: P.M. (Um novo conceito em refrigerator de última geração brota do Deserto)" (Middle part: M.P. [A new concept of fridge sprouts from the desert]), "Segunda parte: D.G. (Depois da geladeira)" (Second part: A.F. [After the fridge]), and "D.F. Depois do Fim (a pedido, ou imposição dos editores)" (A.E. After the end [By request or imposition of the editors]). The second and fourth segments combine the spiritual allusion to Christian history with the language of advertisement slogans and a jab at the editorial market, respectively.

By mingling "religious" and worldly discourses, Bonassi points to the entanglement between religion and the ethos of the marketplace (an allusion that will resurface throughout the text and to which we will return). Using these, as well as other parodic historical signposts, the book creates a mock national historiography of a country referred to as "Civilização Brasileira." (Brazilian Civilization). This mock historiography becomes a counterpoint to the official writing of history that, according to the novel, is a monopoly of the "Governo Nacional" (National Government), which presides over the Civilização Brasileira. The Governo Nacional uses the writing of history not only to cast itself in the best light, but also to justify a series of corrupt and antidemocratic measures. State-sponsored repression is supported by unnamed and yet identifiable external powers: there are several allusions to the "Estados Suínos" (Swine States), a powerful neighbor to the north,[6] and to the "Frente Rústica" (Rustic Front), a reference to the former Soviet Union.

Official historiography is further demystified by belittling its means of propagation: the "little books" (livrinhos) in which it appears. The diminutive form erodes historiographic narrative authority and transforms "history" into a children's story—an allusion underscored by the novel's title. Instead of authoritative historiographical accounts, we have an untrustworthy story. Whereas "truth," including histo-riographic truth, becomes a construct of (armed) power, fiction is the "lie" that corrodes this power.

The novel's plot revolves around a young boy who is abandoned by both father and mother, becomes an orphan, suffers an amorous disillusionment, and consequently goes into self-imposed exile, cross-ing a material and metaphoric wasteland—all in short succession. The protagonist's escape into the desert emulates biblical narratives of Diaspora and exile such as the wanderings of the Hebrews in the desert, Christ's retreat into the desert, or Saint John the Baptist's years of exile.

After several trials with many errors, the protagonist of *O menino que se trancou na geladeira* withdraws into a refrigerator. The appli-ance is a refuge from the outside world. It is a substitute iron womb equipped with the latest survival and surveillance technology. The refrigerator allows the boy to isolate himself, observe his surround-ings, and participate in them vicariously. Locked in the fridge, the anonymous protagonist undergoes a reverse socialization process that leads to alienation rather than a strengthening of social bonds.

After his apprenticeship, he returns triumphantly from his exile—though remaining safely in his mobile and hermetic fridge—and becomes a successful (if corrupt) independent television producer. Specifically, the protagonist creates reality shows that allow him to both pretend to participate in said "reality" and to manipulate it.

O menino que se trancou na geladeira documents how exclusion (literally, the protagonist's voluntary seclusion in the appliance), a met-aphor for differentiated citizenship, is converted into a peculiar form of inclusion. On the one hand, the boy's alienation exposes a causal relationship between the lack of agency and nonexistent community/communitarian ethos. On the other hand, segregation spawns and sig-nals an insurgency that both challenges and reinforces the conditions of differentiated citizenship. *O menino que se trancou na geladeira* documents its protagonist's transition from existential and social abjec-tion into an atomized societal order. In the novel, disenfranchisement transforms citizenship from communitarian involvement to individual-ized, privatized performance. Demands for civil and social rights are circumscribed within the personal realm (Goirand).

Language

Bonassi, who is also a playwright[7] and has written screenplays for both cinema and television, resorts to unusual vocabulary in order to create a Brechtian distancing effect (*Verfremdungseffekt*). The influence of this dramatic technique and of the author's own theater background is broached overtly in the text, with several references—albeit parodic—to Brechtian methods or to Brecht's plays.[8]

Neologisms, intended to transmit the local language (a derivative of the extinct "Guarany-Purunií"), abound in the novel. This language refers to an obsolete culture and parodies a communist-era vocabulary that is inserted within a decidedly neoliberal context. By contrasting the two politico-economic systems, the narrative voice undermines the possibility of any utopian social and/or political construct. In *O menino que se trancou na geladeira*, any type of politics is debunked as a corrupt game that does not affect positive social change.

As part of linguistic defamiliarization, Bonassi changes the spelling of many common Portuguese terms, such as *ervas* (herbs) into *hiyerbas* (*Menino* 111). In other instances, the meaning of certain words is ironically altered. *Amor* (love) becomes *amour*, a "sentimento de Kulpa voltado para os outros" (91).[9] And, significantly, *Kulpa* (i.e., *culpa* [guilt]) is defined as a harmless disease that can, nevertheless, provoke instances of social solidarity (25). Finally, Bonassi also plays with certain expressions, concepts and institutions by parodically altering them. Thus, the canonical medical reference text Manual de medicina legal (Legal Medicine Manual) becomes the "Manual de Medicina Ilegal" (Illegal Medicine Manual) (87), intimating the dire conditions of health-care institutions and professionals that the novel depicts. Many, if not all, the parodic citations refer to Brazil's actual troubles.

Linguistic estrangement is further heightened by the insertion of expressions from other languages, such as Spanish, German, and English, with a Brazilian "twist" (Ex., "*Are you shure?*" [217]). English, in particular, is often employed as a humoristic reference to globalization and to global culture. Hence, for example, a documentary produced by the boy after he finally emerges from his self-incarceration is auctioned at Xotebíys (the luxury auction house Sotheby's) (140).

The lexical manipulations in the novel express a dystopian, globalized reality. For example, allusions to neoliberal globalization—impelled by the powerful Northern neighbor—recur in the text. There are repeated mentions the cultural influence of the Estados Suínos on the "Civilização Brasileira," which is forced to buy (often) obsolete products from this nation. *O menino que se trancou na geladeira* suggests that neoliberal globalization generates traffic of unwanted and/or futile goods that are disposed of in the global margins (Bauman, *Wasted Lives*). In the fictional text, the uneven political-cultural relation between the "Civilização Brasileira" and the Estados Suínos allows for the unbridled influx of the latter's cultural waste products. The "Civilização Brasileira" becomes a dumping ground for global trash, dressed up as cultural commodities.

In sum, linguistic and narrative defamiliarization distances the reader from the narrative. This distance reproduces a fundamental sense of estrangement that permeates how the novel's characters relate to their respective fellows and their milieu. Similar to Luiz Ruffato's verbal and syntactic manipulations, the semantic destabilization in *O menino que se trancou na geladeira* parallels the deterioration of the private and public subject and of her/his hermeneutic and empirical horizons. If, as the novel suggests, language adds to the constitution of reality, then disjointed semantics indicate a disjunctive reality.

Social Structure

O menino que se trancou na geladeira depicts a social configuration marked by extreme—one might say absurd—disjunctions of social and civil rights. The society in which the *menino*[10] lives is composed of three distinct classes: the rich (*ricos*), the poor (*pobres*) and finally, the "IM" (Imprensados no Meio" [Squeezed in the Middle]). In an example of how language intervenes in the configuration of social reality, these divisions are imposed by the government, though they also follow a pre-established order that harks back to a system of old privileges. We learn that the SR (Super-Ricos [Super Rich]) class owes its privileges to slave and sugarcane trade, as well as to more contemporary commerce in hearts of palm and Paraguayan videogames (Bonassi, *Menino* 29). These mercantile activities touch upon the historical economic development of the Brazilian elites. Agricultural oligarchies (slaves and sugarcane) became "postmodern" business elites who deal with variegated goods (organic palm hearts and counterfeit videogames).

Top-down imposition of social divisions occurs not only through the semantic categorization of distinct classes, but also through the distribution of various infrastructural goods, among them tax exemptions and varying types of *cestas básicas* (basic baskets). These *cestas básicas* are a clear reference to Brazil's "Cesta Básica Nacional," which is the bundle of essential products (food, hygiene and household cleaning) that meets the minimum monthly subsistence needs of a single family.

In Bonassi's novel, each basket contains the products deemed appropriate for specific class segments. Whereas the lower socioeconomic segments receive the bare minimum, the Ricos's (rich's) *cesta* is filled with various luxury goods, such as imported alcoholic beverages (*Menino* 17). The "trickle-down" theory that underlies this distribution of assets buttresses differentiated citizenship and, by extension, social inequality. This rigid distinction of social segments extends to other vital services such as access to education, health care, and even potable water. The state promotes social inequalities by legalizing differentiated citizenship through a series of both legal and nonofficial mechanisms.

Speaking of the misuse of the law by Brazilian elites to maintain their privileges, James Holston suggests that due to the unequal distribution of rights in Brazil, citizenship is seen as enfranchising certain social sectors while disenfranchising others (*Insurgent* 19). Holston underscores the paradox intrinsic to this configuration. Instead of empowerment, citizenship (or being a citizen) often becomes equated with a *lack* of agency.

In *O menino que se trancou na geladeira*, nepotism figures prominently among the "official" devices that promote social and civil disjuncture. Favoritism is inscribed into the law in novel's fictional world. Thus, for example, public office is inherited. The hereditary transmission of concessions and divestiture remains within the boundaries of specific classes. With wry humor, Bonassi's text lauds the ingenious configuration that turns preferential treatment into a successful legal practice, suggesting that social and civil inequality are an integral element of the state and how it understands and implements citizenship (Santos).

Repression, Neoliberalism, and Literature

As mentioned earlier, like Luiz Ruffato's *Inferno provisório*, *O menino que se trancou na geladeira* has an unspecified and yet recognizable time frame that includes the 1964–85 dictatorship as well as the country's crises-ridden transitional moments of the 1980s and 1990s. Whereas allusions to the latter punctuate the entire narrative, the former is suggested by passing mentions to repressive governmental tactics such as torture and arbitrary executions.

Alluding to the 1964 dictatorial regime, *O menino que se trancou na geladeira* portrays oppression as a part of everyday life and as essential to social engineering. Parodying the Ato Institucional Número Cinco (Institutional Act Number 5, AI-5), the legislation that ushered in the most repressive period of the Brazilian dictatorship, the novel's narrative voice mentions the effects of the previously mentioned Athos Ocasional Número Hum (Occasional Act Number One, AOH). Despite its general vacuity, this law inaugurates a period of state-sponsored atrocities that claimed the lives of many and weakening the opposition.

The novel's mock classification as a *romance reportagem*, a popular genre during the military dictatorship, accentuates Civilização Brasileira's undemocratic foundations and the collusion between authoritarianism and culture (Avelar, *The Untimely Present* 61–63). Following the impetus of the *romance reportagem*, *O menino que se trancou na geladeira* also proposes to "denounce" the convoluted socioeconomic, political, and cultural conditions of recent Brazilian history. It does so, however, not in the naturalist fashion of the former, but rather through an implausible narrative, thereby undermining the parameters of the genre to which it supposedly belongs. Unlike the *romance reportagem* of the 1970s (61–63), Bonassi's novel does not mask its own conditions of existence. Rather, *O menino que se trancou na geladeira* repeatedly interpolates the reader, pointing to the very constraints that produce the novel and that the text perpetuates.

The *romance reportagem* emerged in the 1970s, during the height of Brazil's military dictatorship, as a means to circumvent the regime's censorship. Initially, the denomination applied to a series published by the publishing house Civilização Brasileira that was edited by Ênio Silveira. Titles were supposed to allude to real life events (Cosson 11). As suggested by the introduction to the series's first book, Carlos Heitor Cony's *O caso Lou* (The case Lou, 1975), the narratives should read as "romanced reality" (Cosson 12).

Taking as a point of departure stories ripped from newspaper headlines, romance-reportagens such as José Louzeiro's *Lúcio Flávio, o passageiro da agonia* (Lúcio Flávio, The passenger of agony, 1975) combined fiction with investigative journalism, all the while suggesting that the latter prevailed. In this way, the narratives brought to the public's attention a violent reality that the military authorities were trying to mask behind the much-touted banner of the "Brazilian miracle."[11]

At its outset, the *romance reportagem*[12] was a hit with the reading public and reviewers alike. Idelber Avelar suggests that the genre's popularity was due in part to the "compensatory substitution" (*Untimely* 63) it offered to Brazil's middle classes. Owing to its mimetic quality, the *romance reportagem* could allay the guilt felt by this sector for having supported the 1964 coup. Avelar explains that "[if] the romance-reportagem ended up accounting for some of the greatest market successes in Brazil during the 1970s, the explanation may be found in this revamping of naturalist claims to neutrality and transparency within an aesthetic of abjection basically modeled after the mass media. It was the romance-reportagem's systematic masking of its own conditions of production that enabled the reader's cathartic identification with a warrior-reporter who seemed to float above all social tensions" (*Untimely* 62).

Nonetheless, the *romance reportagem*'s popularity among cultural critics was soon replaced by a rejection of its mimetic nature. After its initial success, the *romance reportagem* increasingly was perceived as a minor genre, circumscribed by specific sociohistorical and political circumstances (Cosson 27). Its exaggerated realism also contributed to the perception of the genre as being unsophisticated not only thematically, but also stylistically.

O menino que se trancou na geladeira simultaneously maintains certain characteristics of the *romance reportagem* and diverges from the genre. While the novel does not refer to specific headlines, it does take as its point of departure Brazil's recent and contemporary reality—though, in a textual mise-en-abîme, it does not pretend to denounce it (while doing precisely this). Rather, the narrative voice promptly negates any impetus toward social critique. In this manner, *O menino que se trancou na geladeira* renders visible the imposed silences of writing under an oppressive order (be it either political or economic) and deconstructs the premises under which the *romance reportagem* operates (i.e., the prospect of full exposure). Even though the traditional *romance reportagem* claims to uncover a concealed truth, Bonassi's novel admits that this goal is impossible under repressive circumstances. In this context, *O menino que se trancou na geladeira* eschews the hyperrealist, often sensationalist language of the aforementioned genre in favor of a postapocalyptic allegory and, as indicated earlier, an often unfamiliar or "estranged" language.

O menino que se trancou na geladeira lampoons the melodramatic tone of many "romance-reportagens" through stylistic recourses such as the use of exclamation points at key moments. Often, this punctuation appears at the end of nondescript sentences, adding a caricaturesque dimension to the text. In other instances, emphatic punctuation reveals the aleatory nature of certain facts. The death of the protagonist's parents is communicated in this histrionic manner: "seus Pais haviam morrido. Sim! Os dois! Acabaram de morrer!" (Bonassi, *Menino* 67).[13] Exclamation points and truncated sentences highlight the ad hoc tone of the news, giving the effect of the author thinking about this plot possibility and deciding to include it ex post facto. By resorting to humor and allegory, Bonassi undoes the identification between reader and text (or, rather, the narrator of the traditional *romance reportagem*), which lies at the heart of the genre (Avelar, *Untimely* 62).

Exposing the constraints that supposedly determine the narrative, *O menino que se trancou na geladeira* renounces the compensatory substitution underlying the 1970s *romance reportagens*. Bonassi's text does not assuage any guilt, nor does it propose a solution to the crisis it describes. Rather, it forces the reader to confront the deterioration of expectations about social justice—and the role literature plays in the fulfillment of the same. Indeed, the novel indicates that expectations have officially been banned by force of another institutional act (Bonassi, *Menino* 217). Referencing the post-Collor years, the decree points to the advent of neoliberal policies in the 1990s and the erosion of the prospect of state-sponsored social policies that would ameliorate Brazil's economic crisis and its social costs. What remains is apathy (*marasmo*).

As indicated by Avelar, allegories of ruins are fundamental for "postdictatorial memory work" (*Untimely* 2). Through allegory, postdicatorial narratives represent the debris of past violence. Simultaneously, allegorical ruins look into a market-oriented future that wants precisely to forget the historical trauma of authoritarianism and its enduring legacy: the erosion of a material and symbolic collectivity. *O menino que se trancou na geladeira* allegorizes the coming apart of the nation-state—both in its physical dimension (i.e., the disintegration of the infrastructural amenities linked to a given national terrain, such as transportation and recreation facilities, public health, and education institutions, as well as mechanisms designed to protect the physical wellbeing of its citizenry) and within the realm of sociability.

National Ruins

In *O menino que se trancou na* geladeira national ruin is suggested at the semantic level through the use of irony and parody. Both rhetorical devices destabilize signification, tearing at the seams of meaning. Thus, for example, the narrative's exaggerated use of bureaucratic jargon, like its unusual punctuation, accentuates its vacuity and exposes its inefficiency and corruption. The narrative voice explains that in order to increase taxes, "com o auxílio inestimável dos juízes ladrões, instituiu o AOH, Athos Ocasional Número Hum, destinado a '*refrear o desperdício do ócio preguiçoso entre os mais necessitados, bem como dar-lhes um sentido oposto ao do potencial conflito com o Governo Nacional*'" (Bonassi, *Menino* 64).[14] In a parody of bureaucratic language, the narrative voice emulates a stilted administrative terminology and empties it of meaning.[15] Legal temporality ("occasional") adds to the decree's absurdity. Legal meaninglessness is also compounded by the agglomeration of senseless and vague clauses that communicate congress's "occasional deliriums." Ongoing execution of meaningless laws creates a Kafkaesque, panoptic scenario where every individual and public action is supervised and commanded by an anonymous yet ubiquitous and inefficient power. Inefficiency and corruption, masquerading under layers of paperwork and bureaucratic jargon, allow for both differentiated citizenship and the aggressive enforcement tactics of said citizenship.

The interplay between market, infrastructure, and citizenship is a central axis of *O menino que se trancou na geladeira*. As in Ferréz's *Capão Pecado* and *Manual prático do ódio*, and to a degree in Bonassi's *Subúrbio*, in *O menino que se trancou na geladeira* all public infrastructure is either decaying or serves to enable corruption schemes. Despite the Programas de Aceleração do Crescimento's (PAC; Programs to Accelerate Growth) relative success, Brazil still lags behind in the quality and extent of its public infrastructure. The World Economic Forum's *Global Competitiveness Report 2010–2011* ranks Brazil sixty-second in the world in terms of infrastructure (Schwab). A recent report by the *Financial Times* points to the country's deficient infrastructure as one of the principal impediments to Brazil's continued economic growth (Rathbone). The report cites the areas of public transportation and transit, telecommunications,[16] water supply, and basic sanitation as particularly lacking. The *Financial Times* also classifies favelas as an infrastructural problem. According to a 2011 report by Amnesty International, Brazil's latest infrastructural projects—such as the hydroelectric dams of Jirau, Santo Antonio, and Belo Monte, or construction for the 2014 World Cup and the 2016 Summer Olympics—often run afoul of (especially lower-income) human rights. Forceful removals of communities located in the vicinity of planned World Cup and Olympic venues disrupt community life. In terms of access to services such as water, sewers, and public transportation, it is often the same impoverished communities that are affected by poor infrastructural goods.

O menino que se trancou na geladeira describes insufficient and inequitable infrastructure as an indicator of differentiated citizenship. In the novel, both infrastructure and social services are legal privileges of the elites, whose access to infrastructural goods goes beyond the basics and includes maintenance of "hanging gardens" that are irrigated, despite scarce water resources (Bonassi, *Menino* 213).

Economic advantages connoted by hanging gardens—a reference to one of the seven wonders of the ancient world, the hanging gardens of Babylon—underscore the elites' overindulgence, which contrasts with the population's overall pauperization. Babylonian excess suggests the establishment of "evil paradises" (Davis and Monk) created by neoliberal economies.

Inequitable wealth distribution partitions metropolitan landscapes into privatized spaces, dreamlands of consumption (enclosed shopping malls, gated communities, etc.), and the wastelands beyond these. According to Mike Davis and Daniel Bertrand Monk, nowadays, consumption is only accessible to the majority of the global populace via television, since the material world is increasingly divided into different socioeconomic enclaves (xiii). Unjust income allocation impacts not only the urban cartography, but also other social goods, such as health care and education. Both of these goods are part of a larger infrastructural grid that—in Bonassi's novel—is accessible only to a privileged few. In *O menino que se trancou na geladeira*, health, education, and leisure become luxury goods.

Health Care

Quality of social goods such as education and health care correlates to socioeconomic status. Alluding to real-life disparities in the contemporary Brazilian public health care system, the narrative voice describes the fictional counterpart in the novel as riddled by inefficiency and fraud.

Brazil's 1988 constitution instituted the universalization of social rights, including health—defined in the Brazilian constitution as overall quality of life. Established in 1989, the *Sistema Único de Saúde* (SUS; Unified Health System) was created with the intention of generating better access to services and consequently making public health care more efficient.[17] The premise of the program is that health—and health care—are fundamental rights of citizenship. Indeed, in 2007 Brazil's Ministry of Health launched the strategic plan (within the overarching Programa de Aceleração do Crescimento) (Growth acceleration program) Mais Saúde. Direito de todos (More Health: Everybody's Right), which points specifically to such rights, which also include betterment of what the decree terms "quality of life." Building on this proposition, the Lei Orgânica de Saúde, Lei No. 8080 (Organic Health Law, Law 8080) was approved in 1990. This ruling stipulates not only that health is a fundamental human right and that the responsibility of ensuring that right falls to the state, but also that access to health surpasses health care *strictu sensu*. Article 3 of the Lei Orgânica de Saúde specifies that health encompasses adequate nutrition, housing, sanitation, environment, employment, income, transportation, leisure, and "access to basic goods and services."[18] The law further highlights health as a function of public administration and as an integral part of the public sphere, detailing that the state must "guarantee that individuals and the collectivity conditions of physical, mental, and social well-being." In sum, the Brazilian state formally recognizes that health, health care, and the conditions for a healthy living are integral elements of citizenship.

Nonetheless, according to Célia Almeida et. al, the 1989 reform ultimately has fallen short of its objectives: access to services continues to vary according to region and, within these regions, according to socioeconomic status, suggesting the prevalence of differentiated citizenship within this arena. Several factors contribute to the discrepancies in health care. Among them are "underfunding, fiscal stress and lack of priorities for the sector" (131). Public health services in Brazil reflect general social inequality and are dire indeed. Certain regions lack adequate basic facilities or properly trained staff. Even in states with sufficient funding, low-income citizens often have much less access to assistance (155–57).

Lara Luna maintains that the SUS's inadequacy is part of a heritage of differentiated social services dating back to the Vargas administration. Vargas's policies "rewarded" formal workers with social benefits. The rationale was that they contributed to the development of an internal market (308), while informal workers, who were not seen as potential consumers of industrialized goods, did not partake in the same benefits. During the 1964–85 dictatorship, health care became increasingly privatized and market-oriented (308–9). The state began shifting the onus of health care provisions to the private sector, often funding private hospitals and clinics in detriment to public health care.

In *O menino que se trancou na geladeira*, deficient public health care, which is tied to the state's profitability (Bonassi, *Menino* 14) indicates the deficient social rights of a decadent middle class. The precarious conditions of public health care affect the novel's young protagonist from birth. Because his parents belong to the declining middle class, they cannot afford private services, which are synonymous with proper care. Consequently, the menino is delivered at a dilapidated public hospital. His birth is doubly traumatic: first because of the unsanitary conditions of his delivery, which will leave him physically and psychologically scarred, and second because of the incompetence of the medical professionals who work for the public health care system.

Underpaid, under qualified, and on strike, health workers literally rip the infant from his mother's womb. Both the hospital's precarious conditions and medical staff's ineptitude carry into the terrain of health insurance, which, as the text reveals, is ineffective largely because it operates under a purely for-profit rationale (not unlike the medical facilities and personnel).

The protagonist's violent birth segues into a series of episodes of abandonment and neglect (set into motion by the mother's desire to "expel" her progeny first from her womb, then from her life). He first leads a quasi-vegetative childhood, then goes into self-imposed isolation, and finally becomes an entrepreneur of voyeurism. Negligence, at both the private and the public levels (parents and state, respectively), generates in the protagonist an overwhelming sense of unmooring. His passage through the manifold societal institutions whose function is to indoctrinate the child into the hegemonic sociocultural system compounds his bewilderment and isolation.

NGOs

O menino que se trancou na geladeira repeatedly suggests that public services have been taken over by the private sector, or by the alliance between private enterprise and the state in the form of NGOs (ONG in Portuguese). Brazilian sociologist Evelina Dagnino shows how, in tandem with the neoliberal rationale, the state's role in the social contract is increasingly being transferred to nongovernmental organizations. More and more, NGOs are substituting civil society ("Citizenship in Latin America" 10–11). Nonetheless, this substitution cannot occur without the complicity of both the state that "employs" the organizations or allows them to operate and the international agencies that finance them (11). Similarly, George Yúdice maintains that nongovernmental organizations are both co-opted by the state and have the potential to undermine it. NGOs question state-sponsored policies that augment social inequality, but their modus operandi often depends on the support of the same official organisms that they critique.

In light of the liaison between state, market, and nongovernmental organizations, civil society is weakened (Dagnino, "Confluência"). Because NGOs are expected to provide services that were formerly the responsibility of the state (e.g., poverty alleviation), they become progressively disengaged from the civil sphere. Civil involvement gives way to social assistance, and social participation becomes subsumed under the rubric of "solidarity participation" (205). The result is an emphasis on individual voluntarism rather than the kind of collective enterprise that might lead to considerable social change. Dagnino sees in this shift a "depolitization" of the participatory project due to the prevalence of individualized social initiatives (205).

Individualized—or rather mercantilized—social aid is a symptom of a brittle or nonexistent collectivity in *O menino que se trancou na geladeira*. In the absence of social and/or familial ties, the novel's protagonist becomes the ward of a pseudo-nongovernmental organization. In a play on the Brazilian abbreviation for NGO (ONG), Bonassi renames these "Organismos no Governo" (Organizations within the Government; *Menino* 38). Conceived as a charitable institution, the NGO in question provides not only subsistence, but also luxury goods. Indulgence connotes the surplus of social assistance that curtails the recipient's civil involvement. Emphasis on individual rather than collective action is construed in the novel through one particular organization—the NGO Deus Dará (God Will Provide). The NGO's name, Deus Dará, highlights the alliances between the neoliberal state and the nonprofit industry and also emblematizes the disastrous convergence of social aid, lack of civil agency, and a laissez affaire rationality that presupposes minimal direct state interference.[19] To optimize its social and market performance, the NGO is at the same time a governmental, multinational, and paramilitary foundation (Bonassi, *Menino* 38).

The NGO's overlapping facets gain materiality in the paramilitary order that physically isolates Deus Dará's beneficiaries. While receiving the organization's help, individuals are kept in a heavily guarded compound. Charity is exchanged for control. Assistance seekers must conform to the norms dictated to them by the investors of the NGO and by the conditions imposed on the nonprofits by the national government. The recipient's quasi-imprisonment on the NGO's premises stems from and is justified by their immiseration. Impoverished members of society must be put out of sight and out of the minds of the general populace. Poverty equals marginality and obliterates under-privileged citizens from both the symbolic and the material sphere of the nation. Their isolation reflects both the overall social individual-ization and the protagonist's impending seclusion inside the fridge.

Satirizing the function and functioning of NGOs in posttransitional Brazil, Deus Dará is ultimately an absurd construction that is unable or unwilling to transform the social conditions impacting its constituency. Rather, by providing charitable services, the NGO ironically preempts the need for social transformation. Civil society is therefore paradoxically annulled by access to a limited number of basic social rights, such as education.

Education

The same combination of semi-inefficient services and efficient denial of agency plagues the centralized educational system in the novel. According to the SUS's ideological underpinnings, educational institutions are created with the overt intention of forming passive citizens that will not question the status quo. The disastrous combination of mediocre assistance, control, and denial of participation in the public sphere is particularly evident in primary and secondary education.

After fleeing his inattentive mother and evading the heavy security of Deus Dará's compound, the menino enters a government-sponsored educational facility, the Unidades Sintéticas de Educação de Base do Sistema Educacional do Governo Nacional (USÉIBIS; Synthetic Units for Basic Education of National Government's Educational System) (Bonassi, *Menino* 52). The USÉIBIS stand for a bloated bureaucratic system and are emblematic of ineffective state stewardship. These units are an indirect reference to the Centros Integrados de Educação Pública (CIEPs; Integrated Public Education Centers).[20] Similar to the CIEPs, the USÉIBIS are designed as all-day educational facilities established to assist disadvantaged children and prepare them to become productive citizens.

The services provided within the institutional framework of the USÉIBIS (which include not only education, but also food and personal hygiene) are insufficient to guarantee the pupils' healthy physical and intellectual development. Thus, for example, instead of the daily shower provided by the real-life CIEPs, in the fictional USÉIBIS, the vandalized showers only dispense a foul oil-like substance (60). The maintenance of the USÉIBIS's physical and didactic infrastructure, similar to that of other public institutions depicted in *O menino que se trancou na geladeira*, is overseen by incompetent and unsupervised workers, hired on the basis of personal connections. Far from being nurturing social institutions, the USÉIBIS are primarily centers of indoctrination where social exclusion and privilege are taught to the pupils via coercive methods.

Unlike the real-life CIEPs, in which the educational approach was to contextualize the pedagogical material so as to make it meaningful to the students, at the USÉIBIS, education becomes synonymous with inefficiency. Not only are the teachers ill-prepared, but the curriculum is inadequate and generates disinformation rather than molding the pupils into citizens ready to enter the civil and political arenas. Initially designed to serve both the lower and the decadent middle classes, these institutions primarily assist the "classe dos imprensados no meio" (class of the crushed in the middle), since the lower social echelons literally do not have the physical means to "compete" for the limited spaces available in the establishments. The middle class literally outruns their poorer competition, thus obtaining a space *pro méritum* (57).

The novel's narrative voice parodies the concept of merit-based achievement by transforming it into a game of musical chairs for scarce resources. Success, in this context, has less to do with the pupil's intellectual capacity or dedication, but rather with her/his previous wherewithal, which, in turn determines her/his future possibilities (though these are dismal as well). Impoverished children are blamed for their failure to partake in the competitive cycle, thus echoing the dominant noninterventionist ethos. This same logic casts the better-off pupils as more "deserving" of social rights such as education. The competitive rationale that determines the children's behavior results from a consistent lack of resources within the "Templos de Ensino" (Educational Temples), the pedagogical branch of the USÉIBIS.

Primary education, theoretically a collective right of all Brazilians, has in recent decades become universalized. In 2009, 97.6 percent of Brazilian children between the ages of 6 and 14 attended school. Nonetheless, these numbers reveal little to nothing about the adequacy of the instruction received. In 2009, 9.7 percent of all Brazilians were illiterate (down from 10 percent the previous year). In a 2010 *New York Times* article, Alexei Barrionuevo points to Brazil's educational failures as one of the primary obstacles for the country's continued economic growth. Inadequate primary education is particularly evident within the public state and municipal school system, which serves lower-income populations.

Public education in Brazil, as we now know it, dates back to 1824, when the state recognized primary education as a universal right (Akkari). With the 1930 Revolution and the consolidation of an urban middle class, public education expanded in Brazil to serve primarily the aforementioned segment of the population. The lower-income bracket was ignored by the state, which apparently did not view it as a social class per se (Freitas). Lorena Freitas argues that because of their marginality within the labor market, poor citizens lacked visibility vis-à-vis the state and, consequently, also the power to demand their rights. Within this framework, the public education structure ignored the needs of underprivileged learners, as did the health-care system vis-à-vis informal workers.

Until the 1980s, Brazil's public schools catered to the needs of its middle classes, and public institutions surpassed private ones in academic achievement. This picture has changed dramatically since the country's neoliberal turn in the 1990s. The increased shift to market-oriented policies eroded the quality of public education as funding for state and municipal institutions decreased in the context of structural-adjustment measures. Even the 1996 Lei de Diretrizes e Bases, Lei No. 9.934 (Law of Directives and Bases Law 9.934), which mandates that at least 18 percent of the states' and 25 percent of the municipalities' budgets should go toward education funding, did not change this scenario. To the contrary, the law actually had the unintended effect of consolidating regional differences in public education.

Deficiencies in reading, math, and sciences are more pronounced in the public education sector that serves the majority of the country's citizens. In general, students from public schools lag behind those from private institutions in academic achievement. Not only are state and municipal schools underfunded in comparison to private ones, but the former also serve a population that, due to socioeconomic need, must struggle to access education and to remain within the school system.

If education is a "dever da família e do Estado, inspirada nos princípios de liberdade e nos ideais de solidariedade humana, tem por finalidade o pleno desenvolvimento do educando, seu preparo para o exercício da cidadania e sua qualificação para o trabalho" (Article 2 of Lei de Diretrizes e Bases, Lei No. 9.934 [Law number 9.934]),[21] then an inefficient public educational system amounts to a denial of the right to adequate workforce preparation (*qualificação para o trabalho*) and, in more general terms, negates full-fledged access to citizenship. In fact, a recent article indicates that illiteracy and insufficient schooling are some of the primary reasons for social immobility among people who receive the *Bolsa Família*. Among the beneficiaries, 15.8 percent of those 25 years or older are illiterate, 65.3 percent did not finish elementary school, and less than 10 percent graduated from middle school (Monteiro).

Referring Brazil's wanting public education structure, *O menino que se trancou na geladeira* depicts a low-quality system burdened by insufficient funding. Bonassi employs irony to reveal the educational shortcomings. Asked to report what he is learning in the Templo de Ensino, the menino must lie to hide his ignorance.

O menino que se trancou na geladeira ridicules not only ineffectual primary and secondary education. Higher learning is likewise excoriated for either being a tool of state indoctrination or for being irrelevant. The academic system disengages knowledge from social praxis, impeding the fulfillment of educational—and, by extension—civil goals.

O menino que se trancou na geladeira portrays universities as locales where the elites learn how to unquestioningly accept the government's determinations (Bonassi, *Menino* 22). Socioeconomically disadvantaged citizens are excluded from these institutions. The novel implicitly critiques the structure of higher learning in Brazil, where middle and upper classes frequent public universities and the poorer population must pay for higher education at private schools. Brazil's university system hence reinforces the diagram of differentiated citizenship through the allocation of educational privileges.

Mass Media

Mass media plays a prominent role in Bonassi's novel. Similar to educational facilities, it aids in the "formation" of the citizenry by disseminating disinformation. Media is also the means by which the Menino will regain access to the official sphere of the Civilização Brasileira after his "refrigerated" self-exile.

The protagonist's life is steeped in mass media culture from his inception. Both his mother and his father are part of the two-channel, state-run television system that dominates the airwaves and is responsible for upholding the status quo. However, while the TV da Força Maior (TV of the Higher Power) does this in a clearly coercive manner, the TV do Amour (Love TV)[22] subtly alienates the impoverished masses through Biblical soap operas. Reflecting the ideas of the Frankfurt School on the role of media (Horkheimer and Adorno), culture and capitalism, Bonassi proposes a direct correlation between mass media and hegemony. To this mix, religion is added.

The ironically named TV do Amour transmits mainly static "biblical" scenes. These *tableaux vivants* combine religious imaginary derived from the Catholic Bible with emblematic moments of Brazilian and world history as well as highlights of Hollywood classics. The miracle of the fishes is juxtaposed to "Inauguração de Brasileíya" (Inauguration of Brasileíya), "Muro de Berlínyka" (The Berlínyka Wall), and "Apocalypse Now." There is no logic to the choice of scenes, suggesting randomness in programming and viewing. Haphazard grouping evokes the act of zapping, which produces a chain of isolated images largely emptied of narrative and content. Zapping symbolically fragments reality and transforms it into "an object of contemplation" (Debord 12). Indeed, the "biblical" scenes are mere reproductions and do not contain any dogma that endows the images with signification. Devoid of meaning, the imagery both generates and becomes the reality that it supposedly represents; the scenes are simulacra (Baudrillard *Simulacra*). Empty of any content, the televised images provide the ideal tool to (mis)inform their audience, which views the content uncritically.

As stated earlier, media plays an important part in the Menino's reinsertion into the Civilização Brasileira. Upon returning from his exile, the protagonist captures his "reality" cinematically by producing "reality shows," commodifying daily existence through his voyeuristic gaze. Fredric Jameson contends that the substitution of the empirical horizon by simulacra is a sign of the dominance of a late capitalist logic. According to this rationale, the market has permeated every corner of existence.

Reality shows, which are increasingly popular in Brazil (see for example the success of the *Big Brother* franchise in Brazil, aired by Rede Globo and known to Brazilian audiences as *BBB*), provide a sanctioned voyeuristic pleasure and/or a vicarious experience. Alluding to the genre's appeal, *O menino que se trancou na geladeira* reveals how these shows are ubiquitous. Following the concept of shows such as *Big Brother*, the Menino's program erases the line between reality and fiction.

The protagonist films the private lives of the rich and, to a lesser degree, of the poor, and transforms these lives into a public spectacle. He effectively expunges the distinction between the "real" and "showbiz." From the beginning, the novel proposes that the two ambits are indistinguishable and that the Civilização Brasileira is a "society of the spectacle" (Debord) in which images outstrip social interactions, creating a community of isolated individuals (Bauman *Society Under Siege* 168). Paradigmatic is the Menino's affair with the Anciã Desquitada (old divorcée). Their relationship occurs solely at the virtual level—he films her from within his fridge—literally exempting them from direct physical contact.

Their relationship is determined by the reactions and demands of the viewing public. Artificiality is emphasized by how the Menino pays for filming the object of his desires during a striptease session performed by his lover. In exchange for his—and the audience's—cinematographic voyeurism, the protagonist pays the Anciã Desquitada with passes for plastic surgery and silicone injections (Bonassi, *Menino* 165). Both the spectacular nature of the relationship and the trade-in favors that makes this exhibition possible signal the infiltration of affective relations by the logic of commerce.

Reality television is, according to Henri Giroux, the media symptom of neoliberalism. Not only does this kind of entertainment transform life itself into a performance that can be consumed, but it also often is also grounded in a Darwinistic principle (Giroux 595). Shows such as *BBB*, *The Apprentice* (NBC) or *Survivor* (CBS)[23] relay "an insatiable and cut-throat scorn for the weaknesses of others and a sadistic affirmation of ruthlessness and steroidal power. Getting voted off the island or being told 'You're fired!' now renders real life despair and misfortune entertaining, even pleasurable" (595). In other words, reality television bolsters the notion of the subject as a disposable commodity.

Body and Consumption

Within the profit and consumption-orientated social system, the individual body—and human life itself—becomes yet another piece of merchandise that determines the value of the subject's life. Body parts, such as organs, enter the circulation of goods and can be exchanged for other commodities even during the donor's lifetime. This happens to the menino/Menino's beloved, Milâne's father. After being attacked by the "Máphia Rústica" (Rustic Mafia) for not paying his debts, the man has his vital organs mortgaged while he is hospitalized (Bonassi, *Menino* 86). Added to the trafficking of organs, a persistent narrative of neoliberal globalization (Franco, *Decline and Fall*), plastic surgery is also ubiquitous in the novel. Plastic surgery reaffirms how the body has become an integral part of the economic cycle. The individual body becomes an investment that can at once be ameliorated through technology—like the fridge and plastic surgery—or transformed into a multipart retail unit.

Both cosmetic "enhancement" and the isolation of individual organs, the body's commercialization, sever it, isolating its individual parts. It is precisely the body's disassembling that makes it more profitable (Baudrillard *Consumer Society*). Literal and metaphorical bodily dissection echoes the fragmentation of the social body, which no longer is an ambit for/of collective action. Political, civil and/or sociocultural agency becomes consigned to the individual subject who resorts to technology, media, or marketing to ascertain visibility in the society of spectacle.

Refrigerated Insurgency

Within the static and disparate social system that Bonassi's novel describes, insurgency, as defined by Holston (*Insurgent*), is a paradoxical gesture that does not imply engagement with the conditions that cause disjuncture. Instead, insurgency means literal isolation from the public ambit—hence the necessity of the protective refrigerator in *O menino que se trancou na geladeira*.

According to Jean Franco (*Fear and Loathing*), the pessimistic tone that prevails in contemporary Latin American literature signifies the emptying—or weakening—of concepts such as civil and human rights, hegemony, and citizenship. The novel's protagonist either ignores or cannot empirically access citizenship in its liberal sense—that is, as a rapport between the individual and the state that guarantees the former's rights. In Bonassi's text, the state effectively ignores the protagonist, and he, like the character Vicente Cambota in the homonymous story of *Inferno provisório*, disappears into the institutional cracks that are supposed to guarantee his rights as a citizen. In this context, the refrigerator represents not only protection from a hostile environment, but also a paradoxical empowerment that lies in the boy's noninvolvement with a precarious public sphere. An embodiment of absolute egoism and isolation, the fridge transforms the menino into an antisuperhero (Bonassi, *Menino* 120). The narrative voice ironically describes the Menino as a superhero without a mission that would benefit any given group. Instead, his charge is solely to protect himself.

Without a community that can/should be transformed, the protagonist's "rebellion" cannot modify the social conditions that led to his seclusion in the first place. However, in a paradoxical "insurgent" gesture, the protagonist exploits the alienating conditions and transforms them into a mediatized spectacle. Spectacle becomes the venue in which he can "perform" his citizenship: he makes himself visible by transforming others into a mass media exhibition.

O menino que se trancou na geladeira highlights sociopolitical apathy. None of the actions performed by the novel's different characters follows or envisages a broader political agenda. As pointed out by Resende, much of contemporary Brazilian literature does not have a utopian project (93). Like Ruffato's *Inferno provisório* and many other recent Brazilian texts dealing with agency and/or disempowerment and social crises, Bonassi's *O menino que se trancou na geladeira* and *Subúrbio* lack a communitarian utopian horizon. Utopia, as a collective social project, is replaced by individual enterprises, such as the attainment of middle-class status (Ruffato, *Inferno provisório*), the isolation from a disjunctive context (Bonassi, *Menino*), or in a more positive vein, the reclaiming of a geosocial and cultural space in the divided city (Faustini).

The fridge is a paradoxical space of insurgency. Here, the rules and regulations of the Civilização Brasileira—and of its detritus—are employed to both reinsert the Menino into the center of society and to isolate him from it. While Luiz Ruffato points to labor and knowledge ("Era uma vez" *O livro das impossibilidades*) as a mode of insurgency and Ferréz suggests that violence is an expression of both differentiated citizenship and of a paradoxical agency, Fernando Bonassi transforms insurgence into a parody about the conditions of differentiated citizenship (*O menino que se trancou na geladeira*).

The jesting tone is absent from *Subúrbio*, the other novel by Bonassi that this chapter examines. If in *O menino que se trancou na geladeira*, the grotesque was strongly present throughout the narrative, it was mitigated by the text's humorous tone. *Subúrbio*, on the other hand, focuses on inexorable abjection. The novel evokes (sub)urban decadence and violence that ensue from the weakened social fabric. In this respect, *Subúrbio* resembles several of *Inferno provisório*'s stories as well as Ferréz's *Capão Pecado* and *Manual prático do ódio*.

SUBURBAN NIGHTMARES: THE LIMINAL SPACES AND BODIES OF FERNANDO BONASSI'S *SUBÚRBIO*

In *Subúrbio*, citizenship is corroded by multiple factors such as poverty, abandonment, and manifold types of violence. Citizenship—or what remains of it—bears the sign of the abject.[24] *Subúrbio* begs the question about the status of citizenship in the neoliberal episteme. If citizenship arises and is ensconced within the notion of a social contract, then the weakening of this contract dissipates the premise of the citizenry as a group that has both rights and responsibilities vis-à-vis the state and, in a more narrow and direct sense, the community.

Published initially in 1994 and reissued in 2005, *Subúrbio* pinpoints a moment of national crisis. The novel broaches similar themes as *O menino que se trancou na geladeira* and *Inferno provisório*—socioeconomic disenfranchisement, personal and collective disillusionment, in sum, the erosion of social rights. *Subúrbio* is set at a moment in which Brazil is well on its neoliberalizing path, and the landscape that emerges from the novel's pages bears testimony of this process's impact upon the working classes. The modest gains in citizenship that this class accrued since the 1940s are progressively undermined either directly by neoliberal measures (such as augmented labor flexibility) or by the consequences of these procedures (such as increasing poverty). Abjection—material, but also social and individual (the three being intimately connected) is the upshot.

In her book *The Powers of Horror: An Essay on Abjection* (1982), French psychoanalyst Julia Kristeva defines the abject as a concrete and symbolic entity marked by ambiguity. The abject object/subject at the same time attracts and repels those who come into contact with it. This incertitude of the abject defies the articulation of stable identities and, consequently, challenges the production of a firm, dichotomous social normativity that demands a clear separation between desire and repulsion, self and other, and the acceptable and the unacceptable. Abject subjects (criminals, madwomen and madmen, social others) cross from the legal sites to the territories of the nonsocial, arenas where societal as well as cultural regulations become tenuous and fluid. Therefore, abject subjects exist within the confines of society without being a sanctioned part of this structure. From this liminal position the abject subject can destabilize the hegemonic social order and expose its constructed, arbitrary nature. Concurrently, the abject subject can also debilitate the barriers that compose the societal edifice and the individual body.

Abject subjects, individuals who exist beyond the crevices that establish the distinguishing parameters of differentiated citizenship, represent the waste products of said citizenship. These subjects serve as a reminder of the boundaries of citizenship. Their bodies, depicted in Bonassi's fiction as transgressive, deficient, decadent, or hyperbolic symbolize the existence and the transgression of limits. Abjection outlines the conditions that make productive insurgency unfeasible. By creating an abject scenario of the suburban metropolis and its working class denizens, Bonassi doubles back on the concept of insurgency against differentiated citizenship. What remains is a counterinsurgency that operates through contamination and violence. The individual body, a metaphor of the social body, is where transgression and brutality converge.

Abjection is not restricted to the elaboration of individual subjectivities and corporalities. The abject prevails also in the configuration of the social body and in the empirical as well as figurative cartographies that the citizens of this body inhabit. Accordingly, cityscapes are composed of both proper and improper spaces, of the well-illuminated dwellings of the bourgeoisie, and of the "dark" and allegedly dangerous spaces of the subaltern classes. These territories, in turn, allow or impede access to citizenship. Citizenship assumes variegated meanings in different sociogeographical enclaves, or it is annulled entirely.

In Fernando Bonassi's novel *Subúrbio*, the abject is present as a geographic as well as social category. Both aspects of abjection intersect at the crossroads of two different bodies: that of an old man, *o velho*, and that of a young girl, *a menina*. Their bodies are synecdoches for the territory they inhabit: whereas the old man's decaying physique represents the degradation of the suburban terrain, the young girl's violated corpse becomes an emblem of the absence of sociability within São Paulo's crises-ridden peripheries during Brazil's neoliberal turn. If the body, with its boundaries and porosities, emblematizes social configuration (Douglas; Butler), then both the old man's and the young girl's bodies convey a breach in the social contract. *Subúrbio* hence establishes a continuum between the individual and social bodies that points to both entities' disintegration as a result of differentiated citizenship. Through this continuum, the novel establishes a critique of the crisis of community in posttransition Brazil.

The plot of *Subúrbio* revolves around an elderly couple who; albeit still inhabiting the same domestic space, does not share anything beyond the house in which they live. The old man is a drunkard who becomes enamored of a young neighborhood girl. The child epitomizes both ingenuousness and seduction for the elderly man. Besides representing the offspring he never had, she is also symbolic of an idealized past and provides a vestige of hope and emotional attachment in the surrounding grey landscape. As the narrative progresses the relationship between the two characters transforms from an innocent quasi-familiar affair into the nightmare of sexual violation. The novel's denouement is the climax of an ongoing enactment of brutality at both the social (the lack of meaningful civil and communitarian apparatuses that serve to support and protect the social subject) and individual levels (the failure of emotional relations and familial bonds).

Material and Figurative Suburbs

As the book's title indicates, the city, or rather, its outskirts represent one of the primary axes around which the story develops. The novel's title encompasses not only the material dimension of a suburb—the neighborhoods that fringe the central city—but also adverts to its Latin root, the term *suburbium*. *Suburbium* appertains to the locales "under" the city, terrains inhabited by people of lesser wealth and/or sociopolitical standing. As Holston demonstrates, it is in the suburbs of the Brazilian metropolis that differentiated citizenship becomes at once visible and visibly contested (*Insurgent*).

Focusing on the literal and discursive edges of the hegemonic metropolis, Bonassi reclaims this zone from the oblivion of dominant culture, allocating to it an (albeit problematic) agency that most of the human characters within the text lack. Neither *asfalto* (asphalt/center) nor *morro/periferia* (hills/periphery), *Subúrbio*'s urban terrain is inhabited by the figures that straddle the border between these two regions, both financially and symbolically. It is an area marked by social as well as individual decadence, thus illustrating Susana Rotker's contention that "[c]ities too have their ailments, cancerous zones that should be excised, or at least isolated to specific neighborhoods. Modernity divided the large cities into clearly marked areas: high and low, clean and dirty" (18). Modernity established the novel's suburban terrain. It is here, in the city's outskirts, that the working-class population settled during São Paulo's industrial surge. Attracted by industrial jobs and the social mobility these promised, urban centers such as São Paulo experienced, since the 1940s, a large population influx, for which they were not always prepared.[25]

Initially, blue-collar and *Lumpen* tenements, which until the 1940s existed in central urban areas, were relegated to the outskirts (Holston, *Insurgent*; Caldeira, *City of Walls* 213). Located outside the city "proper," the working classes did not benefit from urban infrastructure and, as a result, had only limited or no access to either social or civil citizenship (Holston, *Insurgent* 236). As the city proper developed and the working classes became established in their neighborhoods, communitarian associations sprung up that—through insurgent practice—claimed improvements such as paved streets and sidewalks, electricity, connection to the metropolitan sewer lines, schools, and so on. The periphery became integrated into the official urban cartography as its denizens accessed social and civil citizenship. Meanwhile, the economic margins continued to be pushed toward the conurbation's outer limits (*Insurgent*), continually expanding São Paulo's dimension. However, as the country adopted a neoliberal model, the working-class peripheral areas, together with their residents, experienced a socioeconomic (and hence infrastructural) descent, becoming once again regions of abjection.

Subúrbio captures this postmodern moment, as the gains of the working classes are corroded by the encroachment of neoliberalization and the socioeconomic crisis that ensues from privatization and cost-containment measures.[26] Though, as Caldeira proposes, division is no longer always geographic; it continues to be physical. Modern security technologies and old-fashioned walls replace physical distance (*City of Walls* 213). New segregation patterns highlight differentiated access to social goods, such as schools, hospitals, or adequate leisure spaces. Segregation also superimposes apposite and abject spaces, with the latter being cast as "encroaching" on the former.

The geographic, figurative, as well as economic margins of the city proper represent a grey zone where social regulations become tenuous and/or disappear entirely, providing fertile ground for manifold modes of contravention. Or at least, this is the manner in which the hegemonic discourse tends to represent these areas of the urban topography, transforming them into territories of an abhorrent otherness. They are the geographic enclaves of abjection. Within the neoliberal ideology, discourses of fear proliferate among other commodities, generating, in its turn, new modes of commodification (of the security apparatus, of urban segregation, of private means of transportation and of secluded locales of leisure). Fear both builds on and expands differentiated citizenship. Anxiety about social difference also gives material shape to new forms social and civil disjuncture while coalescing old divisions.

Reverberating the logic of the divided metropolis that is split between "high/clean" and "low/unclean" perimeters, *Subúrbio*'s physical environs evoke urban decrepitude, the ailing "cancerous zones" alluded to by Rotker. The vicinity's corners are imprinted by shadows and mold (Bonassi, *Subúrbio* 13). *Subúrbio* describes the cityscape, both geographically and socially, as a diseased, agonizing organism with only vestiges of a deteriorating urbanity. Basic urban comforts such as street lamps and signage have disintegrated, leaving in their places only rusted blotches that evoke urban leprosy (13). In this ambiance, the past layers of sociability have fused into a dead crust that transforms the polis into a fossil of another era.

Analogous to the ailing urban sphere, the private arena is also diseased in its own way. The outward registers of domestic decadence signal to literal and metaphorical (inter)personal dissolution. As Bonassi's novel purveys the moldering urban and social corpus, it also concentrates on individual decaying bodies. Flaccid flesh, decrepit limbs, and rotting organs become the object of an abject voyeurism as the narrative voice dwells on the minutiae of corporeal degradation. Emblematic of this dissipation is the old man who is keenly aware of his own sagging flesh, an emblem of his encroaching mortality and, at the same time, of his social obsolescence (78). His corporeal deterioration contrasts with his perverse surveillance of "healthy" bodies, such as the young girl's. His gaze constructs her body as the only vital nucleus in the waning scenery.

Sociologist Yves Pedrazzini argues that there is an intrinsic link between social partition, degradation, and violence (100). *Subúrbio* both reproduces and extrapolates from this juxtaposition. Confined to the dismal perimeter of the suburb and the eroding domestic space, the individual and the social bodies in *Subúrbio* become simultaneously the agents and the subjects of abjection. In this duality, the figures that populate Bonassi's text challenge the parameters of the prevailing social taxonomy, since they cannot be defined in exclusive terms of transgression or victimization. Instead, Bonassi's characters are at the same time perpetrators and receptacles of multiple types of violence: psychological, sexual, material, and civil.

The discourses that differentiate between legitimate and illicit citizens and between the proper and the improper city have been exacerbated not only by fiscal inequities, but also by the unrestrained and unregulated growth of metropolitan areas such as São Paulo. In the discursive construction of the metropolis, the conurbation's boundaries tend to coincide with its human "outsiders," who supposedly threaten the metropolitan sociocultural and material makeup.

Since the 1940s, population influx into Brazil's urban regions resulted in the metastasizing of nonregulated, low-income residential developments that lack basic infrastructure such as sewage and electricity. Urban growth, stemming in great part from the migration of people from the interior into the metropolitan centers in search of better work and income, often further strains already economically strapped neighborhoods. Although informal housing projects at times eventually become connected to basic services, these locales nonetheless continue to be frequently burdened by the absence of civil establishments such as schools, hospitals, police precincts, and so on. Without adequate public infrastructure, the underprivileged municipal regions disclose the erosion of the social contract within the larger urban as well as national context.

In São Paulo, socioeconomic divisions are compounded by the city's geographic makeup that thrusts its economically disadvantaged dwellers to the physical borders of the *urbe*. Transit between the center and periphery is frequently an arduous affair due to the inadequate means and the normally expensive cost of transportation. Bonassi's suburban landscape highlights the geographic separation of the *subúrbio* from the rest of the megalopolis by alluding to the increase in the bus fare between one vicinity and another (Bonassi, *Subúrbio* 13–14). The allusion to the differential in bus fare indicates the geographic liminality of the novel's setting, a liminality that, according to Néstor García Canclini, weakens civil participation within a larger national domain because it dissociates the peripheral populace from the centers of legislative power (*Consumers*).

Highlighting the polluted atmosphere in this part of the city, the narrative voice further emphasizes the difficult conditions on the socioeconomic purlieus of the conurbation. Environmental dilapidation is one of the outcomes of a state apparatus that obeys foremost the directives of a neoliberal, globalized economy. Octavio Ianni contends that the preponderance of a globalized market weakens the nation-state and its regulatory power since it follows the dictates of multinational corporations instead of national regulations (and interests) (43).

Accordingly, state policies designed to protect fair wages, workers' rights, and the environment are often circumvented and/or ignored. In *Subúrbio*, the omnipresent smoke spewed forth by the transnational company Mannesman signifies an economic system in which the state forgoes its regulatory power in favor of investor-friendly measures. The result is the degrading of the suburban dwellers' *Lebenswelt*. Dilapidation has both psychological and empirical consequences such as the spread of diseases, which in Bonassi's novel become one the peripheral subject's defining traits (Bonassi, *Subúrbio* 101). Illnesses afflict people throughout their lives. Trapped in an ignominious existence during and after her/his "productive" years, the individual finally becomes reduced to an assemblage of corporeal ailments, a body in distress that resonates its environment's exigency.

Alienation and the hostility generated by the breach in the social contract and the accompanying collective *telos* are repeatedly mirrored in the novel's scenarios. It is significant that the text's settings, which oscillate between the exterior and the interior landscapes of the periphery, do not include any communitarian areas such as public parks, neighborhood associations, and so on. The only ambiance that evokes collectivity is the young girl's school. But even this institution is outlined as a hollow edifice, seen from the outside by the protagonist's voyeuristic gaze (195). All other zones of public gathering in the novel are commercial spaces: the bakery that is also the local bar, the barbershop, and the neighborhood store that sells illegal lottery tickets, for example. These establishments, frequented primarily by male customers, do not provide an adequate venue of communication among their customers but are, instead, an arena where relations of power, both metaphorical and economic, are played out.

The only other public space is the Represa Billings (Billings Reservoir). Planned and built between 1930 and 1940 by São Paulo Tramway, Light and Power Company, Ltd., the Billings Reservoir is São Paulo's largest water reservoir, covering an area of 127 square kilometers. Due to the larger São Paulo metropolitan area's chaotic growth, nowadays the reservoir suffers from heavy metal, industrial, and domestic pollution.

The Represa Billings is also a public recreational area and is where *paulista* families go on the weekends to fish, picnic, and swim. It is in this setting that the old man's crime occurs. In the novel, the familial panorama is emptied of sociability and becomes the theater of violence, a landscape that connotes anomie. At the outset the *velho*'s and the *menina*'s sojourn mimics the leisure activities of weekenders: they rent a paddleboat and eat in the deserted picnic area. But the quasi-domestic interaction soon gives way to a dark parody of familial bondage as the girl is transformed into an object of incestuous and murderous desire, and the supposed safety of the domestic sphere is destroyed. It is significant that the rape occurs as they play "house" (*cabaninha*) by the lake.

Subúrbio further emphasizes the anonymity and the disintegration of the *urbe* in its depiction of means and routes of transit as well as in the itineraries of the novel's characters. The *velho* in particular is a debased flanêur of sorts, alternatively wandering aimlessly or purposefully (when in search of his object(s) of desire, for instance) through various metropolitan routes. Despite the meticulous recounting of the protagonist's urban trajectories, the narrative does not assemble a cohesive map of the city. Rather, Bonassi's text severs the urban body into separate, incongruous pieces, painting the portrait of a monstrous *urbe*.

Frankensteinian dismemberment of the megalopolis is stressed in the procession of jettisoned objects that drift in the river and that the weary old man observes on one of his amblings.[27] The floating garbage speaks of the wasted lives and of the material waste of modernity that "litters" the megalopolis.[28] It is significant that various objects he sees—car tires and windshield wipers, industrial waste, supermarket bags and sneakers—are part of modern consumption. The items' obsolescence encapsulates the coupled messages of disposal and exchange that prevail in the city. Transience, signified by the river's current in which the discarded objects float, adds not only to the idea of movement, a central component of metropolitan life, but also to the notion of disposability of both objects and humans.

Thoroughfares, omnibuses, bus stops, and stations appear repeatedly in the text. Not only do these sites allegorize transit—of humans and of commodities—but they are also (analogously to the polluted river) terrains of flux and instability. Like the private and the commercial domains, the notion of social cohesion formulated by the modern nation-state has all but disappeared. The street is no longer the ambit of encounters between citizens from various backgrounds but has become what Michel de Certeau has termed a "nonspace" (Certeau; Augé). Public spaces are populated by the people who move through the streets, the wasted bodies that are eventually discarded—like the sick body of the old man. Just as the refuse in the river, he too is a used-up and broken-down waste product.

Bonassi's metropolitan avenues expose the failed project of modernity, showcasing the ruins of the "casas dos metalúrgicos cortadas ao meio pela avenida, como cáries que vão pegando uma boca suja sem piedade. Banheiros, quartos, salas, cozinhas. Aquela intimidade junto do meio-fio tinha alguma coisa de fim de mundo" (*Subúrbio* 130).[29] The wrecked tenements enunciate modernity's double failure: On the one hand, the ruins signify the failure of a national *modernizing* project, the attempt to develop a national industry and thereby fortify the national autonomy that was in place until the 1960s. On the other, modernization within the country has been a partial venture at best, as the previously mentioned allusion to the transnational enterprise Mannesman suggests.

Emphasis on the development of a national industry, popular from the 1930s to the mid-1960s (i.e., from Getúlio Vargas's Estado Novo until the 1964 military *coup de état*), has given way to the progressive abdication of the manufacturing sector to the spread of transnational capitalism. The preponderance of transnational corporations also reflects the general trend within neoliberalism that sees the state as an intermediary between global capital and spaces of investment within a given nation. According to this rationale, the state's role is no longer to serve the public good, but rather to facilitate the interests of transnational capital within a given national sphere through the deregulation of markets (Nef and Robles 37–8).[30]

Moreover, the rubble of the subsidized working-class homes augurs the waning of the social security system and, by extension, of the social pact. In *Postmodernity and Its Discontents*, sociologist Zygmunt Bauman asserts that within the present-day neoliberal order, financial communities have replaced civic and social communities, which, in turn, has augmented economic disparities (23).

The rationale of profit transforms the city's social settings as it saturates its main arteries and seeps into its fractures. In light of this, the description of the deteriorating metropolitan landscape in Bonassi's novel also emblematizes the transformation of the modes of production that accompanies the erosion of social rights. The demolished workers' dwellings bring to mind the consolidation of labor rights during Vargas's first tenure. However, the neoliberal model has deteriorated some of these rights in the name of increased labor flexibility, which should equate to incremented productivity. In this arrangement, labor rights—a modern achievement—are considered anachronistic. Entitlements are a hindrance to modernization (Dagnino, "Confluência" 209–10). The ruins of the working-class tenements signify this erosion, while the avenue that cuts through them, exposing the remnants of a dead lifestyle, similar to the contaminated river and the ailing bodies, connotes the traffic of merchandise, the new flexibility of the production process and its attendant debris.

Mass Media

In *Subúrbio*, the permeation of capital into the traditional fields of collective life is further manifested in the presence of several billboards that interrupt the fictional text. Bonassi places marketing intertexts, printed in the format of miniature billboards, into the novel. The announcements promote either dental or jewelry resale services. Their presence in the novel's third and sixth parts disrupts the narrative flow, suggesting the laceration of the urban landscape through the prevalence of a monetized (instead of communitarian) ethics in the public sphere.

In the first instance, the commercial texts suggest the privatization of health care (Bonassi, *Subúrbio* 19). Like in *O menino que se trancou na geladeira*, health is a commodity that can and must be acquired in the marketplace. Health care no longer is the citizen's prerogative. The second instance, a reference to pawnshops, suggests the working class's socioeconomic erosion in face of changed labor and welfare practices. The advertisement appeals to desperation, indicating that the business advertised buys everything from wedding bands to prostheses (22).

Isolated in a landscape in which the signs of consumerism abound but where the collective dynamic has all but disappeared, the subject has to reimagine her/his social identity utilizing a market-oriented symbolic horizon to formulate this identity. Anthropologist Néstor García Canclini believes that in the framework of late capitalism/neoliberalism, consumption is one of the favored sites for the construction of citizenship. For Canclini, the contemporary period distinguishes itself by various "sociocultural changes" (*Consumers* 24), including the citizen's retreat from the public sphere due to a lack of viable civic and political projects. In the absence of congruent political narratives and/or viable venues for civil participation within a larger (e.g., national) scheme, the contemporary individual recurs to the market to position herself/himself within the social corpus.

This organization is delimited by the constraints and by the symbols laid down by the hegemonic economic, social, and cultural episteme and is often transmitted by the mass media. Consumption patterns, conveyed by television and print or in *Subúrbio* through the aforementioned advertisement intertexts, highlight the socioeconomic constraints faced by consumer-citizens. Analogously to rites of consumption, mass media, specifically television, establishes new manners of sociability that substitute the public sphere, which is increasingly seen as "dangerous" (Martín-Barbero 28).

On the conflictive stage of the metropolis, its citizens increasingly insulate themselves within the backstage of the private domain: shopping centers, gated condominiums, individual homes, and living rooms whose "windows" open up onto the flickering panorama of small-screen entertainment and marketable dreams/products. The public spaces of the metropolis are hence abandoned and become dilapidated. James Holston equates the pattern of urban segregation to the erosion of sociability. If the elites deride public spaces as unsafe, contaminated by the undesirable subjects of the lower classes, then the latter perceive these terrains as zones of marginalization (Holston, *Insurgent* 282).

The ruptured sociability of public venues penetrates into the interior, private spaces. Inside the private zones depicted in *Subúrbio*, interpersonal communication frequently turns into an ephemeral commodity. Hence, for example, as the old man and his wife watch television together, the only interaction is between the actors on the soap opera, who engage in a simulacrum of affection. In contrast, the couple is unable to exhibit their emotions or to engage in a meaningful relationship. Their interface is limited to hostile silences or to a broken semblance of a dialogue, interrupted by the mass media images that invade the living room. Their conversations throughout the narrative are monosyllabic exchanges that do not provide an adequate communicative forum. Emotional sterility leads both characters to seek substitutes for their lack of sentiments and interaction. While the old man finds refuge first in alcohol and then in his perverse passion for the young girl, the old woman insulates herself in commercial culture. Specifically, she is enthralled by an advertisement for jewelry that, in its superimposition of romantic clichés, makes her nostalgic for a different, impossible life. The photograph, described in detail, shows the image of an amorous encounter, perhaps a marriage proposal. Every feature of the picture connotes wealth and taste, from the yacht anchored in the background to the couple's flawless necks. But the most important facet is a diamond ring (Bonassi, *Subúrbio* 119) nestled in a velvet case, which condenses all the promises that the picture encloses.

The beauty and the implicit/explicit message of the snapshot differ starkly from the old woman's personal and material circumstances. Unlike the implied relationship between the couple in the photograph, the *velha*'s marital estrangement is compounded by her meager existential conditions. Instead of a pristine beach landscape, the old woman finds herself in a stultifying environment, emblematized by the kitchen, where layers of frying oil cover all surfaces (16). The kitchen, traditionally a space of sociability, is, like the public environment, transmogrified into a decadent area where the only traces of past conviviality are fossilized into the grime that covers everything.

For the old woman, commercial culture becomes a surrogate for emotional, if not material, comfort. In the television programs and their accompanying advertisement spots and in the pages of glossy magazines that tout products as representative of personal fulfillment, the yearning for affection is translated into the desire for specific objects and the messages affixed to them. Disappointed with her lived experience, the elderly woman withdraws into the space of nostalgia and simulacra so that at the time of the narrative, the *velha* spends entire afternoons gazing at the advertisement that appears in an old fashion magazine. Dissociation between image and reality is communicated by the photograph's datedness that contrasts with the old woman's present moment. As the old woman's imaginings meld into the glossy magazine pictures, they lose their anchor in reality, becoming simulacra of her failed aspirations and ambitions. She disappears, so to speak, in the multiplication of signs.

The bankruptcy of interpersonal relations alluded to by the proliferation of mass and commercial culture in the old couple's existence crystallizes further in the description of their living room (Bonassi, *Subúrbio* 18). The once interactive domain of the living room, where both banal and momentous experiences were shared, now is an empty and silent locale. Its blankness connotes the matrimony's barrenness while also insinuating a generalized deterioration of familial ties. The accretion of manifold little quotidian domestic aggressions—the old man's alcoholism, the wife's anger and loneliness, their mutual frustration—creates the rift that leads to the abandonment of a common life project.

The partners' solitude is reflected in the physical ambiance of the house, which instead of a home (*lar*) is "[a] casa, só" (19).[31]

Concurrently, the violence of an existence plagued by the specter of poverty and burdened by personal disenchantment erodes the emotional, if not material, bonds that link the couple and corrodes their humanity. Both characters lack individual traits including a proper name—as do the novel's other characters. Their reduction to the adjectival form: *o velho* and *a velha* bespeaks of their anonymity vis-à-vis each other and in relation to the context in which they dwell. The isolation and existential misery of the elderly husband and wife is reflected in the decadent inside and the outside of their domicile, which is described thoroughly in the novel (15–18).

Homes and Hovels

Subúrbio represents São Paulo's metropolitan outskirts as peripheral not only geographically, but also socioeconomically. Precarious infrastructure, environmental blight, financial necessity, and social violence: these are the spaces where differentiated citizenship takes shape. And even though in recent years state and municipal governments have made efforts to stabilize and ameliorate low-income communities,[32] the sequence of improvements is not always linear (Holston, *Insurgent* 281), and socioeconomic tensions continue to haunt many of these communities. Like the old couple, most of the residents of their vicinity are located at the limit between the quasi-poverty of the lower middle-class and abject misery. The distinction between the two economic echelons is tenuous and, as the narrative suggests, easily (although not voluntarily) crossed.

Holston, citing Brazilian jurists Clóvis Beviláqua and Joaquim Nabuco, suggests that, following chapter 5 of John Locke's *The Second Treatise of Civil Government* ("On Property") (1946) and Hegel's *Philosophy of Right* (1896), citizenship is strongly tied to property in Brazil (*Insurgent*). Therefore, the negation of property implies a negation of civil standing (113).

Subúrbio's characters, principally the old couple and the girl's family, are not homeowners, but tenants. Though the former have resided in their house for decades, the propriety is not theirs and as such, does not merit any investment. Neglect leads to the progressive deterioration of the living quarters. House and couple are metaphoric units of social and individual collapse. Significantly, when the wife decides to leave the marital bed, she transforms the corridor into "her room" (18). The interior portioning emulates the spaces of the *cortiços*.

Teresa Caldeira explains that *cortiços*, akin to favelas, are liminal spaces and are not seen as adequate residential spaces (78–9). Because of their liminality and transience, both favelas and *cortiços* are considered dangerous and polluting locales (79).

While the old couple's home is not a *cortiço* per se, the girl's family resides in a factual *cortiço* (Bonassi, *Subúrbio* 270), a liminal space within the liminality of the *subúrbio*. Like the *velho*'s and *velha*'s house, here too the living arrangement's provisional nature and the tenant's dire financial condition hinder betterments. The *cortiço*'s destitute environment is mirrored in the girl's family's status. They face the continual threat of eviction from even this marginal terrain (270). Eviction from the, albeit makeshift, house signifies expulsion from the realm of citizenship. The girl's family is in constant fear of joining the ranks of the destitute populace represented here by the lack of a fixed address. If, as Holston suggests in the discourse of citizenship property, ownership is linked to values such as "independence, responsibility, rational calculation, legitimacy, and so forth" (*Insurgent* 173), lack of property ownership is synonymous with social illegality and lack of civil agency.

Social and individual estrangement accrues as peripheral residents are caught in the struggle for survival. Anomie is signaled in the tedious weekday routine of the old man, which he repeats for thirty-five years (Bonassi, *Subúrbio* 29). Echoing the disengagement that permeates the daily existence of the working class, the narrative voice meticulously registers the protagonist's quotidian routine. The account of the hollow, everyday activities points to the emptying of the suburban dwellers' existential horizon, as they are reduced to an instrumental function within the machinery of production and consumption. However, while the old man is still inserted within this process, once he retires he will become an outcast from the exchange economy (labor traded for remuneration, which, in turn, will be interchanged for goods) that, in part, defined him.

Crime and Punishment

Beyond the impoverished working class and *Lumpenproletariat* that inhabits the metropolis's outer precincts, the suburb is also the habitat of marginalized figures such as the child bandit Naldinho. Naldinho is paradigmatic of the subjects that fall through the cracks of a fissured social and legal order. Paradoxically, it is precisely his outsider status that confers the youngster a measure of power while concomitantly making him powerless vis-à-vis the hegemonic order. Insurgency, in this context, akin to Ferréz's narratives, stems from and employs disenfranchisement as a strategy. Naldinho's authority (that both attracts and repulses) emanates from the threat of violence, not dissimilar to the menace posed by the corrupt police in Ferréz's texts. In Bonassi's and Ferréz's novels, delinquents and agents of law enforcement are mirror images of the same coercive system.

In spite of his threatening presence, the juvenile offender still retains in him elements of a troubled, discordant childhood. He is "um menino que trazia muitas mortes na cara, como se fosse um bigode ralinho" (Bonassi, *Subúrbio* 43).[33] The adolescent's facial features reveal his societal and personal abjection through the contradictory traits of youth and death, innocence and degeneration. Situated between childhood and adulthood and between the admiration and the abhorrence he elicits, Naldinho is, in his ambiguity, emblematic of the figurative and empirical unstableness that characterizes the urban periphery and the live world of its dwellers. The child bandit is both the victim of his social circumstances and the agent of social destruction. As many marginalized juvenile subjects, Naldinho cannot count on the state's safeguard, be it in the form of social services, financial assistance for his basic necessities, or even legal recourses to protect him. This tense experience of the *urbe* is reinforced by the criminalizing discourse associated with the impoverished youth in many Brazilian urban centers (Adorno 105) that provides the justification for "preventive" and/or punitive measures that often extrapolate the limits of legality in the name of law and order. When Naldinho is forced to show documentation to the police he is informed that his papers are not valid (Bonassi, *Subúrbio* 46). Negation of his legal existence by the representatives of the law effectively evicts him from the precincts of legality and civil order.

For Carlos Alberto M. Pereira, violence, in particular symbolic violence, can change structures of exclusion, generating new forms of visibility. Therefore, when Naldinho, upon hearing that his papers are invalid, tears them up and throws them into the garbage (Bonassi, *Subúrbio* 46), he recaptures a measure of self-determination. He exposes his removal from and, concurrently, his rejection of the state-sanctioned societal realm that, according to Bauman, still retains its modern prerogative of delineating the separation between "order and chaos, law and lawlessness, citizen and *homo sacer*, belonging and exclusion" (*Wasted* 33). Naldinho, comparable to the criminals depicted in *Capão Pecado* and *Manual prático do ódio*, embodies the *homines sacers* that dwell in the city's literal and metaphorical frontiers. It is the discourse of violence that justifies his ambivalent legal status. The discourse of violence that spreads via mass media or that becomes the target of state action transforms the periphery into spaces of exception in which legal *Aufhebung*—this is, the abolishment of the law—is used to enforce the law. Exclusion from law and from the dominant social body transforms the marginal youth into easy prey of various coercive acts and, in turn, can prompt them into transgressing the same juridical system that segregates them.

As James Holston suggests, differentiated citizenship produces an array of social ills, including criminal and paralegal violence (*Insurgent* 283). He observes that while the junction of differentiated and insurgent citizenship often dents "the coherence of taken-for-granted categories of domination that gave daily life its sense of order and security" (303), it also promotes aggressive rejoinders to these destabilizations. Analogous to insurgent practices, the retorts occur at the sites of differentiated citizenship. Among the effects that shape Brazil's disjunctive democracy are "criminal and police violence, incivility in public encounters, criminalization of the poor, indignation at impunity, massive property conflicts, new privatizations of security, and popular support for violent measures of social control" (303). Though disjunctive democracy creates spaces of contestation, this contestation does not always assume a constructive format. Instead, challenges to the status quo can also exacerbate the incivility of both the public and the private realms.

The contingency of sociability and of polity related in *Subúrbio* can be traced first to a tradition of state-sanctioned violence, imposed by the military dictatorship that, in the present, manifests itself in official (i.e., police) violence against the impoverished population. As indicated by Jorge Balán, the "culture of fear" commenced during authoritarian rule has become prevalent, infusing various social spheres. For Balán, nowadays this culture poses one of the foremost threats to democracy. It leads the subject away from participatory venues and into delegating civil agency onto those who proclaim to control violence and to tame the "savage" metropolis. Vigilante justice is but one expression of fearful passivity (Holston, *Insurgent*; Caldeira *City of Walls*).[34]

Second, the crisis of civil society is also a consequence of the weakening of the social state, partly due to the spread of transnational capitalism and neoliberal policies implemented in the aftermath of totalitarian rule. Privatization of public services, such as security, makes them accessible only to a fortunate few. Less privileged social sectors regularly dwell in no-man's terrains where state power is replaced by other forms of legislation, often the *lex talionis*.[35]

In *Subúrbio*, this law becomes evident in the summary lynching of the old man after his criminal deed is discovered. The verdict, passed on by a mob that eschews the discredited legal order, is reduced to one single verb—"Lynch"—repeated several times (Bonassi, *Subúrbio* 291). In a distorted mirror-image of brutality, the climax of pent-up violence and of anger and frustration with the failure of legal order evokes/repeats the *velho*'s own brutal rape and murder of the young girl. Concurrently, the repetition of the verb "to lynch," underscored by exclamation points, confers a measure of elation to the scene. Violence is spectacularized and becomes a perverse performance of community in which the old man is the scapegoat that cures/coalesces—with his blood—a depraved form of solidarity.[36] The paradoxical enforcement of a law beyond the law, which represents both archaic "justice" and a transgression of the legal system, becomes a mode to reclaim some measure of communitarian agency.

As signaled by Pedrazzini, the discourse of fear often casts poor citizens as threats to the established socioeconomic urban center and its residents. They menace the stability and security of the privileged sectors. Paradoxically, this same discourse also penetrates the imaginary of the disenfranchised classes and engenders fearsome "others" of its own. This all-encompassing terror of a perilous other manifests itself in *o velho*'s dread of being robbed (Bonassi, *Subúrbio* 60). Even while *o velho* and *a velha* are in the putatively secure terrain of their home, the preoccupation with crime prowls in the shadows outside, threatening to invade the domestic "heaven."

As the horror of a supposedly dangerous other permeates different levels of sociability, it contributes to the waning of the already precarious urban communitarian spaces. According to Nancy Cárdia, the connection between the erosion of the social contract and violence lies in that the former promotes the latter but is also a consequence of the fear generated by a hostile atmosphere. Correspondingly, in *Subúrbio* the disintegration of familial and communitarian ties manifests itself in rituals of violence which are executed within both the domestic and public realms. Presaging his murder of the young girl, the old man batters his spouse, using her body as the surface on which he etches his anger and his frustrations (Bonassi, *Subúrbio* 71).

Economic and interpersonal abjection and hostility are also extant in the young girl's domicile, a "haunted house" (269) disturbed by manifold ghosts: financial strain, domestic violence, and parental neglect. Her father, a night patrolman who suffers from mental problems, is disengaged from the material reality that surrounds him. In his estrangement, he embodies the general social anomie in which the metropolitan dweller lives and which, in turn, encourages social and individual dysfunction. Her mother cannot fulfill the role of guardian to her offspring either. Each one of the family's members is enmeshed in the struggle of daily survival and, in this framework, there is little room for the formation of sentimental ties. Instead, akin to their social environment, their domestic space is laden with multiple modes of aggression. Beyond neglect, the parental relationship, like the old couple's interactions, is fraught with abuse that also spills over into maltreatment of their offspring: "[o] pai batia na mãe porque sofria dos nervos. . . . Ele brigava com todos. . . . Muitas vezes o menino chorava e a menina também apanhava porque o menino tinha que ficar quieto. . . . A menina até beliscava ele mas aí o irmãozinho chorava mais e mais. . . . Se todo mundo tivesse um quarto o problema era resolvido. . . . Só que a família não tinha dinheiro para mudar de casa" (269–70).[37]

Forced intimacy due to poverty creates a hostile ambiance that inculcates the customs of mutual aggression in each one of the family members, including its youngest ones. Luiz Eduardo Soares pinpoints three predominant modalities of violence in Brazilian society: the economic violence of the elites, the subsistence violence of the subaltern classes, and finally, the all-encompassing and irrational violence of the domestic sphere. For Soares, the latter contaminates all areas of life, though it predominates the private ambit. It affects principally women and children ("Interpretação" 41).

Focusing on the aggression that occurs both within and outside the house, Bonassi ties the threads that link them together, exposing the interwoven fabric of differentiated citizenship and hostility that affects the lives of the disenfranchised working class populace. In order to flee her suffocating environment, *a menina* runs away (Bonassi, *Subúrbio* 271). Her flight, however, does not lead her to a safe space where she can find refuge from her daily tribulations, but takes her instead from the hostile province of the home into the abject terrains of the metropolis.

Predatory Sexuality

The young girl's victimization, first within the family and then outside it, represents the vulnerability of low-income children to the erosion of the social pact. Disintegration of the familial network is compounded by inadequate access to social services (such as day-care centers, suitable schooling, and after-school programs) and their respective protective localities. As a result, young people from/in the metropolitan wastelands often transit in unsafe arenas and frequently become unstable ciphers within the urban imaginary. The *menina*'s symbolic volatility evidences itself in the duality of desire she evokes in the old man. For him, she is at the same time child and woman, granddaughter and sexualized object.

Elizabeth Lowe, in her book about the representation of the city in Brazilian literature, contends that the representation of a hostile *urbe* is tied to sexual deviance (138). Inserting himself into the space of the remiss parents, the old man assumes the part of the young girl's guardian. He shields her from the inhospitable milieu she dwells in and, simultaneously, assumes the role of sexual predator. His sentiments toward her shift from the ambit of desire for parenthood to the realm of amorous interest. In this context, her physicality is gradually transformed from that of an innocent child into one of a seductive object, as is inscribed by the old man's increasingly sexualized stare. He observes "as curvas dos bracinhos, das perninhas, da cinturinha, da bundinha" (Bonassi, *Subúrbio* 283).[38] The narrative voice accompanies the gaze's progression through the, at first, nonsexualized body parts (*os bracinhos*) into the terrain of the sexualized physicality (*a bundinha*). Juxtaposing the diminutive suffix (*inho* and *inha*) with a libidinal discourse, the narrative voice exposes the perversion and violence of this voyeuristic exercise and intimates the impeding assault. The *velho*'s desire is abject as it contaminates the child's innocence with his tainted longing, mingles her purity with his decrepitude, her youth with the death he embodies, and transforms affection into violence. Her body, a paradigm of guilelessness, becomes marked/marred by the old man's ambiguous feelings of parental and sexual longing. Ultimately, the *velho*'s libidinal gaze progressively strips the child of her subject-status, transforming her into an abject object, a familiar yet strange being endowed with both the innocence of childhood and the allure of a sexually mature woman. The child's metamorphosis into an abject object culminates in her murder (the transformation of her living body into a corpse) and in the postmortem defilement of her cadaver by the old man, who penetrates her dead flesh.

As a prelude to the young girl's rape, *Subúrbio* addresses gendered aggression in its description of the *velho*'s voyeuristic escapades. Through a peephole he observes the naked body of his female neighbor. His eye, and by extension the reader's eye, fragments the woman's anatomy, concentrating on its disjointed parts and focusing on its intimacy, in particular *a vala* (literally the ditch, metaphorically the vagina) (63). The *vala* signifies for the male onlooker the symbolic darkness of a female sexuality that both attracts and rebuffs him. *Vala* in this context becomes a synonym for the grave. This association between the female genitalia and death reveals the pull of attraction and repulsion that the sexual organs—and woman in general—represent for the old man.[39] The neighbor's corporeality is thus the abject that the masculine viewer must restrain. Through his gaze, the old man reduces the woman to her sex, transforming her into a mere object of libidinous contemplation/consumption. The obsession with and the fragmentation of the female corpus is reproduced at a linguistic level through the repetition of specific words such as *o cheiro* (odor) and, more important, *a vala*. Repetition mimics the double movement of desire and obsession inherent in this scene.

As the old man observes his neighbor masturbating, her libidinal energy disconcerts the protagonist since, as an object of *his* desire, she is not supposed to possess any sexual yearnings herself. He therefore relegates her into the terrain of a pejorative femaleness by calling her first a "—Vaca-vaca-vaca" (63)[40] and subsequently a "—Puta-puta-filha-da-puta" (63).[41] Reduced to a debased status, the woman is "controlled" by the old man's desire-derision and by his libidinous fixation. Her solitary act is paralleled by his masturbation. As he replicates her movements, the old man effectively invades her private sphere and violates the neighbor. In his orgasm, the protagonist expels from his body the abject desire for this subject-object. When he ejaculates, his lust is reduced to a sliver of sperm that promptly disappears into the sewer (64). His sexuality, being debased from its inception, does not enter a productive emotional or libidinal economy but becomes instead yet another of the city's waste products, disappearing in its abject entrails. The graphicness of the description that emphasizes sliminess highlights the debasement inherent in the old man's voyeuristic exercise, the violence of the gaze transformed into repugnant matter.

In late-capitalist socioeconomic organization, women's bodies are one of the preferred surfaces on which aggression is emblazoned. Destabilization of traditional social arrangements leads to the confusion of established (notwithstanding problematic) gender roles in many societies. Jean Franco asserts that economic restructuring destabilizes traditional male identity by eroding the parameters around which it was constructed, such as labor (*Decline and Fall* 220–21). Emasculated by an economic and cultural logic that aims to maximize productivity and from which he is expelled, the male subject seeks to reassert his patriarchal power by exerting control over the female body. In *Subúrbio*, this dominance is expressed not only in the voyeuristic escapades of the old man (who, when he is looked back at, cannot feel aroused by the naked frame of his neighbor), but also through his rape of the young girl. When violating the child, the old man dismembers her mentally and transforms the girl into a collection of physical parts, an act reminiscent of his earlier voyeuristic appropriation of his neighbor's anatomy. Moreover, as the child protests his sexual advances, he erases her subjectivity and silences her by breaking her neck (Bonassi, *Subúrbio* 283–84).

Sexual crime is, as Rebecca Biron suggests, an attempt at reintegration into the hegemonic patriarchal system. However, this type of crime also connotes the expulsion of the criminal from this same organization. Cast aside from the workforce, unable to establish a meaningful relationship in either the private or public realms, the elderly man resorts to violence as a form of establishing a perverse connection to the girl, and by extension, reinstating his association to the larger private and public organism (the family, the collectivity). For him, the rape signifies a nefarious conjugal union, the culmination of a debased and ultimately deadly "matrimony."

It is significant that the rape takes place in the makeshift "house" that the old man and the child have erected beneath a picnic table in the park by the Represa Billings. Within this scenario, a debased simulacrum of the domestic sphere, the old man transforms *a menina* into a surrogate for familial and emotional ties. Assembled of the rubbish that litters the picnic grounds and that is emblematic of the lost traces of personal and public memories, the makeshift construction is also indicative of the child's obliteration from both the private and the public domains.

The garbage that surrounds the old man and the girl represents not only the disposability of the latter, but also remits to the larger proliferation of waste occasioned by the discourse of modernity (Bauman, *Wasted Lives*). As Nelly Richard indicates, the fascination with the "new," dictated also by the capitalist necessity of creating ever-expanding markets, is paradigmatic of modernity and engenders a multitude of waste products—including "human garbage" (49).

The scene of the rape is strewn thus not only with the objects of a wasteful modernity but also with its subjects. In the scheme of a society that relegates the peripheral youth to the status of debris, the child is just another artifact of an abject socioeconomic order. In tandem to the girl's disposability, *o velho*, due to his age, his alcoholism, and perhaps most importantly his retirement from the workforce, is "evicted" from the space of production and of consumption, becoming himself refuse. In Bonassi's suburban terrain, the old man (similar to Naldinho, the girl's father, and other anonymous inhabitants of the margins) is both the casualty and the executor of the culture of violence that perturbs Brazil's late-capitalist dystopian landscape. Nestled among—or at the edges of—the pockets of prosperity generated by the neoliberal rationale, the abject sites of the *urbe* multiply, and with them, the abject subjects that inhabit said territories, the suburbs of the neoliberal order.

Chapter 3

Practical Handbook of Citizenship

Negating/Negotiating Human Rights in São Paulo's Periphery

It's a chilly July night in São Paulo's sprawling periphery and the bar is already quite full. People drink beer and snack on fried cod fish cakes. Then the function begins. Poet and community activist Sérgio Vaz introduces the artists who will be performing tonight. He explains what the "Sarau da Co-operifa" is and requests silence from the audience. An elderly woman takes the stage and proudly declaims the poem "O navio negreiro" (The slave ship) by romantic poet Castro Alves. Her voice echoes through the drafty space, and the people cramped into the bar and spilling out on the street are tied by an invisible chord to her words, the story, the memories and the emotions the stanzas invoke. Engagement and community are words that come to mind. Community and empowerment through literature— this is what Co-operifa is all about. The Sarau da Co-operifa is but one example of the literary activism that is emerging from Brazil's urban peripheries and creating a space in which the voices of the country's traditionally marginal groups can find expression.

This chapter examines the intersection between literature as a critique of differentiated citizenship and culture as a means of agency in Ferréz's two novels: *Capão Pecado* (Capão sin, 2000) and *Manual prático do ódio* (Practical handbook of hate, 2003). The two novels are set in São Paulo's marginal community of Capão Redondo, where Ferréz resides. Both *Capão Pecado* and *Manual prático do ódio* denounce the disparity of social rights that permeates Brazil's peripheral communities and, like Luiz Ruffato's and Fernando Bonassi's novels, also show how these inequalities create a culture of violence. Similar to Ruffato's setting of working-class homes and hovels and Bonassi's dystopian landscapes, Capão Redondo emblematizes the space of differentiated citizenship.

Ferréz's two novels indicate that socioeconomic and cultural marginalization lead to assimilation of subalternity as an identity. That is to say, the characters of both books feel trapped by their social circumstance, reacting either with a generalized apathy or with violence and transgression. Nevertheless, when read in the larger context of Ferréz's multiple sociocultural endeavors, including his clothing line, 1dasul, *Capão Pecado* and *Manual prático do ódio* transform (literary) discourse on socioeconomic and racial discrimination into a strategy of resistance.

Writing from an "insider" perspective, Ferréz constructs a fresco of life in the *periferia* in which he at the same time reinforces and problematizes the stereotype of the racialized and poor peripheral subject from "within." Though *Capão Pecado* and *Manual prático do ódio* are not testimonials in the traditional sense of the genre,[1] the two novels do contain some of the genre's attributes—specifically its impetus to make certain social, cultural, and political circumstances known to wider, mainly hegemonic audiences and through this knowledge promote social action (Nance 19). If we take this understanding of the testimonial text to the fictional realm, applying it to narratives that share the same or similar goals to *testimonio*, it can be said that the insider perspective in Ferréz's two novels also prompts a project of social justice. The insider perspective both lends "truth" valence to the narrative at hand—it becomes, so to speak, a written documentary—and empowers the writing subject and the community that she/he represents.

Capão Pecado and *Manual prático do ódio* set out to retrieve a measure of legitimacy—civic, social, and cultural—for the marginalized subjects the books depict. In this context, the two novels reclaim—through an insurgent discourse—legitimacy for São Paulo's peripheral communities, both within and outside these neighborhoods. This legitimacy can be translated into instrumentality, as is the case in the various community and cultural initiatives spearheaded by the author. This is to say, cultural insurgency—the combination between literary denunciation and sociocultural action against differentiated citizenship—translates into social agency. In other words, Ferréz's literary endeavors at the same time critique and reinforce negative stereotypes about Brazil's metropolitan peripheries. Ferréz's two novels use hegemonic representations of disadvantaged peoples to undo the notion of a supposed cultural deficit within disenfranchised communities. Allied with other cultural initiatives, literature serves to contest social injustice.

In a posting on Ferréz's blog, the *paulista* writer, activist, and hip-hop artist relates a quotidian incident in the low-income vicinity, on the outskirts of São Paulo, in which he lives. After a long day in the city, he returns to Capão Redondo and finds a "blitz, a polícia revista todo mundo, mão no saco, mão no peito, mão na bunda, pergunta e restrição de caminhos. Estou ficando louco?"[2] (Ferréz, "Depois eu que sou louco"). The scene emblematizes the various forms of official abuse that many underprivileged Brazilian communities endure, a feature of what James Holston designates as "civilly disjunctive democracies," electoral democracies where citizens are subjected to both official and extraofficial violence with immunity (*Citizenship* 81). Lacking proper access to the material and institutional safeguards of citizenship (courts, policy makers, education, public security, etc.), impoverished social sectors suffer the biggest impact of the unequal allocation of civic, political, and socioeconomic rights.

In the previously cited episode, one sees that citizenship is eroded—or flat out denied—at many levels. First, civil citizenship is breached through the police's aggressive invasion of the neighborhood. The police's foray into the terrain of the low-income community signals the symbolic and juridical association of this space with criminality. This correlation provides the ideological pretext for the physical and psychological abuse meted out by the authorities. For sociologist Zygmunt Bauman, the criminalization of the poor, and of the territories they occupy, corresponds to their categorization as abject others of consumer society (*Community* 120).

The poor are both inside and outside the realm of consumption and production; they are foreign bodies wedged into the contemporary social fabric. They provide the cheap labor of the informal economy as producers and also represent what Bauman calls the "surplus population" of capitalist modernity. Nevertheless, these same people are habitually unable to participate in the rituals of consumption that increasingly have come to define citizenship. Exclusion is exacerbated when this populace is also classified as supernumerary to the production process, cast aside from both sides of the economic platform that formulates citizenship.

As redundant subjects, scores of impoverished citizens are interdicted from the hegemonic urban cartography. They are driven to its physical and symbolic margins, the nonplaces of sociability that are rampant in many contemporary conurbations. As residents of such spaces, they are banned from the official civic and social realm. However, the marginalized social segments also remain inserted within the hegemonic sociocultural structure. They provide the negative social and symbolic screen onto which the elites project their anxieties and thereby validate both their prejudices and their privileges. The "surplus" urban population is hence subject to the law[3] and is simultaneously barred from this domain. It can therefore be argued that in the diagram of disjunctive citizenship, the marginal subject is transformed into what Giorgio Agamben has termed *homo sacer*: "The being that stands both inside and outside the legal system, that resides in the juridical and political non-places of the nation, and is in effect stripped of her/his citizenship—and of her/his human rights. *Homo sacer*, and the marginal subject, cannot be sacrificed, but can be killed with impunity" (*Homo Sacer* 8).

According to Agamben, the ban is both an inclusive and exclusive phenomenon that creates subjects which exists outside the law (are "abandoned" by it) (28). *Homo sacer* is proscribed from the figurative and material topography of the city proper. However, she/he also inhabits these spaces as a revenant of sorts that disturbs the "secure" and "unsoiled" terrains of the "city of walls." Agamben asserts that *homo sacer* is linked simultaneously to the figure of the sacred man and to that of the werewolf, a being located between the threshold of the human and the nonhuman. As such, *homo sacer* belongs neither to the realm of the law, nor is he entirely outside of it (105). This is to say, while *homo sacer* must be barred from the polis, she/he nevertheless populates its imaginary and, occasionally, transgresses into the hegemonic city. Both forms of incursions (symbolic and real) spawn and/or corroborate so-called preemptive measures, such as police raids that, as indicated by the incident related earlier, spill into the marginal dominions, the favelas, and the low-income communities in which *homo sacer* resides.

Thus, the *homenes sacers* that inhabit the metropolitan margins are caught in a dual equation of power that corresponds to a double configuration of exclusion. They become the abject object of the upper and middle classes' sovereign gaze. At the same time, they are also excluded from the establishments of power that purport to represent said classes, in this case, the police. So-called transgressive and/or poor subjects in effect do not have a legal status or membership in the civic community.[4]

What distinguishes *homo sacer* is not merely her/his relation to the middle and upper social echelons and their institutionalized powers, but that she/he exists in the tension between two forms of sovereignty: that of official rule and that of the extrajudicial order that controls these metropolitan exclaves (or, depending on the urban geography, enclaves), that is, organized crime (Penna, "Estado de exceção"). Caught between two conflicting and yet paradoxically complementary modes of sovereignty/exclusion—the official law of the *asfalto* and the unofficial law/illegality of the *morro/periferia*, often represented by drug dealers that control these dominions—the marginalized populace becomes a facile target of various forms of victimization from both within and outside the community. They exist in a de facto "state of nature."[5]

In this respect, the police invasion of Capão Redondo described by Ferréz in his blog exposes the dual (geographic and sociolegal) injunction experienced by its inhabitants vis-à-vis the official realm of the city and its authorities. The raid also indicates how the former is linked to the paralegal power that structures the community and extends into the polis. The police's rogue actions sematize Capão Redondo as a no-man's-land, a domain where even though the law is present (in the belligerent physical presence and performance of the police officers); it is invalidated by its presumptive agents. This cancellation occurs via the articulation of an alleged and a real state of exception (Agamben *State of Exception*) that is literally embodied by the peripheral subject who threatens the body/bodies of the legitimate city. This assumed threat allows for the alternation of *bios* into *zoe*.

The unwarranted and (sexually) abusive search of the residents denotes the symbolic negation of political citizenship. The subject is stripped of his or her legislative rights and is reduced to her/his bare corporality. Without *bios*, the state exercises its full authority upon the *zoe*. This is to say, the peripheral subject is in effect expunged from the polis, the political body, for "menacing" the civic body of the sovereign city and the physical bodies of its residents (and the material belongings that surround these bodies).

In the episode Ferréz narrates, peripheral physicality, existing outside the confines of the legal system (that coincides with the boundaries of the "city proper": the middle and upper class metropolis), becomes the object of hubris—in this case, sexualized groping. Groping is a gesture that violates the individual's private sphere as well as her/his personal decorum. The peripheral residents are thus objects of a biopolitics of abjection in which their bodies (*zoe*) become a fundamental vector in the formulation of power—be it legal or extralegal. For Agamben, biopolitics, the politics of the biological, that is, the control of bodies, lies at the heart of sovereignty. And, as indicated by Foucault (*The*

History of Sexuality), biopower is profoundly enmeshed in the history of capitalism (*History of Sexuality* 141). Biopolitics both manages the bodies that partake in the process of production and consumption and proscribes those that are not integrated into this process.

The scene narrated by Ferréz highlights how, in the scheme of differentiated citizenship, marginalized social sectors fall into a grey zone of legality that extends from their bare life to their biological life. Within this spectrum, their physical and legal-political bodies are at once subject to the law (the blitz operation) and not protected by it (as indicated by the infringement on personal rights and dignity). The confluence between bodily and civic disenfranchisement is reproduced within the paralegal realm. Here, the peripheral subjects' bodies are exposed to the sanctioned violence of the criminal powers that, for all intents and purposes, fill in the void of governmental authority that prevails in many low-income communities.

The problematics of differentiated citizenship and unequal/inexistent human rights in Brazil has gained prominence within critical studies and cultural production alike.[6] Several studies attempt to represent, explain, and critique the socioeconomic violence that ensues from civic and material inequality. Specifically the axis of violence, marginality, and urban segmentation has become a staple of sociological and cultural studies and production alike as the crisis of sociability resists being assuaged by social programs that seek to ameliorate Brazil's social gap.

The increment of discourses that touch upon the proliferation of violence due to marginalization has also produced a growing number of testimonials from impoverished urban areas. These texts frequently address the issue of geosocial division, human rights, and citizenship in the fractured metropolis. Several narratives that focus on Brazil's socioeconomic margins—be they fictional, semifictional, or documentary—relate specifically the infringement on the aforementioned rights and offer the reader a perspective from inside the urban ghettos. Some of these narratives attempt to counteract the spectacularization of violence and crises that prevails in the hegemonic media. Texts such as Ferréz's *Capão Pecado* and *Manual prático do ódio* simultaneously counteract and reinforce the characterization of the peripheral subject as *homo sacer*. In this respect, this type of cultural production unwittingly reproduces the dichotomy of inclusion/exclusion that lies at the heart of the relation between sovereign powers and *homo sacer*.

Books such as Ferréz and Ademiro Alves's (Sacolinha) *Graduado em marginalidade* (Graduate in marginality, 2005) aim to call attention to the endemic transformation of the peripheral subject into *homo sacer*. Such narratives center on the rampant violence and lack of sociability that exist within the favela. The stories' focus on exigency unintentionally harks back to precisely the elements that the stories set out to deconstruct. In this respect, *Graduado em marginalidade* and similar books deal with the same symbolic currency as mainstream sociocultural discourse. Violence and criminality become the cultural commodities that circulate both within hegemonic and nonhegemonic narratives, selling either a discourse of marginality or of marginalization.

Considered *literatura marginal* (marginal literature), texts such as *Graduado em marginalidade* are, to varying degrees, documents that, in spite of their ambivalence of representation—or perhaps because of it—denounce social conditions in the margins and voice a program of sociocultural resistance. At the same time, *literatura marginal* also maintains a dialogue with predominant mediations of the favela and its residents, such as hip-hop and graffiti. Like these artistic expressions, *literatura marginal* has an overt social program (Eslava 47).

Literatura marginal and, by extension, *arte marginal* (marginal art, which includes among its expressions rap, funk, break dancing, graffiti, and clothing design), aspire to generate discursive and material spaces of empowerment for members of subaltern social groups. This type of literary expression sets out to establish concrete as well as virtual communities in an arena where social ties suffer the consequences of differentiated citizenship.

The communitarian aspects of both *literatura* and *arte marginal* strive to counteract the dismantlement of traditional social and civic bonds and accompanying individualism. This crisis of sociability reflects both the ongoing socioeconomic gap and processes of globalization that impact the unity of the nation-state in political, economic, and cultural terms (Appadurai; Sousa Santos, "Os processos da globalização"; Hardt and Negri; Bauman, *Community, Wasted Lives, Consuming Life*). Marginal literature and art thus seek to reestablish ties within the fractured terrain of the metropolis, both within the community and with other disenfranchised communities/social sectors. At times these initiatives also transcend the borders of a particular conurbation.

In many texts that belong to this literary modality, individualism is negatively juxtaposed to solidarity and cultural agency is contrasted to vacuous materialism and attendant violence.

Violence is both a cause and an effect of social fragmentation. It reflects the erosion of the public sphere and leads, in turn, to the stigmatization of marginal territories and populations as inherently antisocial. According to Nancy Cárdia, this perception engenders further disengagement from a collectivity, or the investment in what she terms "social capital" (164). *Literatura marginal* engages both discursive and substantive expressions of violence as terrains of contestation and agency.

Reginaldo Ferreira da Silva, also known as Ferréz, is currently perhaps the best-known Brazilian writer-activist to emerge from a socioeconomically disadvantaged milieu. Beyond being a consecrated author, Ferréz is also known as a social activist, rapper, and entrepreneur. His fictional production, which encompasses three novels, a short story collection,[7] and an ensemble of short stories and chronicles of urban life, recounts the difficult daily existences of favela inhabitants in Brazil. Most of his stories are set in his home community of Capão Redondo. Like many other low-income districts around São Paulo, this neighborhood, located in the southern periphery of the city, is home to many poor migrants that came to the megalopolis in search of better living conditions. Many of these people escaped hunger and generalized poverty in Brazil's Northeastern states. Lúcia Sá points out that because of this, Capão Redondo is seen as a "bad" neighborhood (108). Negative bias against residents of Capão Redondo is incremented by the vicinage's violent reputation.

Ferréz's literature dialogues indirectly with his social activism, being in effect one of the various modes through which he seeks to mobilize the residents of São Paulo's periphery against victimization both from the outside and from within the community. Ferréz's writing is one of the iterations of insurgent citizenship that, according to Holston, springs forth in the interstices of disjointed citizenship. On the surface, *Capão Pecado* and *Manual prático do ódio* seem to deny the possibility of reclaiming a functional public sphere and counteracting the state of exception inhabited by the *homenes sacers* of the periphery. Both texts are nonetheless cautionary tales that remit to art as an alternative to the social crisis being portrayed in the novels. Ferréz's literary output suggests that art as a mode of agency only arises from the interactions between fictional production and social engagement, a recurrent theme of *literatura marginal*.

Pursuing art as social agenda, the *paulista* author has become a spokesperson of sorts for marginal literature and the social segments this genre purports to represent. Ferréz is actively engaged in the promotion and publication of other marginal writers, both from Brazil and from other Latin American countries, such as Mexico and Argentina. For Ferréz, culture foments resistance to material and discursive disparities and provides an example of what can be called "globalization from below" (Sousa Santos, "Toward a Multicultural Conception"). "Globalization from below" both defies and provides an alternative to late-capitalist globalization.

For Portuguese sociologist Boaventura de Sousa Santos, globalization necessitates diverse modes of resistance.[8] Those struggling against neoliberal globalization want to transform not only the economic, but also social and symbolic inequities that become exacerbated in the context of both "globalizing localisms" and "localized globalisms" ("Os processos da globalização"). Among the devices of resistance against neoliberal globalization, Sousa Santos includes artistic and literary movements from the global periphery that seek to promote counterhegemonic culture (73).

Ferréz is an active participant in the series "Literatura Marginal," printed by the publishing house LM in conjunction with Ação Educativa[9] under the rubric of "Selo Povo" (People's Stamp). Selo Povo aims to promote and make available books by contemporary marginal authors from Brazil. It has also reedited books by what are considered subaltern writers such as Lima Barreto and Maria Carolina de Jesus, who have been appropriated by the national canon.[10]

Beyond endorsing writers from disenfranchised communities, Selo Povo also strives to make literature widely available to economically depressed residents who normally would not have the means to purchase books and/or have exposure to literary production in general. The first volume published by Selo Povo is composed of chronicles written by Ferréz that, like his fictional narratives, transmit a critical vision of the internal and external tensions that favela residents confront. In Ferréz's view, literature becomes the remedy to the manifold problems confronted by the denizens of the *periferia*. Literature provides alternate modes of identification and empowerment for said populace.

As stated previously, marginal literature wants to create an affirmative paragon of favelas that counteracts their widespread representation as violent, uncultured, and threatening enclaves that unsettle the "civilized" perimeters of the city proper. Such depictions have gained popularity in mass media venues through blockbuster publications such as Paulo Lins's *Cidade de Deus* (City of God, 1997), Dráuzio Varela's *Estação Carandiru* (Station Carandiru, 1999), MV Bill and Celso Athayde's *Falcão: Meninos do tráfico* (Falcon: The children of the traffic, 2006), and Luiz Eduardo Soares's *Elite da tropa* (Elite troop, 2005). The success of these books was partly fuelled by the release of recent films based on the texts[11] and, in the case of *Falcão*, by the homonymous documentary that was aired by Rede Globo in 2006. The aforesaid texts' intention is generally to denounce the deficit in citizenship that promotes criminality (especially the drug trade) within impoverished communities. In contrast, the cinematographic representations, particularly *Cidade de Deus* and *Tropa de elite* (2008, directed by José Padilha), which ensued from the books, convey a spectacle of violence that interpolates its audience, establishing and/or solidifying negative expectations about the *periferia* and, in particular, its young male residents (Pedrazzini).

The discourse of fear propagated by media outlets feeds into and responds to an underlying predicament of sociability in both the metropolis's private and public sphere. It also dialogues with the formulation of impoverished neighborhoods as propelling a "state of exception." In a circular motion, fear produces and/or worsens said crisis, providing continual fodder for narratives of exigency and panic.[12] The rise of social and cultural discourses centered on the threatening presence of others—usually the underprivileged classes that dwell just beyond the real and metaphorical gates of the "city of walls"—not only affects individual social relations, but also influences social policies (Debord, *Society*; Sartori, *Homo videns* Morin *Cinema*). Social policies that respond to violence oscillate between castigation (that transform the peripheral others into agents of mayhem and destruction) and well-intentioned, but nonetheless paternalistic, measures that construct the urban poor as victims without agency.

For Benito Rodriguez Martinez, the mass media delineates the favela population, especially its youth, in Manichean terms, either as helpless victims that need the state's protection or as "agents of their own violence," responsible for their own demise (64). The binary between victims and victimizers serves, according to Martinez, to justify inoperative civil and social mechanisms of citizenship. In accordance to this logic, the favela becomes *homo sacer*'s terrain par excellence.

Whereas films such as *Cidade de Deus*, *Tropa de elite*, and *Última parada 174* (Last stop 174, 2008, directed by Bruno Barreto) engage a voyeurism of the abject that popularizes and demonizes the favela (all the while commodifying the space and its residents in an exotification of violence), they do not—for the most part—have the transformative potential that is sought after by *literatura marginal*.[13] Instead, these cinematographic depictions of the *periferia* reiterate a distance between what is considered the "city proper" and its margins. Such films reinforce the perception of the *periferia* as a terrain of contravention. As a result, the subjacent message of these films seems to be that the subjects that inhabit these urban territories are justifiably barred from access to civic, social, and (at least in practice) political citizenship even though they are fit to be cast as objects of aesthetic expenditure in an economy of apprehension.

Ferréz observes the contradiction between the mass media popularity of the favela and the community's abandonment by social agents (*Cronista* 13). *Literatura marginal* questions this "relegation" of the peripheral subject to the outskirts of the socioeconomic and cultural circumference. Nonetheless, this type of literature also capitalizes on the increased popularity of the "marginal" within artistic circles. As suggested by its moniker, the "marginal" (subject and topic) becomes a distinguishing feature of *literatura marginal*.[14]

Notwithstanding its desire to contest prejudice, marginal literature does not interrogate the existence of walls per se. This is to say, walls are a given in the national panorama. Nor, as implied in many of the texts of *literatura marginal*, is their dismantling necessarily a concrete reality. Rather, marginal literature zooms in on the complexity of what lies beyond the walls, what inhabits the supposedly "dangerous" terrains beyond the enclosures of the polis.

In opposition to the mass media exhibitions of violence that reinforce or promote social neglect, Ferréz details another reality of the favela. In this reality, literary activities are increasingly an integral part of life in the urban periphery, thanks to the outreach of writer-activists such as Ferréz. The author reveals how the diffusion of *literatura marginal* has engendered a spate of cultural activities, such as readings and book releases, that consolidate the *periferia* as a dynamic cultural terrain (*Cronista* 17).

Journalist Fabiana Guedes proposes that *literatura marginal* "replenish" the vacuum of the body politic in disenfranchised communities (37). Ferréz's short story anthology *Literatura marginal. Talentos da escrita periférica* (Marginal literature: Talents from peripheral writing) assembles writings from various peripheral authors. The collection opens with a programmatic manifesto on marginal literature that replicates the characteristics delineated by Guedes and other literary critics. Ferréz highlights the social dimension of this type of writing and rails against the cultural and economic configuration that generates and preserves inequity. He proposes textual production as an antidote against material and symbolic discrimination. The author establishes a dichotomy between *literatura marginal* and dominant culture, which he perceives to be a tool within Brazil's network of differentiated citizenship (*Literatura marginal* 11).

Throughout the manifesto, Ferréz emphasizes the peripheral aspect of marginal literature. The periphery is present not only in the physical locus of discursive production, but also in regard to its epistemic localization. For the author, *literatura marginal* goes against the grain of mainstream knowledge about the subject and sites of otherness: the periphery/the favela/the ghetto. But *literatura marginal* also dialogues with this cognition. For Ferréz, *literatura marginal*, including his own textual production, thus fabricates a contrapuntal reading of Brazil's real and imagined margins/marginality.[15]

Ferréz inserts his literary output and that of the writers included in the anthology within a cultural genealogy that spans both the past and future. This lineage includes the silenced voices of the disempowered in the past and the creativity of future "minority" writers. The texts of future minority writers not only converse with past and present expressions of marginal literature, but their literature is made possible by the struggles that enable the assertion of *literatura marginal*'s sociocultural valence.

The author squarely interweaves his own textual production and his social activism into the gamut of emancipatory gestures that are opening new sites of expression and cultural validation for minority writers and their literature (11). Ferréz underscores that his artistic heritage is firmly rooted in the context of the *periferia*/favela/*gueto* (ghetto) and often assumes either a testimonial or pseudotestimonial mode. His "testimonies" blend it with other narrative genres, such as the documentary, social critique/denouncement, and autobiography (Dalcastagnè, "Vozes na sombra"; Dias; Atencio; Eslava).[16] Indeed, his "insider status" imbues legitimacy upon texts that propose to communicate the "reality" of favela life.

Both academic and nonacademic literary criticism tends to read *literatura marginal* through the binary prism that juxtaposes and, frequently, confronts "authenticity" to "literary quality"[17] (Carneiro). For the Brazilian literary critic Regina Dalcastagnè, this is, however, an artificial duality. Instead, Dalcastagnè proposes that *literatura marginal* indicates a changing field of literary studies. For her, the discipline of literary studies necessitates the same democratization that is occurring—through *literatura marginal*—in the arena of literary production (49). The democratization of the literary panorama and its collective facet are the central tenets of marginal literature, as this genre professes not only to articulate a reality that is both known and unknown, but also to make literature accessible to members of disenfranchised communities.[18]

Ferréz's two novels, *Capão Pecado* and *Manual prático do ódio* situate the conflictive social and private terrains of the favela within a grid of inequitable access to civil and social citizenship. Both books are set in Capão Redondo, a space that emblematizes an almost absolute lack of substantive citizenship. Unlike *Inferno provisório*'s Cataguases, *Capão Pecado*'s and *Manual prático do ódio*'s peripheral landscapes are not inhabited by a working class that hopes to transcend its sociospatial abjection. Rather, Capão Redondo condenses the crisis of citizenship that affects low-income urban neighborhoods and its residents. The social outcasts (criminals, addicts, street children) that populate *Capão Pecado* and *Manual prático do ódio* struggle on the edge of survival. Their social aspirations are often reduced to not being caught in the conflicting web of official and unofficial power, the police and the criminal lords that control the favela—often with the avail of the former.

Capão Pecado and *Manual prático do ódio* represent rampant differentiated citizenship. In this context, insurgence often takes the guise of violence. *Capão Pecado* and *Manual prático do ódio* beg the question of whether the democratization of antinomic citizenship confronts its limits in the impoverished metropolitan locales. It is here that the state of exception finds its most pungent expression. However, at the same time that the novels impart a despondent view of the community, the texts' circuitous dialogue with the *periferia*'s larger sociocultural context and propose an alternative to the dire landscape that appears in the novels. In this sense, they echo Holston's proposition that insurgent modalities of civil, political, and social agency arise in the crevices of differentiated citizenship.

In its dialogic tension between the illustration of despondency and the extratextual modes and spaces of empowerment, Ferréz's novels reflect ambiguous discourse on violence in Brazilian cultural discourse. The sematization of social aggression oscillates between fetish and critique, allegorizing both victimization and agency. Both *Capão Pecado* and *Manual prático do ódio* thematize differentiated citizenship in Brazil's metropolises by criminalizing the peripheral populace and calling attention to the prevalent corruption of the police force. The novels therefore apparently mimic dominant representations of these two groups. Nonetheless, both novels juxtapose generalized criminality with the tentative normalcy of the law-abiding dwellers of Capão Redondo. Even so, these subjects become social outsiders by force of their geographical and economic positioning. Thus, while the original definition of *homo sacer* relates to a subject who committed a crime so heinous as to expel him from the polis (allowing this subject to be killed, but not to be sacrificed), in the two novels, the abjection inherent to *homo sacer* is enmeshed with not only legal contravention, but also material dearth.

Capão Pecado and *Manual prático do ódio* engage the nexus of violence, differentiated citizenship, and the codification of the economically disenfranchised sectors as *homo sacer*. The two novels contest the juxtaposition of these three elements and attempt to produce alternate modes of epistemological and material agency for Brazil's impoverished citizens. In *Capão Pecado* and *Manual prático do ódio*, Ferréz creates a negative blueprint of favela life to, perhaps paradoxically, counteract the criminalization of its residents from *within* and from without the community.[19] For Ferréz, Capão Redondo is allegorical of a broader pattern of marginalization and social redundancy, of a periphery that extends into the entire urban landscape (*Capão* 8). Through the portrayal of socioeconomic and racial discrimination, Ferréz circuitously enunciates a strategy of resistance to said disenfranchisement. By extension, he articulates an alternate perception/practice of citizenship. Paradoxically violence—or at least the literary portrayal of it—becomes an instrument to both contest and reclaim sociocultural agency.

For Enrique Desmond Arias and Daniel Goldstein, violence is tightly woven into to the sociopolitical fabric of many of Latin America's recent democracies. Violence is an integral part of national sociopolitical makeup and of the challenge to new democracies, which are, in the authors' words "violently plural" (*Violent Democracies* 4–5). In this context, the ambivalence of representation that emerges from peripheral writing manifests a larger social phenomenon in which rituals of aggression are prevalent. Violence signifies both hegemonic and counterhegemonic modes of assertion/interrogation that are performed by various types of social actors. Finally, violence has various kinds of victims, both within hegemonic and nonhegemonic social spheres.

Ferréz's first novel, *Capão Pecado*, coalesces the intermingling of violence into a double-pronged aesthetic tool that promulgates social critique and proffers art as a means to retrieve citizenship. Concentrating on the destruction of individual (and, allegorically, collective) hopes, the novel's plot is decidedly fatalistic. Indeed, in its negativity, the narrative serves first and foremost as an admonition that operates at various levels of signification, mingling public and private dramas.

Capão Pecado centers on Rael, a young male resident of the vicinity who becomes involved with his best friend's girlfriend, Paula. This relationship proves to be the downfall of the honest and hard-working protagonist. Ferréz employs the ill-fated love story as an armature that allows him to express a tripartite critique of social predicament. First, Rael and Paula's relationship is a statement against individualism that impedes solidarity and leads to social inaction. Second, the portrayal of life in the favela allows the author to expose the endemic problems that beleaguer the community and that have their roots both within and outside the *periferia*. Third, the exposition of said plight is also a critique of social injustice at a national level. The novel's thematization of differentiated citizenship produces an aesthetic of crisis. Crisis—within the home and the larger community—is the organizing principle of the narrative. It provides the raw material that, paradoxically, serves to articulate a critique of the conditions that create social predicament.

By initiating a liaison with Paula, Rael sins against the first law of the favela: "nunca cante a mina de um aliado, se não vai subir"[20] (Ferréz, *Capão* 66). Loyalty and mutual respect are the two axes of the *periferia*'s moral code. The novel's title—which alludes to various modalities of transgression—comes full circle in Paula's and Rael's betrayal and prophesizes the story's ending, when Rael, deceived in turn by Paula and their boss, commits murder. He is aided by Burgos, the local assassin. Rael and Paula's relationship, premised on the fragile bonds of treachery and hedonism that are replicated in the woman's subsequent liaison with Seu Oscar, and the protagonist's ensuing demise allude not only to the anomic existences that predominate in Capão Redondo, but also to the personal alienation and individualization that feeds this anomic condition. The narrative voice suggests that Paula's affair with her employer is based primarily on material bonds—it affords her middle-class status, apportioning her not only material comfort but also symbolic validation as a resident of the hegemonic metropolis. She and Seu Oscar move to the middle class neighborhood of Jardim Sto. Eduardo (164–5).

Perhaps reflecting the incremented interest in documents that deal with the disenfranchised others that reside on the real and imaginary outskirts of the polis, *Capão Pecado* is in its second edition. Significantly, the first and subsequent printings of the text vary notably. Whereas Labortexto, a smaller publishing venue, issued the text's first edition, the novel's second edition came out of the mainstream publishing house Objetiva. Although the main body of the narrative remains the same, there have been some important modifications in the text's layout and, to a lesser extent, in its content. Several of the non-narrative materials that accompanied the first edition of *Capão Pecado* are absent from its second edition. The editorial changes transform the book's reading experience, considerably diminishing the communitarian aspect that is present in *Capão Pecado*'s first edition. Hence, for example, while the Labortexto edition contains photographs that showcase everyday life in Capão Redondo and feature many of its residents, including the author, the Objetiva version has no images. The snapshots that supplement the novel's first edition were taken by various artists and add to the book's collective quality. They both include the community at large through the pictures and open up the notion of the book's authorship, as the novel's text is complemented by the images and vice versa. Dialoguing not only with the novel's plot, but also with the captions that accompany some of the photographs, the pictures lend a human dimension to the neighborhood and concurrently to the story. Images attribute individuality to the nameless residents of Capão Redondo and, indirectly, to the novel's characters (who are based on several of the vicinity's inhabitants).

Moreover, if we think of the book as a communitarian project not only in terms of its composition, but also in regard to its reception, then the photographs allow for the identification of readers from the *periferia* with the text. The images establish a direct link between fictional story and individual stories. They reinforce Ferréz's conceptualization of literature—and art in general—as integral parts of Capão Redondo's quotidian. In this context, the inclusion of the snapshots adds to the documentary and cooperative dimensions of the text. Images make the text extrapolate from the authorial sphere to include the reading public as well.[21] The inclusive momentum of *Capão Pecado*'s imagistic facet is underscored in the epigraph that precedes the *depoimento* (testimonial) that opens the novel's first section in its Labortexto edition: "'Querido sistema', você pode até não ler, mas tudo bem, pelo menos viu a capa" (Ferréz, *Capão* 19).[22] On the one hand, the allusion to the *querido sistema* (dear system) signals to the impoverished population's lack of access to basic social rights, such as adequate education. Inadequate social rights result in rampant formal and functional illiteracy within these communities. Lack of education obstructs the peripheral population's access to cultural goods, such as literature, that could, at least in theory be instrumental in social change. Inadequate education also hinders the production of culture within marginalized spaces. Finally, deficient education produces incomplete citizens. Without knowledge, the individual is not sufficiently aware of her/his rights and, as a result, can only access the spheres of citizenship in a partial manner. She or he is also more prone to be the victim of differentiated citizenship.

On the other hand, the novel's epigraph also intimates that the dear system does not pay attention to the cultural artifacts that are emerging from within these communities. Marginal communities are not seen as potential incubators of art. Rather, their residents are perceived primarily as producers of transgression. Or they are identified as passive users of bourgeois consumer-culture. Ferréz plays with the title image of the novel, adumbrating and deconstructing the dominant expectations regarding the *favela*. The mere existence of *Capão Pecado* obliquely repudiates the "dear system," even though the novel does regurgitate some of the expectations of this system concerning the favela.

The interplay between refutation of dominant formulas and their reproduction runs throughout *Capão Pecado*. Emblematic is the ambivalent imagery of the novel's front cover. *Capão Pecado*'s cover foreshadows the narrative to follow, but also, to a degree, misleads the reader. In the end, the novel's plot does not focus on youth violence, as suggested by the cover's imagery. Labortexto's cover features a sepia colored photograph of Capão Redondo against which is superimposed the figure of a young boy holding a gun with a black censor bar across his eyes.[23] He stands with his arms stretched out to his sides, in a crucified position. The image of the boy is colored red, insinuating the violence that holds special sway over the favela's youth. This same idea is relayed through the weapon the child touts in his right hand. Yielding a weapon, the boy signifies a menace. However, the gun also transforms the child into a victim of both internal and external violence. He is, in effect, the *homo sacer* that can be obliterated by either the sovereign power of the state (the police) or the drug cartels. Because of the gun, however, his inevitably tragic end cannot be read simply as a sacrifice. Rather, the weapon endows him with a transgressive instrumentality that, nonetheless, is paired with utter lack of agency.

Coercion is further underscored by the boy's metaphorical crucifying. His outstretched arms imply his sacrifice at the altar of social exigency. In this context, the censor bar not only infers the boy's obvious underage status and his engagement in illicit activities, but also allegorizes the child's banishment from the *bios*. He is reduced to a flat image, concentrated on his *zoe*. The boy appears as a two-dimensional being, a cutout figure, from which subjectivity has been drained. His two-dimensionality is emphasized by the collage-like quality of the cover in which the boy's figure appears in the forefront, pasted onto the background of the liminal *urbe*. This lack of depth in the child's outline connotes that, for the dominant social infrastructure, he is an anonymous (anonymity being yet again underscored by the bar across his eyes) and yet threatening figure that can easily be obliterated—reduced to a statistic.[24]

The boy's photograph operates as a social critique, inferring the double structure of socioeconomic exclusion and internal/internalized patterns of violence that promote the participation of favela children in the drug trafficking. This critique is highlighted by the background imagery that shows the dismal (social and urban) infrastructure of the favela and hints at the urban decay that surrounds the young boy. Nonetheless, juxtaposed to its pessimistic content, the image can also be interpreted as an affirmation of humanity within the periphery. The inclusion of the boy's image interlineates the human element encompassed in the narrative and implicitly contradicts the child's erasure from the sociosymbolic horizon of the nation. His exigency is, so to speak, allegorically foregrounded. This centering of marginal(ized) elements is also expressed in various other photographs that are interspersed into *Capão Pecado* and that are organized into two sets. The first group contains color prints, and the second black and white ones. In both arrangements, spatial images are interwoven with those of people, generating a multifaceted picture of the community.

Many of the book's prints replicate the backdrop of the title image, showing the streets and the somewhat precarious infrastructure of Capão Redondo. We also see the faces of several young men, some of them local artists and activists (for example in the two photographs by Pedro Cardilho—"Brown, DJ Lá e Cobra no rolé" (Brown, DJ Lá and Cobra in action) and "C.R., o foco, Cachorrão, DJ Lá, Brown e Cobra" (C.R., the focus, Big Dog, DJ Lá Brown and Cobra)—in which several young men strike a "rap" pose for the camera). Some of the photos highlight the difficult living conditions in Capão Redondo. An example is the snapshot by Teresa Eça of a handicapped and somewhat disheveled man sitting in front of a local bar. His crutches rest besides him. He sits in a hunched position that relays hopelessness and looks away from the camera and into the bar. Despondency is stressed by the accompanying caption "A vida como uma grande decepção" (Life as a great deception/disappointment). The juxtaposition of the photo and its subtitle seem to say that the man's physical condition situates him at the margins of the social structure (Melgaço), a message that is stressed by the fact that the man sits on the bar's threshold, looking in but not partaking in the interactions occurring within.[25] Here, like in Luiz Ruffato's two stories "O ataque" and "Inimigos no quintal," disability signifies exclusion and highlights a structure of disenfranchisement. However, *Capão Pecado* consciously extrapolates the fictional realm by bringing the "real" (i.e., photographs) into the literary terrain.

Contrasted to the picture of the disabled man are various prints that show several of Capão Redondo's children as they partake in different activities. Unlike the boy on the cover, most of these images convey either hope or playfulness as in "Aqui morreu a justiça, mas não a esperança" (Justice died here, but not hope) and "Onde mais serei feliz" (Where else will I be happy), both by Teresa Eça. Each picture shows a young boy smiling at the camera, implicitly contradicting the title image. The pictures of the children challenge the perception of the favela as a space where violence reigns over all aspects of life. Instead, the portraits paint a more nuanced vision of this terrain. Hope coexists with coercion and material deficit (as in "Aqui morreu a justiça, mas não a esperança"). Several of the photographs with children render a playfulness that is, at times, tinged with the harsh conditions of childhood in the urban periphery, as for example in "Onde mais serei feliz." Here the image of the smiling boy is the vortex that triangulates two other pictures, each one showcasing bleak public terrains. Another illustration of the tension between childhood and harsh social conditions appears in Teresa Eça's print "Deixa o menino brincar" (Let the boy play), in which two children play in a broken down car. The print juxtaposes playfulness with decrepitude and, similar to "Onde mais serei feliz," suggests the lack of public and leisure spaces in Capão Redondo that transform debris into recreational spaces/instruments. Indeed, many of the photos depict a lack of either functional public spaces or sound infrastructure. In a photograph by Pedro Cardilho, we see a group of children congregating around and on top of yet another broken down vehicle. The car stands in an empty lot, strewn with litter. Notwithstanding, the potentially melancholy image serves instead to assert the cheerfulness of childhood. The youngsters, although obviously posing for the photographer, still retain spontaneity and seem to have been caught in some kind of game.

As evidenced by numerous photographs, decrepit public infrastructure is paralleled by inadequate private infrastructure. Emblematic are two images by Teresa Eça that exhibit various fragile buildings, including homes cobbled together from discarded building materials. The houses are perched dangerously on the margins of a brook. The image insinuates the danger of flooding that threatens many low-income neighborhoods.[26] The photographic images of the makeshift homes in the first edition of *Capão Pecado* reinforce the social critique articulated in this novel, as well as in *Manual prático do ódio*.

Inadequate infrastructure, especially that of private homes, is a recurrent theme in both *Capão Pecado* and *Manual prático do ódio* and emblematizes the gamut of deprivation confronted by many favela residents. Due to financial constraints, many poor urban dwellers settle into inhospitable urban areas. Often they construct and inhabit fragile housing structures (Fundação Oswaldo Cruz). In *Capão Pecado*, the novel's protagonist describes how many homes in the neighborhood lack (concrete) flooring and therefore do not offer suitable protection from the elements (Ferréz, *Capão* 2nd 78). Adequate flooring is a metaphor for a firm basis that guarantees the stability of the home and the security of its residents. Without this, both are exposed to the (social) elements.

In *Manual prático do ódio*, the narrative voice details how floods and the erosion caused by informal urban development wreak havoc on the precarious housing structures. Strong rains destroy homes built on precarious terrain (*Manual* 204). The scene echoes a familiar reality of dispossession in Brazil's favelas in the wake of natural contingencies that provoke human and ecological catastrophes. Mike Davis contends that hazardous environmental conditions are often preexisting in low-income communities in many developing nations. For Davis, there is an explicit economic reason for settlements in dangerous spaces. Poor residents have few other options but to settle in terrains deemed inadequate by other residents (122). Calamity— either natural (floods, landslides, etc.), or man-made (toxic leakage, fire, pollution)—is exacerbated by the lack of public infrastructure that often afflicts impoverished communities and that, according to Davis, has been aggravated in the wake of neoliberal policies.[27]

Beyond the material repercussions that the lack of flooring has (physical discomfiture), the image also allegorizes the weak familial and communal anchors that both novels describe. Weak social infrastructure promotes anomie and contravention. Most of the characters in *Capão Pecado* and *Manual prático do ódio* come from broken homes, and in the case of the former text, familial disjuncture is the direct (and indirect) cause of social deviancy.

Interestingly, all the photographs were removed from Objetiva's printing of *Capão Pecado*, perhaps in order to appeal to a wider, middle-class public that does not readily identify with the reality of the images or that feels uncomfortable with such a direct confrontation. In effect, the absence of photographs in Objetiva's printing firmly puts *Capão Pecado* within the literary realm. In the same line, the cover has lost its human dimension in the later edition. Instead of the composition of urban landscape and the figure of the young boy yielding a gun, we now have a black background, with the author's name prominently inscribed in a square-type font that segues into a single strand of barbed wire. The wire tapers off on the volume's sides as if it were encircling the volume. Below, in smaller font, is the title of the novel. The centrality of the author's name on the cover erodes the communal element present in the first edition. Instead, Objetiva's cover privileges the perception of the literary text as an individual/individualistic endeavor.

Additionally, the connection between the author's name and the barbed wire favors his role as a spokesperson for a community that lies, so to speak, beyond the purview of the "legal" city. Metaphorically, the barbed wire creates a distance between "us" (the middle-class readers) and "them" (the dangerous characters). Through the fiction at hand, the readers—who purportedly belong to the legal, hegemonic city—are afforded a glimpse into a dangerous universe, into which they would not otherwise venture. The barbed wire not only separates "us" from this perilous terrain; it symbolically protects "us" from an unmediated reality. Without photographs, the novel's characters lose their human dimension and are transformed into two-dimensional beings, mere fictional subjects.

The erosion of the text's communal element also becomes apparent in the elimination of the dedications and acknowledgments that are present in the Labortexto edition. Among the texts that are eliminated from the Objetiva version is one by the rapper Mano Brown, of the *paulista* group Racionais MCs. In *Capão Pecado*, Mano Brown's text opens the first part of the novel. Moreover, the Labortexto edition features Mano Brown's collaboration in the book's creation, mentioning it on the cover ("Participação Mano Brown" [Participation by Mano Brown]). This recognition disappears in Objetiva's printing, as does the long list of acknowledgments that opens the novel. Instead, these tributes appear less conspicuously in the preface to the second edition.

Important in both texts are the *depoimentos* from community members and artists that precede each of the book's five segments and that remain largely the same in both printings. Reflecting the overarching agenda of *literatura marginal*, these testimonials provide a counter-discourse to the hegemonic narratives of marginalization propagated by the mass media and (ironically) to a certain degree, reproduced in *Capão Pecado*'s storyline. The *depoimentos* add to the text's communal character, a point that is broached in the novel's fourth (third

in the Objetiva edition) manifesto. Written by the rap group Realismo Frontal,[28] the text alludes to both the collaborative nature of
Capão Pecado and its collective value: "o grupo Realismo Frontal tem
o imenso prazer de estar participando desta importante obra literária
que envolve a sociedade em geral" (Ferréz, *Capão* 133).[29] Additionally, the testimonials also transform the novel into a polyphonic forum
that is reflective of the diversity of the community and social engagement of many of its members, especially of the ones involved in its
artistic milieu.

Both versions of *Capão Pecado* contain three of the same testimonials (second, third, and fourth), but (as mentioned earlier) in
the Objetiva version, Mano Brown's text is omitted, although Ferréz does acknowledge the rapper's participation in the preface to
the book's second edition. Instead, in the Objetiva version we have
a foreword written by the author that interlaces the text's creation
with his development as a writer. Ferréz likens the novel to a "son"
that has transformed his life and opened new horizons to him (2nd
7). Literature, in this context, does become literally a mode of social
advancement, giving Ferréz entrance into the vetoed spaces of the
middle and upper classes. He relates how the book transformed his
status and how the same person who was not allowed to work as
a janitor in one of São Paulo's luxury hotels now enters this same
establishment through the front door—in order to give a talk there
(7). By entering the affluent and socioculturally sanctioned domain
emblematized by the hotel (literally through the front door), Ferréz
also generates visibility for his community. He assumes the stance of
the organic intellectual.

Among the changes made by Objetiva is also the substitution of
the last *depoimento*. Whereas in the first edition the testimonial is by
the rap group Conceito Moral, in the subsequent edition the author
is Garret, one of Ferréz's collaborators in his clothing line-cum-shop
1dasul. The content of both texts remains generally the same. Both
testimonials assert the power of education and sociocultural engagement while also critiquing unjust social conditions. In this respect,
both the manifesto by Conceito Moral and by Garret replicate the
schema proposed by *Literatura marginal* and not only echo the other
paratexts that are inserted within the novel, but also hint at *Capão
Pecado*'s plot. *Capão Pecado*'s narrative action mingles the ill-fated
love story between Rael and Paula, social denouncement, and autobiographical elements.

There is an apparent dichotomy between the socially oriented
depoimentos and the plot development. The love story between Rael

and Paula ends in an apotheosis of drugs and brutality that not only touches the two lovers but engulfs various other characters. Nonetheless, similar to the variegated images inserted in *Capão Redondo*'s first printing, the concurrence of pessimistic storyline and programmatic texts creates a more gradated version of the social and human makeup of the favela and postulates art as an alternative discourse of empowerment. In this sense, Ferréz's two novels echo the nuanced representation of the *periferia* in Marcos Vinícius Faustini's book, which I will discuss in the next chapter.

The title of Ferréz's novel, *Capão Pecado*, alludes to the legal and social void that flourishes in Capão Redondo and in similar communities. In both of Ferréz's novels, Capão Redondo is the emblematic site of differentiated citizenship. As observed by Rebecca Atencio, *Capão Pecado*'s first edition opens with a poetic mise-en-scène that emulates the camera's zoom. Starting with the infinite space of a concomitantly concrete and abstract "universe," the text ends in a phrase that echoes Ferréz's first solo rap album *Determinação* (Determination, 2003): "Bem vindos ao fundo do mundo" (2nd 13).[30] The zoom's initial openness, signifying the realm of possibility, becomes progressively constricted as it approximates the reality of the favela, ending in the complete denial of the initial hope. In Capão Redondo we have, so to speak, reached the bottom of the social well.

Similarly, *Determinação* opens with sound effects that emulate a gunshot and a carrousel coming to an abrupt halt: violence irrupts into the domain of innocence and play. The juxtaposed sound effects are followed by Ferréz's voice that greets the listener with the same sentence that ends the novel's introductory poem. A further parallelism is established between rap music and literary text in that in the record the salutation transitions into the song "Capão Pecado" and the poem is followed by the book's preface, which serves as a window into the *periferia* and, more specifically, into Capão Redondo.[31]

Allusions to the sociocultural value of rap music resurface throughout *Capão Pecado*. Indeed, the Labortexto edition includes a full-page shot of Ferréz in "rap stance" (right hand forward, in the form of a greeting) at the very beginning of the book. The photograph creates a symbolic approximation between the fictional text and the act of rapping. Both serve to raise consciousness via culture/entertainment. *Capão Pecado* suggests that, for the inhabitants of the *periferia*, at times music (with the extensive and socially conscious lyrics of Brazilian rap) is the only form of hope (Ferréz, *Capão* 2nd 137). Alluding to Brazilian rap's usually lengthy and socially conscious lyrics, the text posits artistic expression as simultaneously a promise and a form of social compromise. In this manner, the narrative voice creates a mise-en-abîme in which the text *Capão Pecado* echoes the song "Capão Pecado," hence establishing a continuum of referentiality between the two artistic manifestations.

Similar to *Capão Pecado*, much of the rap music from the *periferia* is constructed as a denouncement of this milieu's unfavorable social conditions. Lyrics are oftentimes extensive and resemble a narrative with specific actors. The songs frequently retell stories of persecution, lack of agency, and violence. Additionally, the lyrics often establish a dichotomy in which the favela is pitched against the *asfalto* and the police (representing the *asfalto*) against the former's residents. Brazilian rap lyrics also frequently admonish favela inhabitants, in particular its youth, to remain on the "straight and narrow path" and to avoid crime and drugs. In this manner, rap lyrics appeal to the lived experience of its listeners, much in the same way that Ferréz's novels evoke the shared reality of part of their readership.

Capão Pecado's preface complements the dedication to the disenfranchised subjects that dwell in the peripheral sites of the metropolis and frontally addresses the issue of noncitizenship (2nd 11).[32] Ferréz not only calls attention to the deficit in access to the basic commodities theoretically guaranteed by the social contract in impoverished communities, but also elucidates how the scales are unjustly tilted toward the enunciation of the peripheral other as subject to the law but not entitled to the privileges associated with it.

Capão Pecado's narrative opens in media res, with the statements of various unspecified people who live in the neighborhood (2nd 15). The anonymous voices of the exchange emblematize the invisible dwellers of the liminal city. We are never introduced to these nameless beings that fall into the novel's discursive crevices. They vanish from the narrative purview as they disappear from the field of citizenship. Their utterances blend sundry manners of social banishment: criminality, material abjection, and psychological degradation. Drug and alcohol consumption, violence, and indigence are parts of a continuum that envelops the quotidian existences of Capão Redondo and similar communities. Significantly, the excerpt also foreshadows the progressive individual and collective dissolution narrated by the novel. The acts mentioned in the exchange reappear in the plot time and again.

On the other hand the passage is indicative of the neonaturalism that characterizes some of Ferréz's fiction. His prose interweaves documentary and fictional narrative modes. Both are strongly infused by the oral register. Spoken word, and in particular slang, not only echo the reality from which the text emerges, but also lend sociocultural validation through linguistic authenticity. The oral tone of the narrative also reinforces the similarities between rap music and *literatura marginal* (2nd 216), and inserts both cultural expressions into the gamut of artistic tools that can serve to counteract socioeconomic and cultural disaggregation.

Realism in both plot development and language also characterizes Ferréz's second novel, *Manual prático do ódio*. This book attests to the enduring lure of violence as a cultural commodity and the social recognition its aesthetization can afford. Unlike *Capão Pecado*, which was published by a lesser-known press before it was reprinted by the megapublisher Objetiva, *Manual prático do ódio* came out with Objetiva and has been translated into Spanish and Italian.

Manual prático do ódio revolves around a loose-knit group of outlaws who band together for a bank heist. Like in *Capão Pecado*, in *Manual prático do ódio* the main plot is fractured and complemented by the recounting of the lives and tragedies of various inhabitants of Capão Redondo. Alternating between third-person and first-person narrators, *Manual prático do ódio* also has a polyphonous character that, analogous to *Capão Pecado*, reproduces the oral language of the *periferia*. And, like in Ferréz's first novel, in *Manual prático do ódio* slang abounds, lending a patina of verisimilitude to the text, a trait that also is implied in the book's title. The noun "manual" evokes a process of practical apprenticeship. As readers, we are being instructed in the causes of violence that spill into the "safe" and affluent enclaves of the city proper. Our "education" occurs by reading a realist account of the dismal environs that prevail outside the limits of said city.

The novel's exacerbated realism is underscored by the plot summary featured on the back cover: "Todos os personagens deste livro existem ou existiram mas o *Manual prático do ódio* é uma ficção. O autor nunca matou alguém por dinheiro mas sabe entender o que isso significa—do ponto de vista do assassino."[33] The summary is complemented by the author's photograph, standing against a slightly blurred background of what one can assume to be Capão Redondo at night—we see only lights stretching into the distance. Claiming both the novel's fictionality and its documental nature, the synopsis implicitly blurs the frontiers between the two genres and thus purports to sell raw "reality" to its (decidedly middle-class) reading public.

Adding to the novel's "market-value" is the narrative's fast pace. *Manual prático do ódio* unwittingly dialogues with various films that deal with urban crime and geographic segregation, such as *Cidade de Deus*. With its focus on the gang of bank robbers and criminal supporting characters, such as the upstart drug dealer Modelo, *Manual prático do ódio* resembles an action movie with a social consciousness. Adding to the "cinematographic" effect of the novel is its fragmented structure, reflective of the text's multiplicity of narrative perspectives and of the disjointed social context of Capão Redondo. The fractures evoke the cinematic technique of jump cuts, which are common in many action movies of the *Cinema da Retomada*.[34] In addition, the splintering of narrative voices, the constant movement from one locality to another, and the diachronic leaps that punctuate the story in the form of individual memories emulate the conflictive social conditions that the novel portrays in which the criminalization of the poor goes hand in hand with material exigency and social anomie.

Most of *Capão Pecado*'s and *Manual prático do ódio*'s characters either occupy the borderlands of the labor market or the liminal zones of an informal economy that coincide with the boundaries of the polis, or they are on the other side of these boundaries. Several characters are therefore unemployed or engage in criminal activities. Like many of Ruffato's characters, various figures in Ferréz's novels also have fallen victim to drug and alcohol abuse.

Throughout *Capão Pecado* and *Manual prático do ódio* it is evident that the demarcation between legality and criminality is but tenuous. Often the texts' characters cross the two terrains unwittingly. Transgression is frequently a result of improper access to both civic and social rights and generally results in violence.

For Todd Landman, violence stems from a lack of agency due to uncertain civil, social, and economic rights. Deficiency in these domains is heightened by legal and illegitimate state coercion (e.g., in the strip search detailed at the beginning of this chapter) and is supplemented by the equally aggressive responses to socioeconomic and state violence (234).

Capão Pecado and *Manual prático do ódio* dialogue with the favela's tense everyday reality and with the discourse on/about violence that proliferates in popular media and, increasingly, in so-called high culture[35] (i.e., in canonical literary texts such as those by Rubem Fonseca). Both of Ferréz's texts create a catalogue of infringements of citizenship that goes from lack of adequate material and social infrastructure and police abuse to domestic brutality and other modes of contravention, such as drug trade and drug-related assassinations.

Among the many rights that are either neglected or annulled is the access to formal work. In *Capão Pecado*, as well as *Manual prático do ódio*, many of the characters are either unemployed or underemployed. This pattern creates other forms of social exclusion. Lack of employment or subemployment vetoes access to basic socioeconomic rights such as health care, social security, and retirement. The result is continual or increased pauperization of the informal workforce (Gay 204).[36] In *Manual prático do ódio*, the confluence between unemployment and social descent is embodied in the character of José Antônio. His story emblematizes many of the problems faced by the community's residents.

After losing his blue-collar job at the Metal Leve manufacturing plant, José Antônio sinks into a spiral of material penury and psychological depression. His social identification and sense of worth are intimately tied to the work he performed and the economic stability it afforded him and his family (*Manual* 46). For the character, the social visibility that accompanies formal employment is as important as the financial guarantee and the benefits that secure work brings. When he is no longer the "man from Metal Leve," he vanishes from the collective horizon. His unemployment also impacts the realm of the *domus*, tinting it with unspoken *Angst* of pauperization. José Antônio's inability to fulfill the traditional role of "provider" segues into a process of real and imagined emasculation. Zygmunt Bauman observes that in a society that constructs social identities in terms of the performance of production and the theater of consumption, the prefix "un" signifies unemployment as both temporal and atypical (*Wasted* 10). However, if this circumstance becomes permanent, or if work affords only a precarious security, agency and autonomy are eroded and the subject becomes unmoored socially—and, as indicated in the case of José Antônio, also existentially.

Whereas José Antônio's trajectory spans the arc of inclusion to exclusion that configures the society of producers/consumer, going from the pole of formal occupation to joblessness, many other characters in *Capão Pecado* and *Manual prático do ódio* are located in a professional limbo. They are actors of the informal economy, which represents a significant slice of Brazil's economy.[37] Mike Davis observes that the proliferation of the informal economy in what he calls the "Third World" is synchronous with the augmentation of slums in the global south. Taking as his point of departure the global economic crisis of the 1980s, Davis avers that the new existential mode for informal laborers is that of "survivalism" (*Planet of Slums* 178).

Davis outlines how one's participation in the informal economy correlates with the weakening of her/his social, civil, and even political rights. Recently, Brazil's unemployment and informal-employment figures have changed for the better. Nonetheless, for people with little or no formal education, the prospect of a well-paying job still remains precarious.

Like José Antônio, several of the characters in *Capão Pecado* are either out of work or engaged in low-income activities. They are maids, laborers, or fast-food employees. Joblessness and underemployment are symptoms and sources of a larger social malaise that transforms the low-income populace into jettisoned subjects of both the labor and consumer market. Bauman denominates this social segment "surplus population," or individuals who are transformed into hubris as a result of industrialization and, more recently, neoliberal globalization (*Wasted* 7).

In Latin America, the drive toward economic "progress" in the late 1990s and early 2000s translated into economic deregulation and structural adjustment measures. This, in turn, augmented the spread of informal or semi-informal labor, leading to increased socioeconomic insecurity. Enrique Desmond Arias and Daniel M. Goldstein contend that "[p]overty, fragmented families, domestic abuse, fear, insecurity, and the instability of daily life for many Latin Americans form a part of life under neoliberal democracies that have governed these societies over the past few decades: they are part of their structural logic rather than the result of their imperfections" ("Violent Pluralism" 17). As a result of material precariousness, violence in both the public and the private domain also grew.

In *Capão Pecado*, lack of employment is often accompanied by other modes of social and existential ailment, such as aggression and/ or alcoholism, that concomitantly result and worsen the critical condition of joblessness. Paradigmatic is the figure of Carimbé, whose story is a tailspin of degradation that begins when he loses his job as a bricklayer. After several misadventures, he comes to the conclusion that his life is nothing but one great disappointment (Ferréz, *Capão* 2nd 130). Carimbé's assessment remits to the figure of the disabled man in Teresa Eça's image ("A vida como uma grande decepção"), who like Carimbé epitomizes social banishment and its accompanying existential crisis.

Carimbé, however, suffers from psychosomatic and social, rather than physical, disabilities. His initial encumbrance lies with his formal lack of education. Because of insufficient education, Carimbé can only find low-paying jobs (121).

Insufficient or inadequate formal education, one of the bases of citizenship, is widespread in low-income communities across Brazil.[38] Like in Carimbé, much of the adult population of Capão Redondo is confronted with deficient education and a dearth of formal employment.[39] Sociologist Loïc Wacquant associates unemployment with two different types of impoverishment: capitalist (i.e., Fordist) and late capitalist. For Wacquant, the former is associated with a (working) class consciousness and is at once limited to a temporal frame and disengaged from a particular geographical locality; the latter, which Wacquant identifies as the "modernization of misery," is no longer associated with macroeconomic factors and affects primarily already economically disadvantaged communities (*Urban Outcasts* 261). Unemployment and subemployment have also changed the perception of the importance of work within youth groups. Faced by the scarcity of satisfactory labor options, many young people in the favelas no longer see professional life as a central vector of identification, but rather as a mode of accessing consumption.[40]

Several of the characters in *Capão Pecado* linger about without an occupation. Emblematic is Matcherros, Paula's boyfriend, who is described as entirely alienated. He spends his days playing with his PlayStation (Ferréz, *Capão* 2nd 48). While not engaged in an economy of production, characters such as Matcherros paradoxically partake in the cycle of consumption. It is precisely this inconsistency that transforms them into anomic characters. Matcherros participates in his own alienation process, which, according to Brazilian sociologist José de Souza Martins, can be an "active social process" through which the subject compensates for real and perceived deficits (44). In the case of Matcherros, we learn that he ends up entering the criminal economy, like many of his peers, by selling stolen motorcycles.

Through the tragic stories of characters such as Carimbé, José Antônio, and the anomic youths that "hang out" in bars, couches, and street corners, Ferréz constructs a morphology of exploitation and disillusionment. Dismal scenarios of professional failure and personal decadence reappear throughout the two novels and seep into the construction of the geosocial milieu. They translate the economic and existential volatility that envelops communities such as Capão Redondo. However, Ferréz does not cast his characters as unproblematic victims of an abortive system. It becomes clear from the narratives that the responsibility for social exigency is pendular, oscillating between the crisis generated by differentiated citizenship and perpetuated by the victims of this structure. Once again, Carimbé is the prototype for this dialectic of disenfranchisement.

In a vicious cycle, Carimbé's loses his job because of drinking and drinks because he is unemployed. Akin to several of the novel's characters, Carimbé too is a social archetype. He embodies social and existential misery. Being cast out of the system of production and therefore of consumption, he transforms his own body into a metaphor of abjection. He is wrinkled and balding, with bloodshot eyes and cracked lips. His clothing is soiled by mud and urine (Ferréz, *Capão* 2nd 120). Prostrated to the point of complete dissipation, Carimbé is an outcast not only from society at large, but also from the familiar sphere—his relatives despise him and regard him as less than human. Carimbé's alcoholic stupor allegorizes the corrosion of his human condition. Instead of interacting with other people he drowns in the misery of his condition and takes it to its limits.

Following a naturalist creed that is underscored by the equally naturalistic language, Carimbé is paradigmatic of social disintegration. His character's profligacy calls attention to the plights of the peripheral community, haunted as it is by lack of professional and economic opportunities. But Carimbé is also a warning about the dangers inherent in antisocial behavior, such as excessive alcohol consumption. In this manner, both *Capão Pecado* and *Manual prático do ódio* interpolate personal responsibility within the wider spectrum of social disenfranchisement. Both public marginalization and private infraction lead to an overarching sense of anomie that promotes individual and collective contravention.

In *Manual prático do ódio*, Paulo, a character that seemingly has ties to Rael and Paula's story,[41] observes how private and communitarian predicament come together in generalized alienation. He sees a continuum between negligent and unhappy parents, and a generalized sense of hopelessness (*Manual* 77). The confusion of social relations that begins at the familial level extends into other realms and ultimately translates into social and ontological estrangement. For sociologist Alba Zaluar, the corrosion of the social fabric and the crisis of the familial structure contribute to the criminalization of favela youth ("Teleguiados e chefes").

In *Capão Pecado*, the hired gun Burgos is the character that perhaps best embodies the prevalent estrangement from social relations due to generalized anomie and the parallel preeminence of consumption. Like many other characters, Burgos too comes from a broken family. His father is an alcoholic who, after an ill-fated attempt to join a local evangelical church, gets beaten up by its members. This experience terminates Burgos's faith in God. Unable to find solace in his family or in a system of belief and having little prospects of attaining socioeconomic stability, Burgos's personal horizon is restricted to the acquisition of consumer goods, while his empirical scope is circumscribed by the violence that affords him entrance into the sphere of expenditure.

For Bauman, the contemporary subject constructs her/his social identity through the rituals of consumption. She/he defines herself/himself through the commodities (in Burgos's case, mainly vehicles and weapons) that she/he can purchase and becomes herself/himself "merchandise" (*Consuming Life* 57). Burgos is paradigmatic of this rationale. In order to embed himself into the predominant logic of expenditure, he transforms the performance of violence into hard currency. His body becomes a component in the cycle of consumption and, not surprisingly, ultimately a causality in the trade of material goods and coercion. Violence for Burgos is not an instrument of insurrection or a tool of empowerment. Rather, violence is another symptom of the anomie that accompanies the ascendancy of materialism. As observed by Alba Zaluar ("Teleguiados e chefes") and Sérgio Adorno,[42] the supremacy of consumption becomes an integral factor in the formulation of not only social identities, but also of gender identities. Access to commodities signifies forceful virility. Merchandise becomes a fetish of an aggressive economy of identification.

When Burgos's use value expires, he is removed from the debased service economy of violence. Existing outside the official legal sphere, his erasure nonetheless straddles both the juridical terrain and the nonsanctioned arena outside official law. In this grey zone, "Burgos foi pego no flagrante, mas o BO não foi registrado. Os policiais, exercendo todo seu treinamento acadêmico, o levaram para o Guaraci e depois que atiraram em sua cabeça o jogaram no rio" (Ferréz, *Capão* 2nd 141).[43] The missing police report obliterates Burgos as a citizen. Instead, he becomes a mere body, and as such can be killed without further repercussions. His body, the medium of violence, is caught within the biopolitical power of the legal apparatus. At the same time Burgos is made invisible by the same biopolitical power. He vanishes into the polluted waters of the nearby river.

In the novel, the river parallels contumacy and connotes the territory of improper burial and unmourned death—the river is effectively a human garbage disposal heap. By dumping Burgos's cadaver into the waters, the police transform him into a mere waste product proscribed from the flow of goods and services; reduced to *zoe*, he has no role in the economy of the polis.

As suggested by Burgos's execution, *Capão Pecado* and *Manual prático do ódio* reflect on how police coercion and corruption are intertwined and contribute to the spread of violence within low-income neighborhoods and to the generalized disregard of human rights within these communities (Gay). Police corruption, a recurrent theme in Ferréz's two novels, serves to indicate how crime in the *periferia* is tied to the dominant socioeconomic and institutional structure.

Arbitrary violence is a paradigmatic feature of differentiated citizenship and, in the Brazilian context, can be traced, in part at least, to the law enforcement policies of the repressive military regime. Camillo Penna observes that many of the human rights abuses perpetrated against the urban poor after 1985 have their roots in the practices of control instated by the military government ("Estado de exceção"). Like other military dictatorships in South America, the 1964 coup effectively gave the police leeway to torture and "disappear" individuals labeled as "subversive." After the transition and despite the implementation of democratic governance, including the drafting and ratification of the 1988 constitution, arbitrary violence on behalf of the authorities continued. However, after the transition, the focus of arbitrary violence shifted from political dissidents onto the impoverished social segments. Often the upper and middle classes perceive poor and darker-skinned people as a threat to their physical and economic security (Gay; Penna, "Estado de exceção"; Pinheiro; Méndez; Koonings).[44] The suppression of "difference" (in this case socioeconomic and racial) has grown in the wake of Brazil's neoliberal turn. Among other things, neoliberalism promoted the privatization of the security apparatus. Privatized security was accompanied by support for vigilante justice on behalf of various social segments, including the ones most affected by such types of violence.

Todd Landman observes that democratic governance does not necessarily imply equitable allocation of social rights. And when social rights are not easily accessible, both political and civil citizenship are weakened (233). To illustrate this point, since Brazil's transition to democracy, there have been several notorious instances of police violence directed against marginal/marginalized citizens (whose status as such is, in effect, denied in the act of aggression).[45] In many of these incidents, the perpetrators, who were either police officers or suspected of belonging to the police corps, were either not persecuted or were absolved of any wrongdoing.

As suggested at the beginning of this chapter, in low-income communities, police abuse takes many forms, from everyday harassment of favela residents to more aggressive manifestations that result in the death of the peripheral subject, as was the case, for example, in Burgos's murder in *Capão Pecado*. The various instances of police misdemeanor buttress the classification of the peripheral subject as *homo sacer*. Though she/he is criminalized through legal discourse (in the novel, through the police report not filed after Burgos's demise), legal discourse does not serve to protect her/him from abuses of power.

Another episode in *Capão Pecado* provides an example of arbitrary police violence and disregard for the populace's civil rights. Toward the end of the novel, the narrative voice relates a police invasion that is reminiscent of the one described in Ferréz's blog entry. Similar to the real-life abuse detailed in the blog, the fictional episode highlights the legal ambiguity the community's residents confront. The authorities' raid draws on the prevalent discourse that constructs the favela and its denizens as both subject and, concomitantly, as ones excluded from the legal domain. We learn that the trigger for the foray is the message of social critique transmitted by rap lyrics: "Um boteco lá em cima chamava a atenção pelo alto volume do som. As frases dos grupos de *rap* deixavam irados os gambés, que chegaram botando pra quebrar no bar do seu Tinho Doido. . . . O som, antes de ser interrompido por motivo de perfuração à bala, bradou o seu último verso: 'Não confio na polícia, raça do caralho'" (Ferréz, *Capão* 2nd 156).[46] Police arbitrariness is underlined in a circular motion, in which the rap lyrics forecast and explain the scene narrated. At the same time, the incident also reaffirms the song's message. Ironically, the passage employs "police parlance" to represent institutional aggression: the music itself (*o som*) becomes the police's murder "victim" that heroically unmasks its perpetrator.

The police's intimidation of the residents is further highlighted when an officer begins to grope and verbally denigrate one of the passersby, a young woman, whose only response to the abuse is impotent tears. Like the scene narrated in the blog, the woman is constructed in terms of her bare physicality, a notion underpinned in the description that concentrates solely on her sexualized body parts: her buttocks, legs, and breasts (155). Beyond this configuration of physical traits, she is merely an anonymous figure—the narrative voice refers to her as the *morena gostosa* (a sexy, dark-skinned woman). The concentration on the body—the bare life—and its violent libidinal inscription by the authority reveals the biopolitics of coercion exercised on the individual and public corpus of marginal citizens.[47] If during the military regime, dissident bodies became imprinted by the pain of the paralegal torture that was sanctioned by the authoritarian state of exception, then in the current period, torture—and/or infringement of personal rights—is both a sequel of these practices[48] and an expression of the state of exception, dictated by rising crime rates in the aftermath of the dictatorship.

As in the event detailed in Ferréz's blog, the episode in the novel constructs the woman—and, by extension, the members of the community—as indeterminate members of civil society. While her body is subject to the law, that is to say, she must comply with the obligations of a citizen, conforming to the legal system, she nonetheless does not partake in the realm of citizenship. Her civil rights are rescinded by the same law that she must observe. Confronted with physical and psychological abuse, she nevertheless cannot utilize the legal system to contest the maltreatment perpetrated against her by the representatives of the law. *Capão Pecado* and *Manual prático do ódio* reinforce the notion of a differentiated citizenship that structures the spaces inhabited by *homo sacer*, such as the favela or the *periferia*, spaces that Agamben equates to contemporary concentration camps.

For Agamben, the concentration camp is the space where the state of exception becomes an empirical reality and where "bare life and the juridical rule enter into a threshold of indistinction" (*Homo Sacer* 174). But according to him, since the state of exception has become, nowadays, the rule, the camp is not a singular, enclosed space. Rather, it is a disperse reality, enacted when legal order is interrupted and where the police have sovereign powers (174). In this framework, the domain of the favela and similar low-income communities can be read as emblematic of the contemporary territories of the state of exception. They resemble refugee camps, internment sites for illegal migrants, clandestine prisons to which "enemy combatants" are sent under the premise of what has become known as "extraordinary rendition," and many times, prisons that are increasingly designed to attend to the surplus population of the late capitalist economy (Wacquant, "Penalisation of Poverty").

Applying Agamben's characterization of an omnipresent state of exception that generates a multiplication of liminal spaces, Camillo Penna compares Brazilian penal institutions with veritable concentration camps for impoverished citizens ("Sujeitos da pena" 13). The enclosed penal domains are sites where law coincides with bare life. Juridical process transverses these spaces, obliterating the rights of the subjects that must—by force—dwell within their walls. Brazil's overflowing and badly maintained detention centers that hold poor criminals are but an extension of the deprived communities from which these subjects emerge. Similar to the inhabitants of these communities, impoverished prisoners, are subject to a rule of an abject sovereignty—the police force that exerts legal and illegal violence inside the walls of the detention facility and within the boundaries of the favela and the network of contravention that also has a stranglehold on both arenas. Indeed, in many instances, the boundary between these two realms is porous and the two types of sovereignty blend and reinforce one another.

In *Manual prático do ódio*, the police provide drugs to the inmates of various detention houses. They receive the narcotics from Modelo, a local drug dealer, in exchange for protection from both official power and other criminals. And, in the unending cycle of contravention, the police distribute the drugs to various inmates. Caught in between these two forces, the residents of Capão Redondo and similar communities are powerless. Whereas the drug dealers' activities erode the social dimension of citizenship, the police negate its civil aspect by constantly harassing residents and practicing random acts of violence with impunity.

The collision between law and illegality, the stripping of the marginal other's *bios*, and the unmitigated violence exerted on his *zoe* by the representative of sovereign power is related in a particularly gruesome scene in which a young boy is executed by a police officer: "Encapuzado, um operário do Estado, chamado popularmente de pé-de-pato, decide se o menino vive ou não, embora a resposta para os outros 34 que ele já matou tenha sido não. . . . Ele engatilha, é aceito pelo próprio povo oprimido que ele julga e condena, tem em sua mente o que lhe clicam há anos, que a culpa é deles, da raça inferior, da raça que rouba, que seqüestra, a raça que mata, a raça que não segue as leis de Deus, a raça que tem que ser exterminada" (*Manual* 151).[49]

The scene condenses how the marginal subject(s), allegorized by the child, are conceptualized as *homenes sacers* vis-à-vis the dominant echelons and how they are included into a law of abjection but expelled from the realm of civility. Mimicking the pre and early modern spectacle of public executions, the man—who, significantly, is a member of the very community he despises—dons a hood and metes out what he believes to be unmediated justice. His prerogative stems from the authority he represents (even if and because he is trespassing the legal norms that bind this authority) as well as from the very disenfranchised peoples, the extant mass of *homenes sacers*, who suffer parallel forms of arbitrary violence. Police coercion and the elimination of the *homo sacer*, the allowed killing of the subject that exists at the limits of the law, is further authorized by the discourse of "law and order" that abounds in the mass media and that promotes paralegal justice as a means to rein in social chaos. The policeman is impelled to murder the child by a television personality that accuses the "bandits" of all manners of social ills (*Manual* 151). The young boy's assassination is but one instance in an ongoing performance of sanctioned killings within the state of exception. The narrative voice lists various incidents of para-legal violence against poor young male subjects, whose assassinations are part of a performance of the law (154).

If we posit extrajudicial killings such as the one depicted in *Manual prático do ódio* and its real-life equivalents into the framework of human rights, it becomes clear that impoverished youngsters lack these rights.[50] In the structure of differentiated citizenship into which they are typecast, they are invisible subjects. Their invisibility is exacerbated by the erasure of their *bios* from the material and symbolic horizon of the nation through either geographic segregation or the aggressive obliteration of their *zoe* by the sovereign power. This power is embodied by the police, who, in this case, opt for a tactics of incivility that find their reasoning in the culture of fear that taints the urban space.

Notwithstanding the emphasis of transgression and violence (individual and collective) in *Capão Pecado* and *Manual prático do ódio*, positive outlooks are expressed by many characters, as Ferréz is careful to balance the negative representation of the periphery and its inhabitants, especially its young residents, with the positive. Hence, for example, the nihilistic stance of many characters in *Capão Pecado* is contrasted with the engaged and optimistic discourse of other characters, such as Narigaz and, at the beginning of the text, Rael. Paraphrasing the discourse of rap, in this case, of the *paulista* rapper Thaíde (Altair Gonçalves), Narigaz contradicts the conception of the poor as unproductive members of society. He rails against the disengagement of his peers who, instead of seeking socioeconomic betterment, prefer to pursue facile pleasures and thus, unwittingly, fall prey to a cycle of disempowerment. Narigaz, one of Rael's friends, entreats his acquaintances to listen to the Thaíde's teachings and aim to become better citizens by educating and informing themselves. Only through self-improvement can peripheral youth compete with the *playbas* (playboys) who have better access to education (Ferréz, *Capão* 2nd 117). Narigaz's comparison between young men from the favela and from the middle class (*playbas*) has a twofold implication. First, it suggests that the socioeconomic system, including education, favors the latter and, consequently, propagates material discrimination. Second, Narigaz's assessment turns the responsibility back onto the youth of the favela. Instead of investing in their future, the young men engage in self-destructive behaviors. The inclusion of these two opposing stances—alienation versus social consciousness—disallows a reductive perspective of the *periferia*, balancing the predominant view of this milieu with a valorization of the potential encompassed within it.

For Ferréz, art has a fundamental role in the production of agency, be it cultural, material—or personal. Narigaz, for example, also postulates that creativity is the only manner in which to resist socioeconomic discrimination and to "beat the system" (93). Artistic expression is a means by which positive modes of identification (as opposed to destructive ones associated with drug trafficking and other means of contravention) and a communitarian ethos can be propagated.

Ferréz's effort to generate discursive spaces for Brazil's disempowered urban populace extrapolates from the purely textual sphere, extending into other cultural realms and into the terrain of social projects. Thus, for example, the author/rapper and artist/social activist, together with the *paulista* rap group Racionais MCs, has created a community library in Capão Redondo. More recently, Ferréz, in conjunction with the activist group Projeto Periferia Ativa, launched a *brinquedoteca*—a play "library" for children residing in economically disadvantaged areas (Ferréz, "Demorou 10 anos"). He also dwells in the production and consumption of cultural goods (specifically hip-hop inspired fashion items) through his clothing line and boutique, 1dasul. The homonymous name of the fashion brand and shop promote local pride, positing the clothes and accessories produced and sold by 1dasul overtly within the peripheral cartography (as indicated by the adjective *sul* [south]). 1dasul references all the *manos* and *trutas* (brothers) that come from and represent districts such as Capão Redondo.

Contributing to the sense of local embedding and pride is the fact that local residents produce the clothes that belong to the 1dasul label entirely in the favela. The goal of this and Ferréz's other enterprises is to supply residents of low-income neighborhoods with access to cultural goods that will, in turn, furnish them with alternate means of sociocultural identification. His clothes, while providing employment for the community, also serve as vehicles through which the artist can transmit his literary production. Each piece features a textual fragment from Ferréz's oeuvre. The brand's logo is a phoenix, signifying the possibility of transcending adverse social circumstances—as Ferréz has done through his artistic endeavors. In this manner, the garments are a moving text that can be read in different contexts and in different combinations. Art (the literary text) enters the public sphere through the mechanisms of consumption (design), destabilizing the cycle of disenfranchisement implicit in the commodification of citizenship.

Even though *Manual prático do ódio* and *Capão Pecado* are not tales of empowerment per se, both novels depict social injustice and its coterminous violence—be it in the guise of organized crime or be it individual acts of violence—in order to criticize it as a mode of agency. Instead, these two novels contrast criminality with social consciousness and art and as a result present them as viable alternatives to nihilistic transgression. By problematizing the stereotypical association of the racialized and poor peripheral subject, Ferréz retrieves a degree of civic, social, and cultural legitimacy (denied by dominant discourse) for the marginalized subjects of his books and, by extension, his community. This legitimacy is transmuted into instrumentality, as is the case in the various community initiatives spearheaded by the author that, together with his fictional production, translate into external recognition of both the problems and the creative energy of disenfranchised urban spaces, such as Capão Redondo, and their populace.[51] This same stance—that is, art and particularly creative writing as communitarian engagement—appears in Marcus Vinícius Faustini's *Guia afetivo da periferia*. Interestingly, and perhaps signaling Brazil's changing socioeconomic panorama and its attendant cultural implications, Faustini concentrates on his low-income neighborhood but also transcends it. Whereas Ferréz's novels explore and communicate the realities of the *periferia*, therefore suggesting an ongoing geosocial divide within the *urbe*, Faustini transforms the *periferia* into an integral part of Rio de Janeiro. *Guia afetivo da periferia* thus constructs a textual bridge over the divided cartography of Brazil's metropolises.

CHAPTER 4

CARTOGRAPHIES OF HOPE
CHARTING EMPOWERMENT IN
GUIA AFETIVO DA PERIFERIA

In 2014, Brazil will host the Soccer World Cup and, two years later, the 2016 Summer Olympics. The country has started bolstering its infrastructure in preparation for these events. In Rio de Janeiro, where the Olympics will be headquartered, the government has begun building and renovating sports facilities, such as the Maracanã Stadium. In addition to these changes, authorities are also endeavoring to "clean up" the urban centers where athletic competitions will occur. Many of these cosmetic improvements, aimed at promoting Rio's "postcard" reputation, hide the fact that the city is also plagued by a myriad of social woes, such as criminal gangs that control many of the city's low-income communities. Several of these neighborhoods are located along the "Linha Vermelha" (Red Line), the popular denomination for the João Goulart Expressway that links the city's middle- and upper-class Zona Sul to its international airport. As such, the Linha Vermelha offers the first glimpses of the city to its foreign (and to many national) visitors.

The juxtaposition between the expressway and the poor communities that—in certain places literally border it—emblematizes the material and symbolic divisions that characterize Rio de Janeiro. On the one hand we have the flux of travelers making their way into the "Marvelous City." On the other, there are the residents of neighborhoods such as Vigário Geral, Maré, and Parada de Lucas—names that have become synonymous with drug trafficking and other forms of criminality. Taxis, executive buses, private cars, and limousines zoom by the at times ramshackle houses along the Linha Vermelha. In an effort to spare the expected international guests from these not-so-picturesque sights, Rio's city administration has begun erecting soundproof barriers between the Expressway and its adjacent districts. The fence, composed of panels measuring thirty meters in length and three in height, will cover 7.6 kilometers and will encircle entire communities (such as Maré). This infrastructure project communicates the notion that Rio's lower-income districts, considered by its more affluent denizens as dangerous terrains, should be in effect cut off from the city proper. Not surprisingly, the metaphor of the "divided city"[1] has become prominent in recent cultural production dealing with Rio de Janeiro. Films such as José Padilha's *Tropa de elite* I and II (2007 and 2010, respectively) portray a city demarcated by invisible and yet violently palpable borders. But are there alternatives to this imagining/experiencing of Rio de Janeiro and, by extension, of many Brazilian metropolises?

In this chapter I discuss how Marcus Vinícius Faustini charts the city of Rio de Janeiro and, through this physical and discursive movement, creates territories of agency for the narrator-protagonist of *Guia afetivo da periferia* (Affective guide of the periphery, 2009). The protagonist-narrator's journeys counteract the symbolic construction of Rio de Janeiro as a "divided city," partitioned along socioeconomic lines. Rather, *Guia afetivo da periferia* concentrates on communal spaces and constructs narrative bridges between the metropolis's different socioeconomic and cultural terrains. Constructing metaphoric bridges and traversing them, the narrator of *Guia afetivo da periferia* establishes himself as a citizen of the entire *urbe*, not a subject relegated to its geographic and figurative outskirts. Accordingly, it can be argued that the narrator of *Guia afetivo da periferia* performs what Engin F. Isin and Greg M. Nielsen call "acts of citizenship," transformative communal and/or personal actions (2). By theorizing citizenship in terms of acts or agency, they advocate viewing citizens as agents of change rather than merely as passive holders of rights and obligations. In other words, *Guia afetivo da periferia* enacts the city. These urban enactments are a mode of insurgent citizenship. Because *Guia afetivo da periferia* demonstrates how sociocultural agency can be claimed through the act of reappropriating the city, the book differs from the novels discussed in previous chapters. Instead of focusing primarily on differentiated citizenship, Faustini's text concentrates on insurgent practices, communicating a new perception of citizenship—the "right to have rights"—that is, an expression of changed socioeconomic conditions in post-2003 Brazil.

Before analyzing *Guia afetivo da periferia* in more depth, I will briefly delineate the chapter's theoretical underpinnings, specifically the nexus between city and citizenship (Appadurai and Holston) and the conception of culture as an expedient (Yúdice). Additionally, I will detail how Brazil's cultural scene has seen an increment in cultural producers and products that emerge from the urban periphery. Marcus Vinícius Faustini's *Guia afetivo da periferia*, like Ferréz's novels, is emblematic of this phenomenon. At times, these "peripheral" artifacts are mediated through national and international corporations—Petrobras in the case of *Guia afetivo da periferia*—that, similar to marginal/marginalized cultural actors, use culture as capital (though with different objectives). While the lower-income communities and artists employ culture as a resource to gain sociopolitical visibility and, at times, to generate income, national and international corporations utilize culture to boost their public image (and for tax purposes). In both instances, culture promotes positive visibility and can be translated into material benefits.

Culture as a resource for disenfranchised groups often comes about at the sites where disempowerment is at its most visible: low-income urban communities. As indicated in Chapter 3, in these locales, civic and social rights are frequently either weak or nonexistent. Many cultural manifestations in the periphery emerge as a response to the deficit in rights and refer either directly (see Ferréz's novels, for example) or indirectly to said conditions. Since disenfranchisement is closely enmeshed with geography, peripheral artists prominently feature the (divided) city in their work. The prevalence of differentiated citizenship in communities such as Capão Redondo and the cultural responses to socioeconomic and civic injustice suggest how city, citizenship, and cultural production are closely connected.

According to Arjun Appadurai and James Holston, the city—and not the nation—is nowadays the primary arena of citizenship (2). Both national heterogeneity (which has weakened the homogenizing national discourses of the nineteenth and early twentieth century) and the centrifugal effects of globalization have eroded the association between citizenship and the "nation." It is within the urban space that individuals most prominently access their rights. And it is within this terrain that the disjunction between formal and substantive citizenship is often the most glaring. One only needs to think of the contrast between the elite *carioca*[2] neighborhoods of Leblon and São Conrado and their adjacent favelas (such as Vidigal, which literally "divides" the two aforementioned residential areas).

Cities are also the primary stages of what Holston calls modes of "insurgent citizenship." (*Insurgent*). Holston characterizes contemporary cities as a grid in which both "entrenched" and "insurgent" modes of citizenship coexist, albeit tensely. Insurgent practices, that is, the contestation of established social configurations, frequently arise in the locales of entrenched citizenship (33). Insurgent practices assume many formats. While homeownership (e.g., autoconstruction in metropolitan peripheries) is undoubtedly an important factor in this process, being able to claim the city in its material and figurative entirety has also become a preoccupation of disenfranchised social groups, especially marginalized youth. As much as the divided metropolis renders differentiated citizenship palpable, it is also the site where socioeconomic and civic differences are contested.

In the divided metropolis, insurgent citizenship oftentimes uses the same symbolic, civil, and political markers that promote differentiation, and transforms them into a means of empowerment. In this manner, for example, neighborhood associations from São Paulo's periphery have created a new public sphere. Holston maintains that the civic engagement that emerged in Brazil's urban peripheries since 1964 was conditioned by the geosocial segregation of these areas. Isolation gave the community's residents a measure of freedom and drove them to fight for inclusion in the "legal city" (247). He points out that by organizing and educating themselves and by creating networks of community assistance, the neighborhood organizations exposed the state's shortcomings in providing them with necessities for their well-being (248).

Community involvement and outreach has generated a slate of formal and informal projects that see in culture (oral and written literature, graffiti, music, theater, cinema, to name some expressions of this culture) a means to assist disenfranchised neighborhoods. Ferréz's community library and *brinquedoteca*, as well as his clothing line cum boutique 1dasul are examples of such ventures. Also in São Paulo's periphery, the poet and community organizer Sérgio Vaz has created the literary soireé Cooperifa, which, for over ten years, meets every Wednesday night in Zé Batidão's Bar in the Jardim Guarujá neighborhood. Vaz describes the event as a "literary *quilombo*"[3] that promotes art for the sake of citizenship (Vaz, "Interview"). Art for the sake of citizenship is the principle underlying the fictional texts discussed in this book. It is also the philosophy of the majority of *literatura* and *arte marginal*.

Art as agency for disenfranchised communities has also increasingly been incorporated into mainstream culture that sees marginal culture as the "true" expression of a vetoed space and reality. The Brazilian publishing industry, which has seen a resurgence since the mid-1990s, has also capitalized on the interest in "marginality" conveyed through an insider perspective. In recent years, several publishing houses have issued fictional, semifictional, or documentary texts by or about the urban periphery. Objetiva, for example, has reissued (and, as discussed in Chapter 3, altered) Ferréz's *Capão Pecado* and published his second novel, *Manual prático do ódio*. In 2007, Nelson de Oliveira, who had previously edited two anthologies of contemporary Brazilian prose, edited the collection *Cenas da favela. As melhores histórias da periferia brasileira* (Favela scenes: The best stories from Brazil's periphery), which was published by Geração Editorial. Interestingly, the compilation includes mainly middle-class authors, such as Lígia Fagundes Telles, Rubem Fonseca, Alberto Mussa, Luiz Ruffato, Fernando Bonassi, and Marçal Aquino, among others. In the volume's introduction, Nelson de Oliveira justifies this inclusion by arguing for the deconstruction of the traditional clichés associated with low-income communities such as favelas. As the plural *scenes* suggests, Oliveira seeks to move beyond a single perspective about the favela in order to offer a multifaceted vision of these geocultural territories that is transmitted by different narrative voices (16). Echoing this premise is the very meaning that the word "favela" acquires in the book. Instead of signifying solely a material place, "favela" as used in Oliveira's anthology connotes both material and symbolic disenfranchisement and varying forms of insurgency. As a result, not all the stories included in *Cenas da favela* pertain to the favela in the strictest sense of the word. Some, like Ruffato's short story "Ciranda," deal with impoverished subjects that inhabit the metropolitan center. Ruffato's story relates to the idea of favela through its treatment of socioeconomic class, rather than to the specific geographic locale.[4]

The favela has always been a hotbed of artistic creativity, a fact that Oliveira inexplicably obscures by selecting only the three most well-known "organic intellectuals" from the periphery (Carolina Maria de Jesus, Paulo Lins, and Ferréz). Beyond being the birthplaces and ongoing centers of Brazilian rap and funk, musical phenomena that have increasingly gained visibility both inside and outside Brazil[5] in recent years, the favelas and other marginalized communities have experienced a surge of cultural activities that also promote a specific social agenda. Many of the phenomena are linked to literature. People from Brazil's sociogeographic margins are increasingly writing, reading, and talking about (their) literature. Literature, traditionally the domain of the bourgeoisie, has climbed the *morro*[6] and entered the *periferia*.

After the 1985 transition to political democracy and the 1990s economic crisis, culture at the margins has become part of a discourse of rights articulated by disenfranchised social sectors. For these actors, culture is both a material resource that can be utilized and a means to resist neoliberal exploitation. A case in point is the NGO Viva Rio,[7] which boasts an impressive list of national and international institutional affiliates such as the Banco do Brasil (Bank of Brazil), Petrobras, Coca-Cola, and British Petroleum, to name but a few. Viva Rio advances social and intellectual activism in order to create a "culture of peace and social development" (Viva Rio).

Similarly, Rio de Janeiro's local (now gone global) Grupo Cultural AfroReggae promotes social engagement through culture. Culture becomes an instrument to attain not only cultural, but also social and civil citizenship. AfroReggae's goal is to promote culture, inclusion, and citizenship through artistic and educational ventures, with a special emphasis on Afro-Brazilian culture (AfroReggae). AfroReggae is perhaps one of the best-known Brazilian NGOs that use culture as a means of empowerment. The organization has both national and international sponsors (Natura, Banco Santander, Petrobras), in addition to an institutional partnership with the city of Rio de Janeiro. The word "bridges" figures prominently in the group's mission statement. Indeed, "bridges" are a central metaphor in the rhetoric of social empowerment advocated by groups such as AfroReggae, highlighting the idea of moving freely between all kinds of cultural, physical, and social spaces.

For AfroReggae and similar organizations, art becomes a tool of citizenship that makes the peripheral community in question visible to the wider public. The cultural artifacts that such NGOs as well as many individual artists produce seek to highlight creativity instead of violence and community instead of crime. AfroReggae's international projection includes having performed at London's Barbican center for the performing arts in 2008. This performance was co-organized with the English NGO People's Palace Project in the context of its "Favela to the World" project. Also, in tandem with People's Palace Project, AfroReggae toured the British Isles in 2011.

As groups such as AfroReggae and Viva Rio show, artistic expression can become a mode of insurgent citizenship in that it deals at a discursive level with the same factors (race, material and symbolic disenfranchisement, lack of access to social resources) that both promote and result from differentiated citizenship. Insurgency emerges from processes that confront, question, and ultimately alter these forces through textual manipulation. Take for example the poem "Nego ativo,"[8] (Active black brother) by the *periferia* poet Márcio Batista:

Quem me nega trabalho, negó
Não terá outra chance de negar
Negro é homem trabalhador
Todos sabem, ninguém pode negar.
Quem me nega salário, nego
Não terá outra chance de negar
Meu suor tem valor, meu senhor
Senhor ainda se nega a pagar.[9] (Vaz, *Cooperifa* 159)

In the first stanza, the poem takes as its point of departure job discrimination to assert the hardworking nature of the lyrical *I*, thereby converting bias into an affirmation of self-worth. The same tactic is evident in the second stanza, where unjust treatment transmutes into an appeal for fair wages. "Nego ativo" works with elements of differentiated citizenship (workplace discrimination) and reorders them through the manipulation of the verb *negar* and the noun *nego*. The poem's title, which juxtaposes the noun (or verb) *nego* to the adjective *ativo*, hints at its insurgent thrust. We can read the title either as an endorsement of an active, conscious black subject, or as an active saying "no" to the conditions that limit black subjects' participation in the socioeconomic realm.

"Nego ativo" was first published in an anthology organized by Sérgio Vaz, *O rastilho da pólvora* (Gunpowder fuse, 2004), and subsequently reproduced in the collection *Cooperifa: Antropofagia periférica* (*Cooperifa*: Anthropophagy from the periphery, 2008), also edited by Vaz. The title of the volume refers to modernist writer Oswald de Andrade's 1928 *Manifesto Antropófago* (Anthropophagous Manifesto), which proposes the assimilation ("ingestion") of various cultural influences to produce an authentic Brazilian culture. Instead of authenticity for authenticity's sake, the focus of *Cooperifa: Antropofagia periférica* is the recognition of peripheral culture as equivalent to hegemonic artistic expressions. The noun *antropofagia* (anthropophagy) is at the same time a reference to one of Brazil's best-known literary documents and the insertion of *literatura periférica* within the discourse of canonical Brazilian literature. Also implicit is the notion that *literatura marginal* has finally attained Oswald de Andrade's greatest dream: a measure of authenticity that comes from the reworking of inequalities into a creative enterprise.

It is significant that *Cooperifa* was published as part of the project *Tramas urbanas*, sponsored by the semipublic Brazilian energy corporation Petrobras.[10] The Brazilian oil giant's role in sponsoring the book highlights the increasing interest of mainstream readers and critics in "marginal" literary expressions. Of course, Petrobras's sponsorship of peripheral culture can also be interpreted as a clever PR tactic designed to improve its image with the national public.

Tramas urbanas also includes Marcus Vinícius Faustini's *Guia afetivo da periferia*. Faustini's text came out as part of the series *Literatura da periferia Brasil* (Peripheral literature Brazil). The goal of *Tramas urbanas* is twofold. First, it aims to give voice to the artists from Brazil's urban peripheries. The project's website defines the artists in the series as organic intellectuals. The emphasis on the participation of "organic intellectuals" from Brazil's socioeconomic margins legitimizes the series and segues into its second goal: namely, to question hegemonic intellectual standpoints. Similar to *Cenas da favela*, *Tramas urbanas* attempts to challenge stereotypes about Brazil's *periferia*, replacing them with a more nuanced vision of this social and cultural territory. Instead of what film critic Ivana Bentes has denominated a *Cosmética da fome* (Cosmetics of hunger)—an aesthetics that highlights and commodifies violence in the favelas and similar locales—the periphery as a site of valuable cultural production and social engagement is emphasized in *Tramas urbanas*. To date, the Petrobras-sponsored press has published twenty titles dealing with various aspects of life in the *periferia*.[11]

Curated by literary critic Heloísa Buarque de Hollanda, *Tramas urbanas* includes not only narrative texts (many, as indicated by the introduction, with a strong autobiographical bend), but also accounts of social projects initiated by *periferia* residents to tackle specific problems faced by their communities. As a result, the collection includes volumes that deal with initiatives as varied as *Tecnobrega* music and the clothing company Daspu. While the former examines the musical genre that combines techno and *brega* (hick) music, the latter is a fashion enterprise founded and run by Rio de Janeiro's prostitutes. Daspu, a parodic allusion to the luxury *paulista* boutique Daslu,[12] has as its mission to fight for prostitutes' citizenship rights. The label, which since 2005 boasts its own online boutique—*putique* (a play on the Portuguese words *puta* and *butique* [boutique])—is associated with the NGO Davida[13] and uses the proceeds from its clothing sales to promote policies that help HIV/AIDS prevention programs and antiviolence campaigns and that demand sex workers' civil rights, like the recognition of prostitution as formal labor.

Similar to the volume on Daspu, all *Tramas urbanas* projects share a sociocultural engagement with their respective communities and an impetus to deconstruct the negative stereotypes often associated with them. Instead, the volumes of *Tramas urbanas* relay a self-sufficient and creative image of marginalized populations. In this respect, these texts depart somewhat from the traditional formulations put forth by *literatura marginal.* Though sharing the premise of "organic art," the accounts in *Tramas urbanas* emphasize positive agency via cultural production. In the brief presentation that accompanies each of the books, Petrobras underlines the strong correlation between peripheral culture and social action. Culture is not only the medium, but also the means through which visibility and agency is attained.

Though produced by "organic intellectuals" from the urban peripheries, the accounts in *Tramas urbanas* are fully inserted into the circuit of cultural commodities that both attempts to generate agency for disenfranchised social segments and capitalizes on such groups. The narratives respond to the hunger for "authenticity." In the institutional presentation, Petrobras promotes both the corporation and the series as a sponsor of the project by citing Heloísa Buarque de Hollanda, according to whom "mais do que a internet, a periferia é a grande novidade do século XXI" ("Introdução").[14] The keyword is *novidade* (novelty), which in the late capitalist system is the condition sine qua non to marketability (Bauman, *Liquid Times*). By promoting *periferia* culture as novelty, *Tramas urbanas* transforms it into a desirable commodity.[15]

Tramas urbanas illustrates George Yúdice's argument about the expediency of culture—namely that culture is a valuable resource in the fight for sociopolitical and economic rights. The series is also paradigmatic of what Jeremy Rifkin has called "cultural capitalism" (9). Petrobras capitalizes on the cultural production of marginalized communities to generate positive visibility for it. Personal narratives are attached to a communitarian ethos that enables the subject to establish a positive sociocultural identification and affords her/him the means to participate in the sociopolitical and cultural arenas.

In Faustini's geobiographical narrative *Guia afetivo da periferia*, the author sketches his physical and "affective" movements through Rio de Janeiro's cartography. The narrator circulates in both the "visible" and less visible areas of the city and reveals the city's less noticeable spatial and symbolic spaces. Moving between the lower-class *periferia* in the Zona Norte and the more affluent neighborhoods of Rio's Zona Sul, Faustini reproduces the gaze of someone who, due to his socioeconomic status, is relegated to the city's outskirts. Nonetheless, the narrator of *Guia afetivo da periferia* is gradually able to stake a claim to its more central areas, making incursions into the upper-middle class terrains of Rio's Zona Sul and partaking in the cultural performances associated with the middle-class spaces. At the same time, the book's narrator remains firmly rooted in his home community.

Besides having various other cultural roles,[16] Marcus Vinícius Faustini is a theater director with a degree from the Escola de Teatro Martins Pena (Martins Pena Theater School) in Rio de Janeiro. His involvement with the stage dates back to the 1980s, when he participated as a teenager in amateur drama. The political engagement that inspires his cultural activities and that underlies *Guia afetivo da periferia* also stems from this time period. In the 1980s he was the vice-director of the Associação Municipal de Estudantes Secundaristas (AMES) (Municipal association of secondary school students). It was during his tenure that Rio de Janeiro's students attained the right to the *passe livre* (free public transportation in Rio de Janeiro). Faustini's early political engagement indirectly infuses *Guia afetivo da periferia*. When, for example, the narrator finds out that a girl that he is dating lives in the Vila Militar (military housing), he promptly breaks up with her since his political formation clashes with anything that has to do with the military—and by extension, the dictatorship (28). Paradoxically, the narrator offers us this information in the chapter "O Hangar do Zeppelin" (The Zeppelin hangar), a visit that fulfills the childhood fantasy of participating in a war (28). The juxtaposition between childhood war fantasy and pacifist adolescent intimates a development that runs parallel to the narrative's spatial charting.

In 2004, Faustini combined his political activism and his theater background. At the invitation of Rio de Janeiro's city government, he became the director of the Teatro da Cidade das Crianças (Children's city theater). From this platform he launched the NGO Reperiferia. The NGO promotes artistic expression from the periphery while using art as a pedagogical tool (Reperiferia). Beyond theater productions, the venue also hosts musical spectacles (invited luminaries include the musical group AfroReggae and the theater company Nós do Morro), promotes local culture (as for example graffiti artists), and offers "creativity workshops" such as theater, cinema, music, dance, and circus classes. Reperiferia's ultimate goal is to show that artistic engagement can be economically viable. Thus, for example, the participants of the Teatro da Cidade das Crianças are supposed to be "taking their first steps toward professionalization" (*Reperiferia*). In order to advance this objective, the NGO arranges internships at Brazil's media conglomerate, TV Globo, and also offers internship opportunities at the Teatro da Cidade das Crianças.

Similar to the success of other NGOs centered on cultural activities and empowerment such as AfroReggae,[17] Reperiferia's success has led to it expanding from its initial community of Santa Cruz into the municipalities of Nova Iguaçu and São Gonçalo, both in the Baixada

Fluminense. It has also expanded its scope to include audiovisual production. In 2006, the NGO, under Faustini's coordination, created the Escola Livre de Cinema de Nova Iguaçu (Free Cinema School of Nova Iguaçu), the first completely tuition-free audiovisual school in the Baixada Fluminense. Reperiferia promotes culture as both a symbolic and material entity. This same conception underlies Faustini's first book-length text, *Guia afetivo da periferia*.

Marcus Vinícius Faustini's text is part memoir, part travelogue, part Bildungsroman, among other genres. In the book's preface, sociologist Luiz Eduardo Soares highlights the "polysemic" nature of the text ("Prefácio"). For Soares, *Guia afetivo da periferia* establishes an active, intertextual dialogue with both national and foreign intellectual figures, literary and philosophical texts, cinema, and other cultural artifacts. Soares refers to the Brazilian poets Carlos Drummond de Andrade and to German philosopher Walter Benjamin, among others.[18] The text's prolific juxtaposition between high art and mass culture testifies to the narrator's background and erudition and helps him to access the different sociocultural realms of the *carioca* metropolis. Each reference is a signpost in the textual cartography drawn by the narrative voice.

As the book's title suggests, the author wants to give us a personal, affectionate tour of his neighborhood, or rather, of the material and symbolic space that composes Rio de Janeiro's periphery. The periphery of *Guia afetivo da periferia* is a figurative terrain that not only encompasses the low-income vicinities of the Zona Norte, but also extends throughout Rio de Janeiro and includes parts of the more prosperous Zona Sul.[19] In this sense, the "periphery" of Faustini's book captures the proposal obliquely spelled out in the series's title *Literatura da Periferia Brasil*. By omitting the preposition and the definite article between *periferia* and *Brasil*, the entire nation becomes composed of margins. "Periferia Brasil" proposes to annul the dichotomy implied in the word "periphery." Without a center, there are not outskirts. Consequently, in *Guia afetivo da periferia*, the entire city composes the territory that Faustini's guidebook aspires to cover.

Guia afetivo da periferia opens with a shot of Faustini in school uniform, seated in front of a large Brazilian flag. The boy's head cuts into the motto *Ordem e Progresso* (Order and progress) that is emblazoned across the banner. The image contains no complete words, just the trace of the vocable *ordem*, suggesting both an ordering and a truncating of the narrative that follows. Other photos intercalate pictures of the city, family snapshots, and images of cultural icons such as the 1980s musician Stevie B. Indeed, the author uses pop culture and, to a degree, high culture (there are several references to Nietzsche, Proust, and other writers and poets) to express both a time frame (the 1980s in the case of Steve B.) and a sociocultural consciousness that includes both the Zona Sul and the Zona Norte. Throughout the text, references to "high culture," traditionally associated with Rio's upper- and middle-class neighborhoods of the Zona Sul, are juxtaposed to manifestations of popular culture that emblematize the city's lower-income communities (as for example funk dances). Taken together, the photographs included in the text make up an album and contribute to the "biographical" makeup of *Guia afetivo da periferia*.

Beyond conveying a personal view of Rio de Janeiro's public spaces, Faustini's narrative mapping of Rio de Janeiro imbues its urban terrains—and particularly its peripheral neighborhoods—with new social and cultural meanings. *Guia afetivo da periferia* transforms the movement through Rio's cityscape into an assertion of the right to have rights that underpins insurgent citizenship. For Holston, insurgent practices ultimately seek equalization of differences through the recognition of "universal equality, dignity and access" (*Insurgent* 249). Though relayed through an individual perspective, the demand for the "right to have rights" in *Guia afetivo da periferia* symbolizes the entrance of increasing numbers of people into the sphere of citizenship—and as such, into the contemporary polis. In this framework, *Guia afetivo da periferia* also captures the gradual modification of Brazil's socioeconomic structure as more and more people access the sphere of consumption, thus entering the domain of substantive citizenship.

Since 2003, with Lula's ascension to the presidency, Brazil's middle class has undergone a process of consolidation and expansion. Middle-class expansion occurs as people from lower-income strata gain access to the C classes. In 2010, approximately 31.9 million Brazilians ascended to this status. The growth of the C class is largely due to employment growth (67 percent); social policies, such as the *Bolsa Família* (17 percent); and finally, improved social security (15.7 percent) (Villaverde). The result is a changing pattern of consumption and—as Holston has indicated—of citizenship, with the new middle class demanding their right to have rights.

In *Guia afetivo da periferia*, the narrator's comings and goings signify the public spaces that he occupies as civic and cultural arenas in which various urban subjects can partake in the social contract and in the social goods implied in said pact. In Faustini's text, Rio de Janeiro is no longer solely the *cidade partida* (broken city; Ventura), divided between the hegemonic center/Zona Sul and the marginal periphery (both the *morro* and the Zona Norte). Rather, the *carioca* metropolis becomes a patchwork of different parts that are sewn together by the narrator's physical dislocations, by his gaze, and by his textual voice. It is a city that can be claimed by heterogeneous social sectors.

Navigating the city, the narrator traverses its disparate terrains and explores its symbolic and material geography. It is within this larger map that he finds (quite literally) a rostrum on which to reflect and represent his experiences in his home community. In the segment titled "Beco da Lúxuria" (Alley of lust), Faustini describes how he discovers in the city the means to become himself—and hence, to express what he is. The alley—the location Martins Pena Theater School—contains everything that makes the narrator-protagonist whole. In this alleyway he learned to reconcile "body, word and territory" (30). The conjunction of the distinct parts that form his identity—body, language, and sociogeographic positionality—only occurs when the author physically and emotionally distances himself from his originary place of identification: the periphery. When he reunites his bodily (private) and sociogeographic (collective) terrain with the larger metropolitan territory, he acquires a voice: the text that we are reading. Faustini advocates writing as an answer to geographic, social, as well as existential disjuncture. Writing is the vehicle for physical and imaginary urban locomotion and reconciliation.

Guia afetivo da periferia not only straddles different genres but textually unites various urban sites. It also scrutinizes and conjoins the city synesthetically. Cultural markers are juxtaposed to the sounds, tastes, and smells that the narrator encounters during his strolls: "Caminho por todo o centro da cidade: Alfândega, Candelária, Praça XV, até chegar ao Palácio Gustavo Capanema. Gosto de cruzar aqueles pilotis e sentir a vento ba-tendo na cara. É tão bom como pedir um guaraná Convenção e um cachorro quente na praça do Curral Falso, em Santa Cruz" (66).[20] In this excerpt, the narrator lexically emulates the sensation of wind hitting his face (*ba-tendo*). To this impression, he juxtaposes the taste of a soft drink and a hot dog consumed in another area of the city. He does not privilege either sentiment, but relishes both equally (*tão bom*), equalizing the city's sentimental terrain.

Each zone contains its own array of sounds, smells, and colors. These elements both distinguish particular areas of the city and fuse them together. In the heading "839" (a reference to a late night bus), the narrator creates a poignant description of how the periphery's public spaces (in this case Campo Grande's bus station) coalesce into the manifold metropolitan faces. As he waits for the 839 bus that will take him home, the narrator observes how elements paradigmatic of many popular public spaces (street vendors selling counterfeit DVDs and food, the smell of urine) (33) are complemented by a street vendor reading Dostoevsky's *Notes from the Underground* (1864), an unlikely book in the hands of a street seller who normally reads Paulo Coelho.[21] The synesthetic mosaic reinforces the idea of bridging disparate metropolitan geosymbolic spaces. Indeed, the bus station itself is a transitional space that allows the narrator and other urban denizens, to access far-flung places.

Transportation is an important theme of *Guia afetivo da periferia*. Like many of the *periferia*'s residents, the narrator relies primarily on public transportation. Transportation communicates the *periferia*'s varied social composition. Consequently, there are different modes of circulating in the city. The public bus is compared to vans.[22] For the narrator, traveling in vans becomes an "obsession" because they are faster and more comfortable. Vans are also a moving stage where the fascinated narrator observes the performances of drivers, conductors, and other passengers. But vans are also more expensive. Ironically, in order to satisfy his desire to use more upscale public transportation, the narrator must work in a series of odd and, at times, somewhat embarrassing jobs that range from impersonating Santa Claus in a supermarket to a stuffed animal in a mall (36). For the narrator of *Guia afetivo da periferia*, transportation is an amphitheater in which imagination and sociability are performed.

In the kombi that takes the narrator from Cesarão to the Estação Santa Cruz we encounter the suburban fauna of street vendors, preachers, and workers (48). This mainly working-class group contrasts with the middle-class punks from Méier, or the bohemian customers of the bar Amarelinho that the narrator comes across in his excursions to the Zona Sul. The vans and buses that transport the working-class residents from their employment in the Zona Sul to their homes in the Zona Norte or to Rio's other outlying neighborhoods pose a contrast to what the narrator terms "mise-en-scène Miami Beach" (39). In this "mise-en-scène," the middle and upper classes that frequent the beaches of the Zona Sul purport to recreate an international (North American) leisure style, thereby identifying with a global cultural imaginary.

Inside the buses going from the Zona Sul to the Zona Norte, an impromptu community arises that transforms the trip into a celebration of the end of the workday. The late-night enjoyment defies the weariness of long work hours and promotes sociability instead of the isolation that comes from mechanical and/or exploitative labor practices. In this sense, the late-night trips become acts of citizenship insofar that they disturb the drudgery of everyday life and labor with creativity, producing a new communitarian forum (Isin and Nielsen 10). The bus is a microcosm of the *carioca* periphery and transports the reader—its literary passenger—into this space.

As a "guide," the book's detailing of spatial dynamics is fundamental. *Guia afetivo da periferia* opens with the narrator's recollection of Santa Cruz and positions him firmly within the territory of the *periferia*. Santa Cruz is the stage where he enacts social and cultural citizenship. His project, to create an "affective map" of Rio de Janeiro's periphery is, as the adjective in the book's title indicates, twofold. On the one hand, *afetivo* (affective/affectionate) is synonymous with "personal." Faustini transmits to us *his* perspective of the *periferia*. On the other hand, the descriptor demonstrates the author's emotional attachment to this space. Faustini resignifies the *periferia* as a positive space by exposing the sentimental bonds that connect him to Santa Cruz. For him, this neighborhood is central. It is his home and the place where he calibrates his urban experiences. By making Santa Cruz the (affective) core of his urban experiences, the narrator inverts the dichotomy that privileges the Zona Sul as Rio de Janeiro's cultural and social axis.

Guia afetivo da periferia also alters the prevalent perception of the *periferia* as a dangerous zone. Rather than situating this area outside the limits of the city proper and therefore reinforcing the notion of liminality, he connects the Zona Sul to the Zona Norte through the Avenida Brasil, Rio's largest thoroughfare and main traffic artery. The book contains three images that either depict or refer to the avenue and signal the expressway's connective importance. If *Guia afetivo da periferia* constructs metaphoric bridges between Rio's different socio-geographic areas, then the Avenida Brasil creates the material link that allows the narrator to traverse the city materially and symbolically from one end (Santa Cruz) to the other (Barra da Tijuca, Ipanema). This avenue becomes the artery that guides the author, and us, into Rio de Janeiro's various districts and their idiosyncrasies.

Speaking about his connection to Ipanema, the narrator affirms that he first became familiar with the nocturnal side of this district. During this time he pinned for the sun-drenched version of the neighborhood, represented in film and literature (44), while also being intimidated by this space. Ipanema, an upper-middle-class neighborhood that suggests a sophisticated bohemian lifestyle,[23] is at the same time familiar and foreign to the young peripheral protagonist. Like any *carioca*, the narrator-protagonist is privy to the imaginary surrounding the famous district. Yet, he does not personally partake in the empirical reality that generates this imaginary. This unfamiliarity with a space that he knows through cultural references displays the sociocultural divisions that characterize Rio's geosymbolic cartography. When the narrator-protagonist finally begins frequenting Ipanema during the daytime, he recognizes certain similarities between this area and Cesarão, specifically, the commercial stalls on the beach that remind him of the homes in Cesarão (44). The resemblance between the two spaces demystifies Ipanema for the narrator and transforms it into a familiar (both in the sense of "known" and "domestic") arena. The narrator-protagonist is as at home in the same landscape that saw the emergence of Bossa Nova as he is in Cesarão. Like his comparison between the pleasure of feeling the wind on his face in Rio's center and the hot dog with Guaraná in Santa Cruz, the likeness between Ipanema and Cesarão erases value judgments that privilege either space.

The idea of bridges or connections is reinforced by the variety of imagery that is included in the text that creates a symbolic bridge linking the periphery to the center and beyond.[24] These images reproduce the narrator's—and the reader's—physical and imaginary routes. As with the narrator's mapping, neither center nor margins are privileged in the photographs. We find, in close textual proximity, the Candelária church (131) and a skating ring in Cesarão (136–37). Both are urban monuments, each with its particular connotation and use. Each becomes important in the book's composition and reading.

The map utilized by Faustini emerges from his private memories that, woven together, reveal a patchwork of Rio's, and by extension, of Brazil's present and recent past (dating back to the 1980s, when the narrative begins). In the back cover comments, Heloísa Buarque de Hollanda asserts that Faustini coins a new literary mode—that of the "memory of the present." *Guia afetivo da periferia* uses the memorial mode to delineate a trajectory within the present. Various black and white photographs that cover different epochs in the author's life and different locales enhance the book's memorial quality. The snapshots mostly show the narrator's childhood years. There are two photos of him as an adult: "Eu na escola de teatro Martins Pena" (Me in the Martins Pena Theater School; 72–73) and the image that closes the book, of the narrator at the time of publication. The opening (Faustini in school uniform in front of the Brazilian flag) and closing images underscore the notion of personal development, of a Bildungsroman.

Like many writings that emerge from the urban periphery, *Guia afetivo da periferia* focuses on the individual's formation and offers it as an exemplary tale. In his examination of contemporary Brazilian marginal literature, Marcos Zibordi maintains that this genre often combines biography and autobiography (73). *Guia afetivo da periferia* both follows this trend (partially assuming the [auto]biographical stance) and departs from it. Most marginal literature implicitly posits identification between the narrative voice and the community from which the narrator/author comes from by reproducing the linguistic register of said community.[25] Language and storyline demonstrate the empirical roots from which the text grows. As Chapter 3 shows, slang generally abounds in this type of literary production. At the same time, marginal literature also aspires to what is conventionally defined as "literariness." In many texts of the genre, one finds highly formalized sentences and/or turns of phrases, or even syntax juxtaposed with colloquial speech (Zibordi 74). Emblematic of this phenomenon is *Manual prático do ódio*, where literary and vernacular language and jargon appear repeatedly and concurrently.

By contrast, *Guia afetivo da periferia* eschews slang and imitation of the oral register in favor of a language that, although not formal, clearly conforms to standards of written Portuguese. Nor does Faustini resort to literary flourishes in his text. The book's language is straightforward, although not exempt from poetic passages. Describing his journey from Ipanema to Santa Cruz, for example, the narrator draws on Machado de Assis to relay the sentiment of the trajectory: "Sentado no meio-fio, esperando a van de madrugada, vendo o mar bravio como o que engoliu Escobar, eis a Ipanema que se repetiu durante anos para mim" (39).[26] The reference to Machado de Assis's canonical novel *Dom Casmurro* (1899)[27] both inserts a lyrical note and introduces an ironic tone into the excerpt. The narrator is aware of the old-fashioned terminology (*mar bravio*) that he employs and uses it to gently poke fun at his own words while also validating his literary voice/experience. At times, the book's language evokes a personal journal with literary pretensions. As such, *Guia afetivo da periferia* both fulfills the "authenticity" requirement of marginal literature and departs from it. The text straddles two discursive modes, crossing over from the periphery to the center and back.

Guia afetivo da periferia is written in the first-person singular, which imbues the text with an intimate tone that incorporates the narrator and the reader. The narrative intimacy also includes the author (Faustini), who is at the same time inside the account and outside it. Though Soares includes *biografia* (biography) as one of the possible genres under which *Guia afetivo da periferia* can be classified, the book is not a biography or even an autobiography in the traditional sense of the word (i.e., a person's life story). The identification between narrator and author (i.e., Faustini) is unsettled partially by the anonymity of the former. At all times, the narrator refers to himself by the first-person singular pronoun (*eu*). Therefore, though we assume that the narrator and author are the same person, the narrator can also be an independent persona that the author impersonates. And while the text is an account of the narrator's life, it reveals only certain fragments of his existence, leaving out other important moments (as, for example, his schooling, his first love, etc.). Taken together, the different episodes that compose the larger narrative of *Guia afetivo da periferia* are like mementos that the narrator unearthed from his mnemonic archive. Consequently, though (auto)biographical, the text ultimately surpasses the constraints of this genre. *Guia afetivo da periferia* is at once a singular chronicle and an account that can reference many life stories.

Unlike most bio or autobiographical texts, *Guia afetivo da periferia* does not follow a chronological order, but rather a sentimental one. This affective structure is, in turn, divided into three main chapters. Each includes nondiachronic subchapters that describe different time periods. The only chapter that appears to refer to one specific epoch is "bússola," which is limited to the narrator's childhood years. "Bússola" (compass) can thus be read as a metaphoric compass that will retrospectively guide the narrator and the reader through the cityscape. In this manner, *Guia afetivo da periferia* not only provides us with a physical itinerary, it also offers us an affective map and a handbook of everyday conduct—thus the noun *guia*, which can mean both "guide," "handbook," or "guidebook."

"Meu território" (My territory) suggests the narrator's endeavors to stake out a geographic and affective territory in the city. His territory runs parallel to the urban areas in which he acquires a measure of agency, be it through his education (the theater school Martins Pena, [downtown Rio de Janeiro]) or a "cot of his own" in an apartment in the Rua Pedro Américo. Correspondingly, this chapter zig-zags throughout Rio de Janeiro's geography, starting in Santa Cruz, the narrator's home base, passing through the artsy Santa Teresa neighborhood, and ending at the Rua Pedro Américo, in the middle-class neighborhood of Catete.

The chart suggests the narrator's recognition of the city and of himself. Reflected in this map is his development from childhood to adulthood that is accompanied by his movement from the parent's home to his own living space. The narrator's autonomy at the end of the chapter is emphasized by his acquisition of a table lamp, an exotic item for someone of his socioeconomic status (93). The lamp serves as a companion in his nightly readings and creates a bond between the narrator and his roommate, a former political prisoner. The light draws a circumference inside which the older man tells his story to the younger one, who, in turn, recounts it to the reader. The roommate's story condenses national history within a specific space. After being imprisoned and tortured, his persecutor frees him at the corner of the Avenue Presidente Wilson and Antônio Carlos Street. The protagonist's roommate takes him to this spot, where history disappears in the flux of everyday life (96). The city's fluidity partially erases the past while creating other spatial narratives (including the one we are reading) that contain their own histories.

"Primeiros mapas" (First maps) relies on the geographic and emotional signposts established in "Meu território" and focuses on particular experiences within certain metropolitan areas. The chapter therefore charts a sentimental rather than physical diagram of the metropolis and of the narrator's life. Significantly, "Primeiros mapas" begins and ends on the "street." Streets are both imaginative and emotional conduits. The chapter's first segment recounts the narrator's desire for a dog, which is coupled with his apocalyptic cinematographic plans: he wants to "explode" the city and watch its demise accompanied by a dog (101–2). Fictionalizing the city allows the narrator to appropriate and inhabit it in its entirety, even when he is constrained to the limited areas of childhood, such as his immediate neighborhood.

In the chapter's final segment "Autoviação" (Self-roads) the narrator once again claims the urban landscape, but this time the movement is reciprocal: the city permeates his imaginary as he traverses it. At the end of "Primeiros mapas," the narrator reflects on the construction of an imaginary cartography that allows the subject to traverse the metropolis: "O que passa na cabeça das pessoas que cruzam a cidade pela madrugada dentro dos ônibus? Será que a cidade invade o lugar de seus pensamentos? Como cada um constrói a sua Autoviação?" (140).[28]

Faustini, who hails from Rio de Janeiro's Zona Norte, grew up in the Baixada Fluminense and in the Cesarão,[29] a subsidized housing project in Santa Cruz, in Rio de Janeiro's west side. Here, Faustini spent his later childhood and adolescence. The Baixada is situated on the outskirts of metropolitan Rio de Janeiro. It is an independent municipality, though in Faustini's book this district melds into the general description of Rio de Janeiro's periphery. Santa Cruz, on the other hand, is a borough associated with the larger metropolitan Rio de Janeiro area, and in Faustini's book, it becomes the nucleus from which the narrative emanates.

The narrative ripples from Santa Cruz's nodal point. *Guia afetivo da periferia* begins with the description of the author's sweltering childhood summers soon after he moves to the new neighborhood (23). Superimposed onto this reminiscence is the earlier memory of the "first" childhood years (*primeira infância*) that Faustini spent in the Baixada Fluminense. The juxtaposition situates Santa Cruz as the present and the Baixada as the past and contrasts the urbanity of Santa Cruz with the almost rural character of the Baixada. In effect, the author's residence in the Baixada is in the Chacrinha (little farm), in the municipality of Duque de Caxias. Faustini's recollections of this place have a rural tint to them—such as dirt roads—that contrasts with the decidedly metropolitan ambiance of Santa Cruz. His family's move to Cesarão signifies a socioeconomic improvement. Here the family can own their own home.

Like the majority of residents from the Baixada and from sub-divisions such as the Cesarão, Faustini too comes from a lower socioeconomic background. Similar to the characters in Ruffato's books and in Bonassi's *Subúrbio*, Faustini and his narrator belong to a precarious working class. They are part of the *classe média baixa*, people who live at the borders of socioeconomic disenfranchisement but who still maintain a tenuous middle-class status.[30] This standing is demonstrated by the small luxuries that are found in the narrator's home: a second-hand fan, a child's record player, and the old VW that the narrator's stepfather owns.

Complementing these items, the narrator describes the family's frugal shopping and eating habits. Despite their limited resources, the narrator's parents are proud to have a well-stocked pantry filled with variegated foods: cooking oil, rice, beans, and so on (111). The foodstuffs are not only utilitarian; they become decorative objects that enliven the domestic space and spawn sociability. Conversations take place over the pantry's arrangement and contents. The narrator's family customarily displays their wares to guests, thereby transforming the pantry into a showcase of middling material comfort.

For the narrator, the products his family buys emblematize both the world outside of the domestic sphere and a certain aspiration for socioeconomic status. Indeed, the canned foods that don the kitchen shelves in low-income homes such as the narrator's reflect an idea of the "modern" propagated by Brazilian television. Consuming the products touted in advertisements for "Sardinhas 88" and Swift Ham asserts the customer's participation in the modern economy as much as owning a car. But of all social markers, homeownership is the most valuable. Property, especially in the liberal concept of citizenship, is a significant measure of social and civil belonging.

The family's move from Duque de Caxias to Santa Cruz is prompted by the prospect of financial stability, of bettering their socioeconomic status. Homeownership is the metaphor for—and concretization of—both economic solidity and ascension. Homeownership, at least theoretically, guarantees the family's social positioning among the working classes. It is worth a 38-caliber gun and the VW (which are exchanged for the house) (50–51). Lúcio Kowarik avers that home-ownership is a form of insurance against unexpected crisis (30). Homeownership not only denotes stability and permanence but also represents the potential of improvement through autoconstruction. It therefore can become an outward symbol of social ascendancy. Similar to the segment "Fim" in Luiz Ruffato's story "A expiação" (*Mamma, son tanto felice*), autoconstruction goes in tandem with urbanization. In *Guia afetivo da periferia*, autoconstruction is denoted by the yellow tiles that are added to the backsplash of the kitchen sink. Urbanization arrives in the form of a paved street in the neighborhood.

The paved street becomes the epicenter of community life. Resi-dents celebrate this hallmark of urbanization with barbecues on the newly improved thoroughfare. Pavement also changes the constitu-tion of childhood games, creating new forms of entertainment. In other words, urbanization transforms not only the neighborhood's physical milieu, but also its forms of sociability. Improvement of pub-lic space in tandem with the autoconstruction or upgrades in homes integrates the periphery's inhabitants into the larger framework of the city and strengthens their sense of citizenship (Holston, *Insurgent* 23). Holston equates the urbanization of Brazil's urban peripheries to a narrative that spans the arc between disempowerment and enfran-chisement. And the denizens of these spaces "read everyday changes in their neighborhoods—each new setting of tile, appliance, sofa, and second storey, each new health clinic, school, paved road, and sewage line—as installments in this narrative of the transformation of subal-tern life" (156). Not surprisingly, the first paved road in the narrator's community becomes the centerpiece of sociability (*Guia* 148). When the residents promenade on the street, they become part of a different city, one in which public infrastructure is less precarious and where, therefore, the populace has better access to social citizenship. More than a mere street, the paved road is a symbol of urban rights.

Just as the paved street creates a new domain for the performance of citizenship, home improvements impart a new significance to the domestic sphere. For the narrator, "[a] possibilidade de asfalto na nossa rua só perdia para a alegria de minha mãe quando a pia da cozinha recebeu azulejo amarelo na parte superior da bica" (*Guia* 148).[31] The transformation of the sink impacts the narrator's relation to the kitchen. Instead of being a merely utilitarian space, this area gains a poetic dimension prompted by the "luz do sol que entrava pelo basculante [refletindo] nos pingos de água do azulejo amarelo" (149).[32] Holston indicates that the houses in Brazilian urban peripheries denote not only the socioeconomic status of their residents, but also designate their owner's stories (*Insurgent* 168). In *Guia afetivo da periferia*, homes have a valence not only according to where they are located, but also according to their contents.

A case in point is the opposition between the metal grater used by Dona Creuza, the narrator's mother, and the plastic grater that his "rich" aunt has. This "rich" aunt lives in Laranjeiras, an upper-middle-class neighborhood in the Zona Sul. For the narrator, who spends some of his childhood vacations in Laranjeiras, the plastic kitchen utensil connotes modernity and affluence, which are reinforced by other objects in the apartment: the three-in-one sound system and a telephone. However, what most impresses him is his aunt's bathroom, which is tiled from floor to ceiling. Unconsciously, the narrator compares the sparse triangle of tiles in his own home to those in his aunt's bathroom and believes her to be a "millionaire" (*Guia* 167). The bathroom tiles become the symbol of socioeconomic status as they signify financial betterment that, in turn, transmutes into home improvement.

Unaware of the social divisions that crisscross the urban landscape, the narrator is surprised to hear his aunt's address referred as *favelão* (big favela; 167) by other residents of the Zona Sul. The demystification caused by this comment induces the narrator to reflect about social status and spatial meaning: "De tia rica e excêntrica, passei a percebê-la como a primeira filha de minha avó a tentar romper intelectualmente o ciclo a que esta família está determinada" (168).[33] For the young boy, the aunt's social striving, reflected in her address and living conditions, translates into agency. Significantly it is this aunt who teaches the narrator to navigate the city's streets. She bequeaths to him the possibility of also becoming empowered by inhabiting the metropolitan landscape.

As suggested earlier, in *Guia afetivo da periferia* empowerment is also synonymous with homeownership. The home is another signpost that not only denotes material possession, but is also a symbol of being an integral part of the urban landscape. Holston suggests that homeownership posits the subject firmly into the realm of citizenship.

He indicates that this is especially the case in regard to subdivisions, such as the first constructions of the Cesarão.[34] Subdivisions stand in contrast to favelas in terms of both physical and moral "orderliness" (Holston, *Insurgent* 172). Unlike favelas, they are an index of their residents' participation in civil society (173). The distinction between the regulated and "secure" terrains of the subdivision and the "disorderly" and precarious territory of the favelas is underscored in the heading "Acordes da Dilermando Reis" (The chords of Dilermando Reis).

Dilermando Reis is the address of the narrator's grandparents and one of his aunts, who reside in state housing (*Guia* 177). From the windows of the apartment, the young narrator can observe the surrounding landscape, which includes the favela do Jacarezinho. On rainy days his pastime during his visits to his grandparents is to watch as the favela's shacks are destroyed by the rising waters (*Guia* 177). The narrator establishes a clear distinction between himself and the *favelados*, at whom he pokes fun ("Surfando no rio, né, favelado?" [177][35]). While he and his family reside in the secure zone of the subdivision, the favela residents inhabit an unstable terrain, both materially and symbolically.

Sociologist Lúcio Kowarick refers to the disenfranchising conditions under which the urban poor live as *espoliação urbana* (urban plundering, urban exploitation). Exploitation creates the necessary conditions for the formation of a disempowered workforce that will feed the labor needs of metropolises such as Rio de Janeiro. The working class that inhabits the periphery, as well as the favelas, performs the menial tasks shunned by the more affluent residents in the metropolis.

Despite the real (i.e., the proverbial train tracks) and imaginary boundaries that separate the apartment on the Dilermando Reis (and similar housing complexes) from the adjacent favela, the limit between the two areas is porous. Both the favela and the housing complex are home to the exploited working class mentioned in the previous paragraph and discussed in Chapters 1 through 3. They are the late-shift employees at the McDonald's of the Zona Sul (*Guia* 38) or gas station attendants, among other low-paying activities.

As violence in urban Rio de Janeiro intensifies, the favela's "disorder" intrudes into the subdivision's ordered terrain. The gun shots that increasingly are fired from the former space leave their physical mark on the latter. However, sites such as the Cohab's apartment on Dilermando Reis still contain the promise of a certain comfort that is nonexistent (or at least invisible) within the favela. Accordingly, the heading's title "Acordes da Dilermando Reis" refers to the ringing of the grandparents' phone in their apartment and to their conversations with their far-flung children. The telephone, a much-coveted commodity, is only available in the zoned—that is, "official" urban areas. In this context, the "notes" of the title are the sounds of familial sociability and of lower-middle-class homeownership.

But *acordes* also evokes the chord of melancholia that the changing social conditions strike in the narrator. The bullet marks he finds on the building conflict with the domesticity of his family's apartment (178). The juxtaposition between the familial and the outside spaces accentuates the wistfulness of this segment. A photograph of the narrator's grandfather speaking for the first time on the telephone (179) further highlights the sense of nostalgia for a more peaceful time. The grandfather sits in an armchair in what appears to be a living room. The living room features lower-middle-class taste and coziness: in the background we see a flowered curtain blocking the outside view and therefore creating a protective barrier against the increasingly violent outside space. Against a wall a shelf contains a myriad of bibelots such as porcelain cats, a decorative tea service, and framed photographs. The shelf is a memorial shrine where the family showcases its remembrances (photographs) and the collection of gifts and small splurges—the tea set is a popular wedding gift, for example. On the side table that flanks the armchair is the phone and an imitation hurricane lamp atop of a doily. All the objects in the photograph connote neatness, thus showcasing Holston's argument of the "orderliness" of subdivisions. The image exudes hominess, tidiness, and modest comfort achieved through constant labor and discipline and stands out against the veiled disorder of the adjoining favela.

In *Guia afetivo da periferia*, the *periferia* is an arena of domesticity inhabited by working class men and women. Emblematic is the narrator's description of Cidade de Deus. *Guia afetivo da periferia* features the reverse side of the images propagated in media of the now famous housing complex. Instead of the violent daily life depicted in the course of Paulo Lins's book and highlighted in Fernando Meirelles's and Kátia Lund's homonymous film (2002), the City of God that appears in *Guia afetivo da periferia* is described through the eyes of a vacationing child. Wonderment and enjoyment replaces violence in this picture, just as working men and women substitute the thugs of Lins's and Meirelles and Lund's *Cidade de Deus*. While the narrator's uncle sells peanuts on the Praça Saens Peña in the Tijuca neighborhood, his cousin is apprenticing to become a massage therapist. Despite being almost blind, she travels from Cidade de Deus, located in Rio's west side, to Glória, in Rio de Janeiro's Zona Sul. The periphery's primarily working-class population represents the working ethic of Jessé Souza's *batalhadores* who, according to him, ascend the social ladder thanks to hard work and self-reliance (*Os batalhadores* 50). By emphasizing the everyday life and labor of Cidade de Deus's residents and their connections to Rio's Zona Sul, the narrator is able to transform the periphery into an ordinary neighborhood, linked to the larger conurbation by employment and leisure.

As films such as *Cidade de Deus, Tropa de elite,* and other recent productions suggest, urban violence is generally associated with Brazil's peripheries or with its favelas. Nonetheless, in *Guia afetivo da periferia* violence occurs primarily outside the *periferia*, not within its perimeter. Living in the periphery, the narrator's exposure to violence is mostly limited to the televised news and the occasional beating he receives from his stepfather for misbehaving (*Guia* 132)." Violence is largely exterior to the narrator's community. For the narrator violence is an abstraction until it gains materiality and intrudes into his consciousness as he drives by the Candelária Church on the morning after the killing of eight street children on the steps of the house of worship. For him, the scenario of the tragedy evokes ambiguous feelings. On the one hand, "violence" remains an intellectual abstraction, a "capitalist evil" as depicted in Marx (which he already read despite his young age). On the other hand, violence, particularly this episode, has a profoundly personal impact. The dead children bring to mind his own brush with hostility: "ali, na Candelária, um pivete havia arrancado do meu pulso um relógio Champion . . . Lembro de ter-me esforçado para não me sentir vingado. Vingança foi uma palavra que aprendi nas novelas" (132).[36]

Not only is this type of violence atypical in his community, but also its symbols—as, for example, the police—are unfamiliar for the narrator. The police's absence from the community generates a peaceful image of the periphery that goes against the grain of predominant depictions of this geosocial terrain. By establishing the *periferia* as a terrain largely removed from the hostility that permeates other metropolitan areas, Faustini produces a counterdiscourse to the general stigmatization of this community as a dangerous and chaotic terrain.

Guia afetivo da periferia seeks, through narration, to offset the violence that permeates Rio's material and imaginary geography. The narrator admits that he never liked the "excess of reality" that impregnates Rio's urban imaginary (74). Writing is the antidote to the surplus of reality that—due to its excessiveness—ultimately becomes unreal. Instead of evading reality, however, the narrator proposes to seek poetry in the metropolis's daily rhythms. According to him, this experience can be found in everyday scenes such as those exemplified by Rio's street vendors. The narrator observes beauty in everyday actions such as "quando você é um camelô e arruma fileiras amarelas e vermelhas de bombons Serenata de Amor sobre a lona de plástico azul da calçada, imitando a vitrine da loja de roupa de grife atrás" (74).[37] The scene transforms the quotidian gesture of a street vendor arranging his wares into a moving poem and the aesthetics of violence give way to an aesthetics of the everyday. Beyond extracting beauty from everyday rituals, the gesture performed by the *camelô* (street vendor) suggests a microinsurgency. His merchandise copies the arrangement of the high-end goods positioned behind him. The reflection forms an interface between the two types of commodities, and the barrier between the swanky boutique and the canvas on the street weakens. Both spaces are fused into the larger metropolitan landscape.

Maclei, a young street vendor, performs a similar "insurgent" gesture. The boy sells sweets in Rio's central district and when someone refuses to buy his ware, he deploys a creative stratagem. Flashing a box at the failed buyer he explains that the acronym I.C.D.F means "Instituto do Cavalheiro com Deficiência Financeira" (Institute of the Gentleman with Financial Disability; 76). Maclei has a precise strategy. Whereas money that is deposited in the box goes to his own expenses, the cash that he receives from the purchase of sweets is destined to help the family.

Maclei is one of the innumerous impoverished kids that roam Brazil's metropolitan centers, eking out a living by selling goods or begging. Many times, these children are lumped together into the category of dangerous street kids who pickpocket passersby. However, *Guia afetivo da periferia* centers on the creative strategies that the children employ to pursue—to a measure—positive goals (in this case, Sunday excursions). Maclei transforms the normally thankless labor of street commerce into a performance that mingles irony and social appeal therefore circumventing the normal repudiation that middle- and upper-class *cariocas* and other residents have toward these children.

Even though the narrator-protagonist of *Guia afetivo da periferia* emphasizes the connections that exist between Rio's different socioeconomic spaces and the commonalities that link their inhabitants, urban division is not entirely absent from Faustini's text. Though *Guia afetivo da periferia* aims to bond the symbolic schisms that scar the metropolitan body, divisions are apparent in the long distances that the narrator has to travel from Santa Cruz to Rio's Zona Sul. Faustini also broaches social stratification in his description of the central neighborhood of Santa Teresa. "Maritacas de Santa Teresa" (79–81) shows two panoramas of this artistic vicinity. Both sceneries have at their core one single house that divides the landscape into two. The exterior vista belongs to famous artists and foreign tourists, who seek the simulacrum of a historic past in its cobblestone streets (79). The other vista gives the perspective of the "hidden" yet advertised Rio de Janeiro of the favelas. Partly because of its proximity to several favelas,[38] Santa Teresa has seen an increase in crime in recent years, frequently due to a spillover of the conflicts between warring drug-trafficking groups or between criminal organizations and the police. Though *Guia afetivo da periferia* casts a glance to the surrounding low-income neighborhoods, it focuses on their communitarian aspects. The narrator observes (and recommends that the reader observe) a group of capoeira practitioners that climb the Aarão Reis street toward their homes in the favela or an elderly black woman who strenuously also returns home. And if this is not enough to touch the viewer/reader, he tells them to watch how on Saturday mornings a group of kids descends the Aarão Reis, led by an elderly black gentleman whose eyes "explode with affection" when he looks at the children (80). *Guia afetivo da periferia* proposes that Santa Teresa's two sides are not separated, but conterminous. In different ways, middle-class residents, tourists, and inhabitants of the low-income neighborhoods claim the areas of the picturesque city as their own, transforming the space. By juxtaposing the neighborhood's two facets, the book's narrator validates both and creates poetry through their dialogue.

Social divisions and differentiated citizenship are also apparent in social interactions and in police bullying. Especially for lower-income residents, who are often darker-skinned youth, police harassment is a common experience. Police harrying reflects the perception of youths from the Zona Norte and from the favelas as an irritant—a "pollutant" (Yúdice 122)—within the upper-middle-class areas of the Zona Sul. Accordingly, sociogeographic space is divided into territories that often implicitly exclude poorer residents (122). This has led to some violent attempts by peripheral youth to appropriate the off-limits zones of the middle and upper classes. Yúdice mentions the 1990s *arrastões* (flash mobs) as examples of insurgent performances that "contaminated" the beaches and their immediate vicinity in the Zona Sul.

Aware of the negative typecasting of peripheral youth, the narrator recognizes that his urban excursions are only possible because of his own "invisibility." Being lighter skinned, he does not fit the profile of the "threatening" suburban youth. One incident highlights how invisibility both circumvents and reinforces social exclusion. In an outing through Santa Cruz's neighboring district of Paciência, the narrator and his friends experience social and racial profiling personally: "Em Paciência, eu e meus amigos fomos uma vez parados pela polícia. Só um deles tomou tapa na cara. Ele era negro. Eu era invisível. Era como se não estivesse ali" (*Guia* 78).[39] Paciência, which is located in Rio de Janeiro's east side and is adjacent to Santa Cruz, is a lower-middle class neighborhood, not so different from Santa Cruz itself. However, even in this area, darker skin color evokes prejudice and leads to differential treatment. Though he is not perceived as a potential delinquent (unlike his black friend), the narrator in effect also does not exist as a civil and social subject. He is "invisible."

Guia afetivo da periferia does not denounce the police nor, by extension, social discrimination and violence, in the same manner as many other peripheral texts. Instead of directly decrying abuses, the narrative circumvents the negative visibility afforded to the peripheral subject by mainstream media largely through the creation of a discourse that establishes him as an active participant in city life.

In order to attain a measure of visibility, but without becoming too conspicuous, the narrator emulates the consumption rituals of Rio's more affluent classes. Clothes, a mark of distinction (Bourdieu), are the canvas onto which he can paint an alternate social identity. The narrator explains that he would buy brand labels to sew onto the exterior of his nondesigner clothes. For him, the tags represent a virtual entrance ticket into the social spaces of the middle classes. When someone looked at him suspiciously in a public space, he would flaunt the tags to show that he was a "decent" person" (*Guia* 79). Being "decent" (both morally and physically) is concomitant with the signs of expenditure. These transform the narrator from either a menacing or invisible subject into an inhabitant of the hegemonic urban sphere. Consumption, or in this case the performance of it, is as indicated in previous chapters—tantamount to citizenship. The visibility the clothes afford the narrator entrance not only to the city, but also to the middle class's inner sanctum, the private home. When he visits a friend in the affluent neighborhood of Barra da Tijuca, he prominently displays the emblem of his consumption (the sewn-on tag) (79) to the suspicious janitor. The narrator, conscious of the power expenditure holds in the imaginary of social exclusion, manipulates the signs associated with consumption to his advantage. There are traces of parody in this gesture that destabilize the meaning of consumption. According to Jean Baudrillard, if the precession of simulacra is tied to late capitalist rationality, then *Guia afetivo da periferia* transforms simulacra into products of consumption (*Simulacra and Simulation*).

Expenditure reappears throughout the narrative as an indicator of social aspirations and of social constraints. In the segment titled "Calçados" (Shoes; 123–24), the narrator pairs specific types of shoes with certain paths and activities: "Com o All Star, cruzava a cidade e participava de passeatas. Com o Redley, desfilava na praça do Curral Falso, em Santa Cruz. Com um Commander, ia para shows punk na Praça da Bandeira" (123–24).[40] Each brand connotes a different positionality. The All Stars allow the narrator to blend into the middle-class and student-movement crowd and emulate a fashionable carelessness. Redleys denote the surfer chic that became popular in Brazil in the mid-1980s, and the Commander's reflect the chaotic pleasures of punk culture.

Later, the clothing labels and the shoes are replaced by cultural capital and the city becomes inhabited by the ghosts of writers past (Manuel Bandeira and Joaquim Manuel de Macedo, among others). Their appearance also operates as an expression of distinction. Culture produces legitimacy and allows the narrator to contest the grid of urban exclusions that characterizes Rio's symbolic geography. Specifically, cultural agency and insurgency occurs through the medium of reading and writing. *Guia afetivo da periferia* is, in its entirety, a document of cultural insurgency. The book transforms the periphery into a sociocultural space, thereby eschewing its characterization as a marginal terrain. Writing is the act the permits the narrator to remain within this sociocultural territory and to transcend it.

The leisure activities cited earlier and the narrator's employment of consumption indicators suggests that culture is intimately tied to the circulation of capital. In a segment titled "Economia" (Economy), Faustini transforms his books and vinyl records into financial commodities that facilitate circulation. Cultural products are the currency that allows him to traverse the city when he is unemployed. He sells them to buy food, drinks, or to pay for shows (*Guia* 55). One cultural product is exchanged for another. Similar to his weekend pursuits, Faustini's tastes in books and music are eclectic: Steve B. is juxtaposed to the Brazilian punk group Sub. For the author, the prefix "sub" communicates a sense of inclusion. Alluding to words such as *suburbano* (suburban) and *subempregado* (underemployed), but also, by virtue of its use, to punk culture, the prefix encompasses the author's many identities as they hover between the varying geosocial metropolitan realms.

Though the narrator remains emotionally bound to the *periferia*, he also transcends this space and becomes part of what Angel Rama calls the lettered city (Rama). For Faustini, culture is indeed a fundamental way to access citizenship, not only through his narrative, but also beyond the text that he writes. Like many other texts that emerge from and thematize the socioeconomic margins of Brazil's metropolises, *Guia afetivo da periferia* places a premium on education. Early on, the narrator discovers that good grades go in tandem with certain liberties, such as staying out longer in order to play. Education is a ticket for him to circulate (albeit in limited fashion) through the city, laying the groundwork for his future urban exploits.

The childhood rationale is replaced by a veritable hunger for knowledge that is only trumped by the physical hunger the narrator sometimes experiences—and which leads him to sell his beloved books and musical recordings. For Marcos Zibordi, education (or, in more general terms, culture) is depicted as a precious good in many peripheral writings (76). In *Guia afetivo da periferia*, the cultural signs that the narrator intersperses throughout the text both indicate his erudition and emblematize how to transcend the geosocial limitations imposed upon the periphery and its residents.

Appropriation of culture becomes a mode of insurgency in that it allows the narrator to sidestep physical, financial, social, and individual barriers. Hence, for example, he copes with a bout of tuberculosis that impedes his urban excursions by reading Marcel Proust's *Remembrance of Things Past* (1913–27). Proust's novel, which hinges on evocation, generates a set of memories of its own in the narrator, who associates it not with a *Madeleine*, but with a specific locale: a second-hand bookstore where he buys his texts (*Guia* 65). This detail reinforces the connection between literature, the city and the narrator's desire to become part of the larger urban landscape.

In another example of how culture is instrumental for personal development, we learn that the narrator's sexual initiation dialogues with his cinematic formation and is also linked to a geographic itinerary. In order to satisfy both his intellectual and his libidinal drive, the narrator ventures outside his community, exploring the city as he explores French cinematography. He initially invites girls to see foreign films and then, when this strategy is not particularly successful, he begins to ask out girls he meets in these sessions (83).

Movement outside the community denotes the narrator's need for distinction, which is promptly recognized—and repudiated—by the objects of his desire. Distinction is both a desirable condition and a problem that the narrator must solve by not only seeking a different scenario for his amorous conquests, but also by searching different, more understanding romantic targets.

Ironically, though he looks for possible girlfriends outside the perimeter of the *periferia*, he ends up meeting a young woman from this area. Like the narrator, she also is seen as "different" because of her intellectual tastes (82). If the suburbs are the background against which their romance develops, its primary stage is Rio de Janeiro's center. Appropriately, the first meeting between the narrator and the young woman from the periphery occurs after the screening of *The Lovers on the Bridge* (1991, directed by Leos Carax) at the Museu da República, in the middle-class Catete neighborhood. Similar to the characters in Carax's film, the narrator and his girlfriend explore Rio de Janeiro's streets, charting an artistic cartography. Their excursions take them often to the Rua do Lavradio, a cultural and bohemian nodal point of Rio de Janeiro's center. Walking around this historic street, the narrator can exhibit his knowledge of the city's past while also inserting himself into its present by using urban history as a backdrop for his amorous adventures. At the same time, his companion also guides the narrator in other urban points of interest—he discovers Clarice Lispector in their mutual wanderings. Significantly, their relationship ends when the young woman must take a job at a McDonalds in the upscale district of Barra da Tijuca. Her employment hinders their strolls through the literary/cultural city, limiting them into the prosaic journey from the Zona Sul to the Zona Norte. The trajectory from one part of the city to the other is the setting for the romance's ending. The final scene of the relationship occurs in a *Frescão* (executive bus) that covers the route Castelo/Santa Cruz and becomes, for the narrator, a mise-en-scène of a French film. In this final encounter and its fictionalization into a make-believe screenplay, the dichotomy between center and periphery becomes undone. Both territories become stages for the reenactment of the narrator's fantasies.

Partaking in the metropolises' different social and cultural venues, the narrator assumes different personas, depending on the context—he emulates punks in Méier, participates in funk dances in Cesarão, and drinks beer at the iconic Amarelinho (48). By frequenting diverse entertainment venues, the narrator destabilizes his social identification. As a result, he effectively accesses and/or multiplies his cultural rights that include "the right to engage in cultural activity, to identify with the cultural communities of one's choice" (qtd. in Yúdice 21). And culture has, in recent times, become a valued commodity in the constitution and performance of citizenship (Yúdice). It is therefore no coincidence that the narrator's path includes so many cultural signposts. They create spaces of inclusion. In this context, his trajectory—and especially his mediums of transportation—are also integral parts of the "Friday night" experience. Vis-à-vis the account of his Friday night activities is a photograph of the empty train car in which the protagonists returns on Saturday morning to his home. The image insinuates the feelings of not only loneliness and exhaustion, but also satisfaction after an enjoyable activity—or activities.

The narrator's pleasurable urban explorations are contrasted with the routine of work in low-paying jobs or the tedium of unemployment. Faustini dedicates a heading of *Guia afetivo da periferia* to demonstrate the importance of work in the periphery. In "Deus e o trabalho" (God and work; 127–8), he equates employment to a religious credo, ascertaining that from an early age, all his family members were either working or looking for work." Work is the index of "decency" (127). Like many members of his family and like most *batalhadores*, the narrator too begins working early on. His labors are another signpost in the mapping of the city and dovetail with his perceptions of other workers who populate Rio de Janeiro's cartography. Like his strolls through the metropolis, his work, from a short-lived stint as a forecourt attendant at a gas station in the Zona Sul to his employment as a Baush and Lomb contact-lens salesman, also takes him to various points in the city. On one occasion, he uses his walks to climb to the top floor of the high rises where the doctors' offices are located. From here he surveys the city, metaphorically appropriating it. These outings are also artistic explorations of sorts that inspire him and approximate him to cultural icons such as Allen Ginsberg (148), and thereby remove him from the drudgery of labor.

In conclusion, *Guia afetivo da periferia* bridges the center-periphery dichotomy that has become a staple of contemporary Brazilian fiction dealing with the city. In addition, the book reveals other facets of the sociocultural and human dimensions of Rio de Janeiro's and, by extension, metropolitan Brazilian peripheries. Instead of centering on violence and on exclusion, *Guia afetivo da periferia* depicts the *periferia* as a communitarian space that serves as a platform for civil and cultural engagement—as evidenced also by Faustini's work in Reperiferia, and other similar venues.

Guia afetivo da periferia offers a guidebook/handbook to the metropolis's physical and geographic outskirts and integrates these zones into the larger urban grid. In so doing, the narrative brings the *periferia* into the center of the city. But the movement is not unidirectional. The narrator's gaze changes as he absorbs the sights, sounds, smells, and the cultural components of Rio's Zona Sul. What ensues is a hybrid perception of the city that sees both its disjunctive dimensions and becomes a mode of insurgency for the culture and the denizens of the periphery. In this sense, the "guidebook" is a form of autoconstruction of cultural citizenship that emerges precisely at the sites where peripheral culture is devalued or negated.

Guia afetivo da periferia evidences a new self-perception of Brazil's low-income population as an integral part of the country's citizenry. An important aspect of this self-perception comes from cultural validation. Culture is both a tool of insurgent citizenship and the expression of newly gained substantive political, social, and civil rights. Like *Capão Pecado*, *Guia afetivo da periferia* indirectly dialogues with the author's other cultural endeavors, such as the project Reperiferia. *Guia afetivo da periferia* proposes the individual trajectory of empowerment as a "map" for collective agency and for the recognition of socioeconomic and geographic communities (exemplified in the book primarily by the narrator and by the residents of Cesarão) as full-fledged Brazilians citizens.

Epilogue

On January 1, 2011, Dilma Vana Rousseff assumed Brazil's presidency. The daughter of a Bulgarian immigrant father, Dilma Rousseff (or, as she is commonly referred to in Brazil, simply Dilma) comes from a very different background than her predecessor, Luiz Ignácio Lula da Silva. Unlike Lula, whose family belonged to the ranks of impoverished Northeastern migrants who came to São Paulo and Rio de Janeiro searching for better living conditions, Dilma grew up in an upper-middle class family in Minas Gerais. After immigrating to Brazil, her father, Pedro Rousseff, became a successful entrepreneur who contracted for Mannesman. Her mother, Dilma Jane da Silva, is from a traditional *mineiro*[1] landowning family. During her childhood, Dilma studied at a private boarding school and learned French and piano. In 1964, Dilma entered the Colégio Estadual Central, a hotbed of Belo Horizonte's student opposition to the dictatorship. She became increasingly politicized and joined the armed resistance in 1967. She was imprisoned in 1970 and remained in detention for 2 years where she was at times tortured.

Campaigning on the promise to eradicate extreme poverty in Brazil, Dilma has vowed to follow in Lula's footsteps in what pertains to social policies. Not only this, but she has pledged to expand these social policies. Brazil's thirty-sixth president has continued popular social projects such as the *Bolsa Família* and the *Sistema Único de Saúde*. Six months after her ascension, Dilma launched *Brasil sem Miséria* (Brasil without misery), a program, intended to help 16.2 million Brazilians with a monthly income of R$ 70 or below. In the inaugural discourse of the *Brasil sem Miséria*, Dilma stated that the state has the duty to eradicate poverty ("Programa Brasil sem Miséria é lançado nesta quinta-feira em Brasília" [Program Brazil without misery is launched this Thursday in Brasília]). Beyond extending food and education assistance, *Brasil sem Miséria* is also slated to create infrastructure that will help low-income citizens.[2] Additionally, Dilma vowed to continue with the construction of low-income housing through the *Minha casa, Minha vida* plan, forecasting the construction of 2 million homes.

Under Lula's administration, approximately 28 million Brazilians were able to emerge from extreme poverty due, in part, to programs such as *Bolsa Família*. Since 2003, 5.9 million families have stopped receiving aid through the program, 40 percent of them because they were able to better their income. However, with 16 million families still living below the poverty line, Brazil has a long way to go in creating an egalitarian society.

Recently, social inequalities have been highlighted in the context of the preparations for both the 2014 Soccer World Cup and the 2016 Summer Olympics. The official promotional videos (such as the one directed by Fernando Meirelles for the Olympic Committee)—both the one used to pitch Rio de Janeiro to the Olympic Committee and the one used to promote the city after it was chosen for the event—highlight the idea of Rio as a harmonious and leisurely city. Additionally, the videos show a decidedly middle-class city, with its shantytowns conveniently erased from the camera's purview. One could of course argue that this is a given in any advertisement that seeks to emphasize the positive aspects of a certain locale. Nonetheless, the images do suggest a dual trend in the infrastructural projects associated with the 2014 World Cup and the 2016 Olympics. On the one hand, federal, state, and local governments are investing in infrastructure and social projects designed to improve social conditions in low-income zones. On the other hand, however, these same governmental branches are destroying poorer communities and forcefully relocating their residents.

In Rio de Janeiro, Brazil's urban postcard, several favelas are reaping the benefits of metropolitan renewal. A December 2010 article from *The Guardian* reports that in preparation for the games, communities such as Rocinha and Complexo do Alemão—better known for their drug traffic-related violence—were going to see a radical restructuring. According to the essay, "In several giant, drug-ridden favelas work has already begun. Walkways, cable-cars, roads and swimming pools are springing up in areas such as Rocinha, Manguinhos and the Complexo do Alemão, a gritty sea of redbrick shantytowns that was recently 'conquered' by thousands of security workers following intense shootouts involving helicopters, armoured personnel carriers and tanks" (Phillips, "Favelas to Get Facelift"). Beyond integrating the favelas into the surrounding city, these projects want to strengthen community ties—both within the favelas and outside them. Projects such as the ones described by *The Guardian* are part of a larger plan to integrate the "divided" city. One of the spearheaded programs in this initiative is the *Morar Carioca* (Living Carioca) program.

Funded by the federal and state governments, *Morar Carioca* was created in June of 2010. Its goal is to urbanize all of Rio's low-income communities by 2020 and thereby promote social integration through urban integration. *Morar Carioca's* webpage delineates the program's main aspects: social inclusion, environmental conscious-ness, and access to housing and integration between low-income communities and their surrounding areas (Secretaria Municipal da Habitação). Integration and development of stronger communities is seen as a way to counteract the criminality that frequently plagues favelas and that often spills over into the hegemonic city. In other words, urbanization is a means to buttress civil and social citizenship in spaces where traditionally the access to these rights is/was either precarious or nonexistent.

Nonetheless, despite the city's efforts to develop the physical con-ditions of poor neighborhoods, the upcoming athletic events have also disrupted, rather than improved, the social and material infrastructure of several other low-income vicinities. Many poor neighborhoods are being hidden from view by literal walls (see my discussion of the Linha Vermelha in Chapter 4) while others are experiencing a restructuring as homes and business are either demolished or relocated to more remote—and hence less conspicuous—areas.

In March of 2010, the Geneva-based Centre on Housing Rights and Evictions (COHRE) criticized the Brazilian government for the forced removal of low-income residents from their homes in prepara-tion to the upcoming World Cup and Olympics (COHRE). COHRE also pointed out that financial compensation for displaced people was often insufficient.

In some poor neighborhoods, infrastructural changes are disrupt-ing not only the physical, but also the social fabric of these locales. Thus, for example, in October of 2010, a shopping complex that operated for over 20 years in the community of Restinga (in Rio de Janeiro) was demolished without previous notice to owners or resi-dents in order to open space for the Transoeste Expressway.[3] Along the same route, the Favela da Restinga will be partly demolished. Finally, close to the Maracanã stadium, several inhabitants of the Favela do Metrô (built in the late 1970s) had their homes destroyed without prior notification (Jinkings). Residents describe the commu-nity as having been beautiful and a great place to live. Citing Jorge Bittar, Rio's housing secretary, *The Guardian* reports that in place of the favela, the city's administration plans to build "[c]ultural centres, tree-lined plazas and a cinema" (Phillips, "World Cup Demolitions"). Paradoxically, the projection of future spaces of sociability (cultural centers, parks, and entertainment venues) erases the existing communitarian ties of the Favela do Metrô. In the wake of the demolitions, *The Guardian* describes a dystopian landscape of abandoned and rat-infested homes, debris-littered streets and air thick with the odor of human waste. Patrick Wilcken, a researcher for Amnesty International in Brazil, describes how social deterioration accompanies the wrecking of homes. Drug addicts moved into the demolished residences and "plagues of rats and plagues of cockroaches that basically force the rest of the community to move, often in very, very unfavorable circumstances" (qtd. in Phillips, "World Cup Demolitions"). These scenes negate *Morar Carioca*'s goal: to integrate the city by improving the living conditions in poor vicinities. At the same time, in a twisted confirmation of the program's agenda—namely that infrastructural improvements will better social relations in the city—the destruction of communities such as Favela do Metrô introduces, or exacerbates, social ills such as drug consumption and the abandonment (or lack) of public spaces.

What does the juxtaposition of social programs designed to eradicate intergenerational poverty and improve the infrastructure of poor communities and lack of respect for low-income communities and their residents tell us? How can we read these seemingly contradictory developments? Perhaps the answer lies in the ongoing culture of disjunctive citizenship that characterizes Brazil's democracy. Though the 1988 constitution clearly states that Brazilians have the right to housing (Article 6), this right can be interpreted in a broad sense. Forced evictions due to the upcoming athletic events do not necessarily leave homeowners without a roof over their heads. But relocations, which can move families up to 50 or 60 kilometers away from their original residence without necessarily taking into account the residents' communitarian ties, employment, and transportation needs, in sum, what could be considered their social rights, do leave people socially homeless. In this case, disjunctive citizenship operates in a paradoxical manner: it gives access to one set of social rights (housing) while disrupting other rights: those of sociability, of using and being part of the city.

Even though Brazil's impoverished communities are still one of the primary sites of disjunctive citizenship, they are also the locales where insurgent practices are creating new arenas of empowerment. An example is the community of Diadema, in the ABC *paulista*. According to a recent *New York Times* article on the art show "Design With the Other 90 Percent: Cities," organized by the Cooper-Hewitt National Design Museum, in the 1980s, 30 percent of Diadema's population lived in slums. The city's crime rate was 140 crimes per 100,000 residents (in the 1990s), a figure that indicates lack of or weak sociability. After the government awarded the right of land-tenure (for up to ninety years) to residents, they became engaged in projects intended to better their community. Decisions on the city's budget were made in consultation with Diadema's inhabitants. Their involvement in the community and the pride of ownership that came with having a home changed the city. The article states that nowadays only 3 percent of the population lives in favelas and the crime rate has dropped to 14.3 incidents per 100,000 residents (Kimmelman). Civic engagement, a result of homeownership, created a communitarian ethos that ultimately counteracted the violence that resulted from weak social ties. Similar developments are taking place in underprivileged communities across the globe. The article cites examples from Thailand, Colombia, Venezuela, and Uganda. Cynthia E. Smith, the show's curator, explains that solutions to infrastructural, social, and environmental problems in informal settlements and similar communities are to be found—to a great degree—within these locales and are facilitated by their residents. Transforming disenfranchised communities through insurgent practices,[4] establishes terrains of citizenship in low-income areas, thus offsetting disjunctive citizenship.

As suggested by the books analyzed in this manuscript, the idea of citizenship, and how it is unevenly distributed and accessed in Brazil, has become a popular topic in the country's contemporary literature. Furthermore, unequal rights are commonly tied to a fragmented and socioeconomically disparate urban cartography. Novels and other literary texts that depict the mechanisms of segregation in the country's conurbations often seek to expose the socioeconomic disparities that led to these divisions in the first place, as well as the negative consequences of geosocial divisions (interpersonal and criminal violence, drug and alcohol abuse, prejudice, to name but a few).

By bringing the "marginal" city into the hegemonic (i.e., middle- and upper-class domains, such as bookstores, universities, literary festivals, among others) it could be argued that texts such as Luiz Ruffato's *Inferno provisório*, Fernando Bonassi's *O menino que se trancou na geladeira* and *Subúrbio*, Ferréz's *Capão Pecado* and *Manual prático do ódio*, and Marcus Vinícius Faustini's *Guia afetivo da periferia* establish (textual) bridges between the two cities. These bridges are configured differently however. While some are constructed through a dystopian discourse that underlines the disjunctures in citizenship and in the city, others propose textual crossings that suture the fragmented urban landscape. Either mode of narrating denounces the unequal distribution of rights that still afflicts low-income Brazil-ians. Nonetheless, whereas Luiz Ruffato's, Fernando Bonassi's, and to a degree Ferréz's novels articulate agency as a critique of these conditions, Marcus Vinicius Faustini's text creates empowerment by focusing on the city as a terrain of (possible) sociability. In a way, *Guia afetivo da periferia* proposes the city as an *Agorá*, even if a fragile one. This shift from literature as a mode of "negative" insurgent citizenship (i.e., mainly denouncement through a "literature of disenchantment") to a "positive" insurgency (i.e., the reclaiming of the city as a space of sociability) reflects Brazil's recent socioeconomic developments, the growth of its middle class and, with it, the augmented cultural and civic self-consciousness of this emerging middle class. Finally however, notwithstanding their differences, all the texts discussed in this book have one thing in common. Namely, all the books examined reflect the growing demand of less affluent and/or impoverished Brazilians to be recognized—and treated—as full-fledged citizens.

NOTES

INTRODUCTION

1. Voting is mandatory for Brazilians 18 years and older, and optional for those between 16 and 18.
2. The Diretas Já campaign was a popular mobilization supporting congressman Dante de Oliveira's proposed amendment to have direct presidential elections in 1985. It marked the country's redemocratization and was supported by various social segments such as trade unions, political parties, and students, among others. Ultimately the amendment was defeated and indirect elections were held in 1985.
3. *Inferno provisório*, Luiz Ruffato's five-volume cycle, begins in the 1950s. However, many of the socioeconomic developments that are illustrated in the narratives forecast the neoliberal crisis of the 1990s.
4. In his essay "As ideias fora do lugar" (Misplaced ideas 1973) Schwarz points to Brazil's fundamental discrepancy between the adoption of a liberal political ideology and the continuation of slavery as the main economic model.
5. Camille Goirand identifies three key moments in the development of citizenship in Brazil: the postabolition period, clearly influenced by the liberal tradition, Vargas's populist agenda, and finally the decade of democratic transition (1980–90).
6. An example of the expansion of political rights is the right to vote for illiterates, which was implemented for the first time in 1985.
7. See, for example, the creation of *habeas data*.
8. Lei No. 10.048 (Law 10.048), from November 8th, 2000, stipulates that priority in assistance will be given to "[a]s pessoas portadoras de deficiência, os idosos com idade igual ou superior a 60 (sessenta) anos, as gestantes, as lactantes e as pessoas acompanhadas por crianças de colo terão atendimento prioritário, nos termos desta Lei" (people with physical handicaps, people 60 years and above, pregnant and lactating women, and people with toddlers) (Constituição Brasileira). This and all translations in the text mine.
9. The constitutions are from 1824 (monarchy), 1891 (old republic [*República Velha*]), 1934, 1937 (New State [*Estado Novo*]), 1946, 1967 (military dictatorship) and 1988 (new republic [*Nova República*]).
10. In 1985 Tancredo Neves was elected president. However, he died before he could assume power. His running mate, José Sarney, a member of

the governing party (ARENA) during the dictatorship, assumed office in 1985.

11. "I.—build a free, just and solidary society; II. guarantee national development; III. eradicate poverty and marginalization and reduce social and regional differences; IV. promote the general wellbeing, independent of origin, race, sex, color, age or any other forms of discrimination."

12. The "new" middle class, or *Classe C* is composed of people who have left the ranks of the poor (*Classe D*) and have achieved better financial conditions. They stand between the traditional middle class and the poor. Usually, members of the Classe C earn between R$ 950 and R$ 1,400.

13. Holston states that "cities provide the dense articulation of the global and local forces in response to which people think and act themselves into politics, becoming new kinds of citizens. In the process, cities become both the site and the substance not only of the uncertainties of modern citizenship but also of its emergent forms" (*Insurgent* 23).

14. Holston observes that "[a]lthough these elements [political rights, access to land, illegality and servility] continue to sustain the regime of differentiated citizenship, they are also the conditions of its subversion, as the urban poor gained political rights, became landowners, made law an asset, created new public spheres of participation, achieved rights to the city, and became modern consumers. In such ways, the lived experiences of the peripheries became both the context and the substance of a new urban citizenship" (*Insurgent* 9).

15. Examples would be Italian and German immigrants to Brazil, who suffered discrimination upon arriving in the country. Once they entered the mainstream, descendants of these groups showed bias against other ethnic minorities (recent immigrants from Paraguay and Bolivia, for example) or socially disempowered segments.

16. This is perhaps because today 80 percent of Brazilians live in cities (Caldeira, *City of Walls*; Holston, *Insurgent*).

17. For an in-depth discussion of the formation of São Paulo's periphery, please see Teresa P. R. Caldeira's *City of Walls: Crime, Segregation and Citizenship in São Paulo.* Caldeira explains how since the 1940s until recently, São Paulo has developed according to a center-periphery model. While the upper and middle classes tend to inhabit more central areas, poorer communities are located in the city's peripheries. This urban model came about as poorer families moved to the city's outskirts, where land was cheaper. Their relocation was, in turn, made possible by an expanded bus system that transported the periphery's residents to their workplaces, often in the center of the city.

CHAPTER 1

1. "I do not want to be an accomplice either of the misery or of the violence, products of this country's absurd concentration of income. Because
   of this I propose, through *Inferno provisório*, to contemplate the last 50
   years of Brazil's history, when we observe the consolidation of the economic elite's power, which began immediately after World War II with the
   country's industrialization and with the forced displacement of millions
   of people to the peripheries and slums of São Paulo and Rio de Janeiro."
   This and all translations in the text mine.
2. Though *Inferno provisório* has five tomes, in this chapter I concentrate
   only on the first four.
3. There are of course exceptions, such as Aluísio de Azevedo's naturalist
   novel *O cortiço* (The slum, 1890) and Patrícia Galvão's (Pagu) *Parque
   industrial* (Industrial park, 1933).
4. In a 2006 interview with Heloísa Buarque de Hollanda and Ana Lygia
   Matos, Ruffato describes how his own origins shaped his writing and how
   it became important for him to portray Brazil's almost invisible blue-
   collar working classes. Ruffato states that he tackled the representation of
   the Brazilian proletariat in a programmatic manner (Ruffato, Interview by
   Heloísa Buarque de Hollanda and Ana Ligia Matos).
5. An example would be Marcelino Freire, who in his trilogy *Angu de
   sangue* (Blood gruel, 2000), *Balé ralé* (Ballet riff-raff, 2003), and *Contos negreiros* (Slavers' short stories, 2006) highlights different forms of
   violence: urban/social (*Angu de sangue*), gender (*Balé ralé*), and racial
   (*Contos negreiros*).
6. Though containing some of the traits of the proletariat as defined in
   Marx and Engel's *The Communist Manifesto*, the proletarian subjects of
   Inferno provisório generally lack the "revolutionary" potential ascribed to
   them by Marx and Engels. If there is an attempt to change their conditions of existence, the novel's characters do so in a manner that approximates what Holston calls "insurgency." This is to say, *Inferno provisório*'s
   characters, rather than topple the existing social system and its modes of
   differentiated citizenship, at times chip away at the social disjunctures
   from within the very system that creates them. Insurgent citizenship in
   Inferno provisório will be discussed in this chapter. Partly, the lack of
   revolutionary potential can be attributed to what sociologist Zygmunt
   Bauman calls "liquid modernity." Liquid or fluid modernity liquefies
   "the bonds which interlock individual choices in collective projects and
   actions—the patterns of communication and co-ordination between
   individually conducted life policies on the one hand and political actions
   of human collectivities on the other" (*Liquid* 6). While Holston does
   suggest that insurgent citizenship taps into collectivities (as for example
   neighborhood associations), the insurgent citizenships that emerge from
   the fictions analyzed in this book indicate a more individualized type of
   action, though these can, at least at a symbolic level, have implications

for a larger group, as suggested in the manuscript's last chapter on *Guia afetivo da periferia*.

7. In *The Communist Manifesto*, Marx and Engels define the *Lumpenproletariat* as the "dangerous class" (92). Unlike the proletariat, the *Lumpen* do not have a revolutionary potential. Rather, due to their miserable socioeconomic conditions, this class plays "the part of a bribed tool of reactionary intrigue" (92). In *Inferno provisório*, we find characters that fall into both the proletarian and the *Lumpenproletarian* classifications. Thus, for example, several characters promote the interests of the local bourgeoisie by campaigning for them in exchange for material favors. See for example the character Seu Jeremias in "Sulfato de Morfina" (Morphine sulfate; *Mamma, son tanto felice*). In order to obtain a scholarship for his son, Seu Jeremias becomes an electoral canvasser, mole, and hired thug for the local political boss (*Mamma* 35).

8. The stories Ruffato alludes to are, respectively, "O alemão e a puria" (The German and the Indian), "Aquário" (Fish tank), "A expiação" (The penance), and "O segredo" (The secret).

9. Marisa Lajolo calls attention to this "lineage," observing that the book takes up incomplete threads, sowing new passages and yet never entirely completing the narrative fabric (103).

10. This genealogy is partially extended in Ruffato's latest text, *Estive em Lisboa e lembrei de você* (I was in Lisbon and thought about you, 2009). Ruffato wrote this novel in the framework of the Brazilian publishing house *Companhia das Letras' Amores expressos* (Express loves) project. *Amores expressos* sent 17 Brazilian writers to 17 different cities in the world, where they stayed for a month. During their sojourn, the authors had to maintain a blog that detailed their experiences and, upon their return, they had to write a "love story" in novel format that took place in their respective metropolises. Ruffato went to Lisbon, and his book—about a Brazilian immigrant to Portugal—refers back to characters in *Inferno provisório*, such as Zé Pinto.

11. The stories are "Ritual" (Ritual), "Fim" (End), and "Tocaia" (Ambush).

12. In this respect, *Inferno provisório* gives continuation to the project delineated in Ruffato's first novel, *Eles eram muitos cavalos* (They were many horses). In this text, the author depicts one day in the busy megalopolis of São Paulo, composing a disjointed panorama of life in this city through different narrative lenses. In her study of the novel, Samantha Braga compares the narrative to a bricolage in which various elements are amassed into a precarious unit. Braga postulates that the novel is arranged as a series of "flashes" that, together, create a narrative mosaic (130). The same technique of bricolage is evident in *O livro das impossibilidades*, although the materials present in the volumes that compose this cycle are, perhaps, less haphazard than those that appear in *Eles eram muitos cavalos*. Since both the former and the latter are texts about the city (or about cities), one can argue that the greater consistency of

"flashes" present in *Inferno provisório* reflects the bigger homogeneity in the urban makeup of Cataguases as well as echoes the consciousness of the predominately proletarian characters in the novel. In contrast, *Eles eram muitos cavalos* incorporates perspectives from different social strata.

13. Discussing *Inferno provisório*'s linguistic composition, critic Karl Erik Schøllhammer classifies the cycle's five volumes as a hybrid of the regionalist and the collective novels, as the five texts combine the impetus to portray a particular reality and the drive to expose the generalized problematics of working class disentitlement (83). Ruffato, however, takes issue with the characterization of his work as "regionalist." His objective is not to portray a specific regional culture but rather a social class that transcends the boundaries of a geographic region.

14. According to a recent study, 2 in every 10 young Brazilians between the ages of 15 and 17 (approximately 18 percent of the population in this age group) are not attending school. Among people 18 to 25 years of age, 68 percent are not in school. Many of those who have dropped out of school are young people from a poor background and/or those living in rural areas (Máximo).

15. "Order and Progress" is the motto emblazoned on Brazil's flag. It reflects the positivist ideology that influenced the country's initial Republican period, during which Brazil's current flag was created.

16. Ruffato explains that when he thought of writing about Brazil's lower middle class, he became aware that the novel format was inadequate for the project since this genre is associated with the bourgeoisie's worldview. In light of this his "precarious" narrative form (between the novel and the short story) wants to transmit the precariousness of Brazilian society, where "everything needs yet to be done" (Sanglard 2). Narrative fragmentation also undermines a comprehensive view of the (*Lumpen*) proletariat depicted in *Inferno provisório*'s five volumes, hinting at the multifaceted reality that the novels capture only provisionally.

17. *"Remember comadre, that time that, It seems that this year it is not going to rai, Dona America's dog, yeah. . . . "* Throughout the book, all quotes will reflect the typography of the original texts unless otherwise noted.

18. The oscillation between consciousness and unconsciousness is suggested in the epigraph that opens the story: "A morfina é um analgésico narcótico potente destinado especialmente para o controle da dor aguda que não responde aos analgésicos tradicionais" (Morphine is a potent painkiller used especially in cases of extreme pain, when traditional sedatives are not effective; Ruffato, *Mamma* 27). Pain here is imbued with a dual meaning: it signifies the physical pain caused by the tumor that is devouring the woman's body, and it also connotes the psychological pain of loss (of her husband) and abandonment (by her children). Morphine dulls both these sufferings.

19. Speaking of the indicators that influence poverty, political scientist Lúcio Kowarik ascertains that, beyond the triangle composed of education,

professional qualification, and income, other factors also impact pauperization. Among them, he points to what he denominates the "biological factor," which, in the metropolises of underdeveloped industrialized countries, particularly affects women, the elderly, and children. They are more impacted by socioeconomic exclusion because of factors such as lower wages and laborer status (81).

20. Cataguases is also representative of Brazil's cultural modernization. In the 1920s, Humberto Mauro, the pioneer Brazilian filmmaker, began his cinematographic career with his "Cataguases Cycle." The association between Cataguases and an incipient national film production links the town to a definite modern cultural expression—mass media discourse that has played an important role in the formulation and diffusion of national sociocultural identities. Furthermore, the correlation between Cataguases and cultural modernity is also present in the town's most famous literary group centered around the *Revista Verde* (Green periodical), a modernist publication founded by Rosário Fusco, Francisco Inácio Peixoto, Henrique de Resende, Âscanio Lopes, and Guilhermino César in 1928. This short-lived periodical linked Brazil's geographical interior to the cultural manifestations and aesthetic ideology of the Week of Modern Art (1922). As such, the *Revista Verde* attests to both the reach and the fascination of a utopian, nationalist modernist ideology within the Brazilian cultural sphere.

21. One of the characters in *O mundo inimigo*, Bibica, who works as a prostitute before becoming a laundress, is able to pay for her son's medicine because her clients, men who work in Cataguases's industry, are getting paid (Ruffato, *Mundo* 101).

22. "He arrived late again. Goodbye and good luck! Out there are lines of people looking for work!"

23. Getúlio Vargas inaugurated this economic program in Brazil, developing the country's industrial park in São Paulo's outskirts and creating state monopolies for oil, automobile manufacturing, mining, alkalis, and steel production. The project reverberated in policies implemented by Juscelino Kubitschek, João Goulart, and to an extent the military junta that took over in 1964.

24. The Brazilian "economic miracle" lasted from 1968 to 1975. It was preceded by an anti-inflation program (1964–67) that led to an economic recuperation. During the "miracle" years, Brazil had very strong economic growth rates (some at 10 percent). However, these growth rates did not reflect equitable income distribution. Upper and middle classes benefited from the economic bonanza by being able to consume more industrial goods, while working-class salaries were capped.

25. Angelina Peralva observes that the transformation of the financial landscape in Brazil lead to massive unemployment, which in recent years has decreased significantly, although much of the labor force is active in the informal sector. Peralva associates rising unemployment with economic

difficulties resulting from modernization and globalization. These have generated unemployment rates of around 20 percent in certain industrial zones (compared to 7.6 percent nationally in 1999) such as the ABCD Paulista (the industrial zone around Greater São Paulo) (27).

26. José de Souza Martins observes that the devaluation of labor was the means by which Brazil became more competitive in the global market. But it also transformed the market into a trigger for social protests. According to him, this combination of factors transformed the working class into "the excluded." The worker's identity thus changed into that of the "periodically excluded familial laborer" (34).

27. Caldeira affirms that "from the 1940s to the 1970s, both Brazil and the metropolitan region of São Paulo changed in dramatic but paradoxical ways: significant urbanization, industrialization, sophistication and expansion of the consumer market, and diversification of the social structure were accompanied by authoritarianism, political repression, unequal distribution of wealth, and a hierarchical pattern of personal relations. In other words, Brazil became a modern country through a paradoxical combination of rapid capitalist development, increased inequality, and lack of political freedom and respect for citizenship rights" (*City* 43).

28. "girls and boys bronzing by the Rowing Club's pools."

29. "mother washing clothes, her colorless eyes, the skin burned by many suns."

30. "a man . . . who is . . . very rich . . . somebody who will take me . . . who will take me away from here . . . from this hole . . . I am going to find a very rich man, very rich."

31. Cesare Andrea Bixio's song "Mamma, son tanto felice" deals with the return of a son to his ageing mother. The lyrics speak of the former's nostalgia toward his mother and for the past.

32. Italians, especially from northern Italy, migrated to Brazil beginning in 1875. However, the bulk of the migratory flux occurred between 1887 and 1902 (Trento 15). During this time, the number of Italians arriving in Brazil exceeded that of Italians settling in Argentina (which, together with Brazil and the United States, was the primary destination for Italian immigrants). While 685,000 Italians settled in Argentina, Brazilian authorities estimated that 949,000 came to Brazil. The data compiled by Italian authorities puts the number of immigrants at 685,000 (16). In 1902, after reports in the Italian press about poverty faced by many Italian immigrants in Brazil, the Italian government issued the Prinetti decree, which forbade subsidized immigration to Brazil. This led to a drop in the influx of Italian immigrants to Brazil. Nonetheless, though in reduced numbers, Italian immigrants continued to arrive steadily until the 1920s. The conditions faced by the Italian immigrants in rural areas were far from optimal, often leading to further impoverishment. As a result, many either returned to Italy, immigrated to other American nations (especially

Argentina, Uruguay, and the United States), or migrated into urban centers such as São Paulo and Belo Horizonte.

33. "the Eve that would populate that world empty of voices."

34. One only needs to think about Brazil's "founding document," Pero Vaz de Caminha's letter to the king of Portugal on the occasion of Pedro Álvares Cabral's arrival in what is now Brazil's Northeastern coast.

35. "handcuffed by countless umbilical cords, leaving her helpless, wasting away in a room with bolted doors and windows, from where she came out, 35 years, stiff, covered in a tablecloth, so birdlike that even the wind attempted to caress her in her last journey."

36. A recent study ranks Brazil twelfth worldwide in murders of women. Every two hours, one woman is killed in Brazil (Redação Revista Fórum).

37. "a family, everything we never were."

38. "Mother, were you happy with my father?"

39. A 2010 report by the Fundação Perseu Abramo and the Serviço Social do Comércio shows that every two minutes, five women suffer violence. The study concludes that 7.2 million women over 15 have experienced aggression. Furthermore, the same survey indicates 8 percent of Brazilian men admit to having beaten a woman, 48 percent to knowing someone who has, and 25 percent to knowing a relative who batters his partner. Finally, according to the report, "2% dos homens declaram que 'tem mulher que só aprende apanhando bastante'. Além disso, entre os 8% que assumem praticar a violência, 14% acreditam ter 'agido bem' e 15% declaram que bateriam de novo, o que indica um padrão de comportamento, não uma exceção" (2 percent of men declare that "some women only learn when they are beaten." Furthermore, among the 8 percent that admit to violence, 14 percent believe that they have "acted well" and 15 percent say that they would beat again, indicating a behavioral pattern, not an exception) (Tavares).

40. Analyzing patterns of violence against women, anthropologist Maria Luisa Heilborn traces the roots of this aggression to a perception of male supremacy that underlies Brazilian and, according to her, Latin American identity. Heilborn maintains that *machismo* is based on the idea of male power and prestige and attendant control over women. In its extreme version it implies a denigration of women, often through violence (95).

41. Jelin observes that "the privacy of family life appears to justify the limitation in this space" (180).

42. "Those eyes, blue as pools, that were also fiery sparks. Those blue eyes that could gaze lovingly and that could also strangle with hate."

43. Holston notes that the movement of migrants to the urban periphery is motivated by the desire for homeownership and the independence and security that such property connotes (*Insurgent* 174).

44. Holston observes that the development of the periphery via autoconstruction is paradoxical. He asserts that "settling the periphery to build

a house of one's own is itself a spatial paradox: each instance of autoconstruction reproduces the periphery, pushing its leading edge farther into the hinterland; but in so doing, it brings the center and its promise of a different future that much closer to the individual house builder. Furthermore, as each autoconstructing family develops, the entire neighborhood evolves" (*Insurgent* 166).

45. "*And the children and progress came: Josué, electricity, sanitation, and running water; Jairzinho, pavement and an addition with two more rooms; Orlando, supermarkets and stores and another story with a bathroom; Rute, health center and a room of her own.*"

46. "The siren! The planes! The bombs! Closer by: the train wagons, their whistle. The yellow fleece pajama gets scared, urine trickling down its legs. Uuuuuuuuuuuh! Shizophrenic arms hurriedly seek protection under the trees. . . . The head explodes into a thousand pieces. Warm milk, Simão?"

47. Holston maintains that property ownership and, more specifically, autoconstruction signify "the kind of commitment to and imagination about the future that property ownership, especially that of land, engenders" (*Insurgent* 173).

48. Unlike most of his other stories, the accounts compiled in *Vista parcial da noite* contain specific dates, suggesting that periodization is particularly relevant in this book. In particular, the following stories mention precise years: "A homenagem" (The homage, 1973); "O ataque" (The attack, 1972); "Cicatrizes" (Scars, 1970), and "O morto" (The dead man, 1975).

49. *Vista parcial da noite* occurs within the period of the AI-5 (Institutional Act Number 5), declared by the military president Artur Costa e Silva. The AI-5 recrudesced political oppression by implementing measures such as the abolition of *habeas corpus*, declaring the illegality of political meetings, enforcing censorship, closing the National Congress, allowing the federal government to intervene at the state and municipal level in defense of "national security," and asserting the immediate legality of all executive orders.

50. The ubiquity of a state of exception that maintains total control over its citizens' bodies is broached in "O ataque" and in the volume's last narrative, "O morto," in which a traveling circus owner/performer is interrogated by Cataguases's police chief and murdered under suspicious circumstances. The man, who remains on the outskirts of the city and is hence both within the purview of its laws and outside it, is but one of the manifestations of sacredness that appear in the book. Moreover, exceptionality and the control that it "justifies" are alluded to by the repression of workers by the police chief, who prides himself on his authoritarian posture, which he considers "paternal" (Ruffato, *Vista* 139).

51. I am using this concept as delineated by Jürgen Habermas in *Theory of Communicative Action* (1984–87). Since Cataguases's economy is part of

a capitalist modernity, the *Lebenswelt* of its inhabitants is thoroughly influenced by a system that includes not only the relations of production and consumption but also the institutions of school and church.

52. Recent studies suggest that violence has increased mainly in Brazil's medium-size cities and rural areas, whereas some larger urban centers are seeing a diminishing of delinquency.

53. "At *Mineiro* Road he loaded and unloaded merchandise into the trucks that came from Rio de Janeiro, São Paulo, Belo Horizonte. 'It messed up my back . . .' . . . On a boat he dredged sand from the Pomba River. 'The cold ruined my joints.'"

54. Lorena Freitas, in the essay "A instituição do fracasso. A educação da ralé," suggests that insufficient citizenship begins within the realm of schooling. According to Freitas, public schooling in Brazil is plagued by "institutional ill-will." This is to say, social capital, including education, is available to those with access to economic resources, which guarantees power, including in social relations. This pattern is established through institutional practices (294–95). In the context of *Inferno provisório*, this ill will is particularly evident in the teacher's aggressive behavior toward her pupils.

55. In 2009, there were 4.3 million children and adolescents working in Brazil. This number is down from 2008, when the country had 4.5 million child laborers (Melo, Lins, and Carvalho).

56. "Father!"

57. "Vicente's name was not Vicente."

58. "then the miniscule bright red spot, perhaps a Cat's Claw scratch or a mosquito bite . . . morphed into painful sores that, budding on his right leg, provoked spasms at any movement, his mouth tensed, his forehead in a frown, his pores exhaling a putrid odor."

59. That this access is precarious at best becomes clear in the last tome of *Inferno provisório*. The story "Outra fábula" (Another fable) completes the story of Luiz Augusto (Guto) the central character of "Era uma vez."

60. "strangled the month that had not yet ended."

61. "[of] that man that, one day he swore . . ."

62. "Who is your favorite actor? 13. Tarcísio Meira *14. Tarcísio Meira* Who is your favorite actress? 13. Regina Duarte *14. Renata Sorrah.*"

63. At the time, Tarcísio Meira was the main character in the soap operas *O homem que deve morrer* (The man who must die, 1971) and *Irmãos Coragem* (Brothers courage, 1970). Regina Duarte performed as Patrícia in the soap opera *Minha doce namorada* (My sweet girlfriend), a role that gave her the title of "Brazil's sweetheart" (Namoradinha do Brasil). Renata Sorrah also participated in two soap operas in 1971: *O cafona* (The tacky one), in which she plays Malu, and *A Próxima atração* (The next attraction), where she is Madalena. In both instances, she is trying to marry into money.

64. "*everything is missing: jobhouseschoolcolleaguesmotherfamilypeace: everything.*"

65. "The back hurts, punches hits kicks jerks slaps whacks wallops blows to the neck beatings whacks thrashings headbutts tramplings, the doctor said that he would order an x-ray, he is still waiting."

66. According to an article in the online newspaper *Cadernos IHU Online*, during Lula's tenure (until the 2009 economic crisis) the number of poor people (earning up to R$ 137 per month) fell by 43 percent, from 50 million to 29.9 million (Canzian). The reduction of impoverished citizens is attributed to social programs, the increase of formal employment, and the increment of the minimum wage.

67. "*Nílson*, pat on the shoulder, *do you remember me?* Did he? One week that changed an until then certain destiny that, from season to season, consumed his sleepy days and led him to the sameness experienced by parents, siblings, friends."

68. In the last volume of *Inferno provisório* the story is completed. The narrator of "Era uma vez" has both achieved some of his goals and experienced a series of failures.

69. "build an addition, buy a fridge, lay hardwood floors, paint the walls, build another addition to rent out, pour a foundation, grow, find one's place in the world, fill it out . . . money is not lacking."

70. "Maybe she was happy. Come to think about it, maybe not. But she did not think about it."

Chapter 2

1. Eliza Reis explains that during Vargas's populist dictatorship, as well as during his constitutional administration, "[to] be entitled to welfare benefits one needed to have a formal job contract. Health assistance, sickness and maternity leaves, pension funds, retirement benefits, and all other existing forms of social protection were regulated along with work rights defined by job categories" (174). Lack of formal employment implied reduced access to social rights.

2. Souza signals to the dual processes entailed in Brazil's modernization. On the one hand, modernization creates new social classes that are able to accede economic and cultural capital. On the other, this same process engenders a class of people that have neither economic and cultural capital, nor the social, moral and cultural qualifications that would allow them to gain this capital (*Os batalhadores* 25). This is to say, socioeconomic exclusion makes integration into modernity possible.

3. "Are you hearing this noise? / The iron grip. Still the old man: / This one . . . / The old woman returned and sat still in a corner. In the same place. He looked at her brow. The old woman could not longer help herself: / Me? / Yes / No / And since the old man doubted what she said, he asked again to make sure: / What?" (60).

4. The novel's narrative voice ostensibly calls attention to this rationale by admitting that "[e]ra necessário fazer alguma coisa, qualquer coisa que se

fosse sob pena dessa novela interminável ficar parada e esgotada, dando prejuízos a todos os envolvidos no processo de produção gráfica de conhecimento" (it was necessary to do something, anything . . . if not this endless novel would be in danger of being paralyzed and exhausted, thus generating losses to all those involved in the printing process of knowledge") (Bonassi, *Menino* 133). The necessity to act, even if action is cancelled out by meaninglessness, drives writing itself.

5. "provide everybody with a little scarcity, so that many became collectively exasperated."

6. Estados Suínos bears a striking syllabic resemblance to "Estados Unidos" (United States) in Portuguese.

7. Among Bonassi's theatrical productions are "Presos entre Ferragens" (Caught between hardware, 1990, directed by Eliana Fonseca); "Um Céu de Estrelas" (A starry sky, 1996, directed by Lígia Cortez), which was adapted from Bonassi's homonymous novel and received Best Text in the Jornada Sesc de Teatro; "Apocalipse 1,11" (Antônio Araújo 2000), which Bonassi produced along with the Teatro da Vertigem and was inspired in the Saint John Bible's last book; and *Como me tornei estúpido* (2007, How I became stupid Beth Lopes), which is the adaptation to Martin Page's "How I Became Stupid" and was produced along with the Companhia Estúpida.

8. For example, Bonassi references Brecht's *The Caucasian Chalk Circle* (*Der kaukasische Kreidekreis*, 1943–45, 1948), although completely removing the reference from its original context. In the novel, the "risco de giz caucasiano" (Caucasian chalk outline) serves to separate two parts of one country: *Iênem do Leste* and *Iênem do Oeste*, an obvious reference to North and South Yemen.

9. "a sentiment of guilt directed at other people."

10. References to the character change throughout the text. He first starts out by being the *menino*. Subsequently, he becomes the Menino. The noun's capitalization references the protagonist's formative voyage and the newfound assertiveness that come from this process (Bonassi, *Menino* 109). In this chapter, the main character's "name" will follow the novel's spelling.

11. According to literary critic Heloísa Buarque de Hollanda, the *romance reportage* reacted against the regime's "sugar coating" of the country's socioeconomic conditions. Beyond silencing political dissent, censorship erased the true material conditions of the period, in favor of the preponderance of Brazil's "economic miracle" (*Impressões de viagem* 95).

12. In Brazil, the *romance reportagem* had its official start with the publication of unconventional reports in the newsmagazine *Realidade* (Reality) beginning in 1966. That same year, Truman Capote published *In Cold Blood*, perhaps the best-known text of the genre. Combining journalistic prose and a penchant for sensationalism, the Brazilian *romance reportagem* broached the social reality of the country under the censorship of the military regime (1964–89).

13. "his Parents had died. Yes! Both of them! They just died!"
14. "with the invaluable help of dishonest judges, the government decreed the AOH, Occasional Act Number One, intended to *'stop the waste of lazy idle time among the neediest and to give them a goal opposed to that of a potential conflict with the National Government.'"*
15. The passage parodies the Brazilian government's proclamations and measures that, by law, are published in the *Diário Oficial da Nação* (Official diary of the nation).
16. *The Global Competitiveness Report 2010–2011* places Brazil as sixty-seventh in transportation and sixty-fifth in telephony worldwide.
17. On July 6th, 2011, president Dilma Rousseff officially approved the *Sistema Único de Assistência Social* (SUAS; United Social Assistance System), which distributes and coordinates the responsibilities of social assistance between the union, states, and individual municipalities. The SUAS continues and develops some of SUS's policies, especially in the areas of assistance to mothers, children, adolescents, and the elderly (Falcão and Flor).
18. Article 2 of the Lei Orgânica de Saúde clearly states that it is the state's duty to "care" for its citizens, allowing them to lead a healthy existence. Accordingly, the regulation decrees that "[a] saúde é um direito fundamental do ser humano, devendo o Estado prover as condições indispensáveis ao seu pleno exercício" ([h]ealth is a fundamental human right and it is the State's duty to provide the necessary condition for its full exercise).
19. The name of the NGO does not have religious connotations, but is rather a reference to the arbitrariness of help provided by this organization.
20. The CIEPs were created during the 1982–86 tenure of Leonel Brizola and Darcy Ribeiro as governor and vice governor, respectively, of Rio de Janeiro.
21. "a duty of family and state, inspired in the principles of liberty and in the ideals of human solidarity, it has as its objective the full development of the pupil, his preparation for the exercise of citizenship, and his qualification for the work force"
22. The TV da Força Maior and the TV do Amour allude to Brazil's two largest television networks, Rede Globo and Rede Record, respectively. Both channels are right-leaning. Globo was founded in 1965 by journalist Roberto Marinho and has been influential in shaping the country's opinions in both the political (it supported the military regime, Collor's election. and his impeachment campaign) and cultural ambits. Nowadays, Globo is Latin America's largest television network and the world's third largest commercial network. TV Record was created in 1953 by Paulo Machado de Carvalho and is Brazil's oldest television network. Nowadays, Record belongs to Bishop Edir Macedo, founder of the Universal Church of the Kingdom of God.
23. All the cited shows are also aired in Brazil. Therefore, though scholars such as Giroux analyze the North American context, their conclusions can also be applied to the Brazilian frame of reference.

24. I would like to thank Emanuelle Oliveira and Christina Karageorgou for the opportunity to publish a shorter version of the second part of the chapter in article format in the *Vanderbilt E-Journal of Luso-Hispanic Studies*.

25. On October 1st, 2007, the United Nations (UN) published a report linking violence and unregulated urban growth in São Paulo. According to the UN, São Paulo, with 0.17 percent of the world's population, is responsible for 1 percent of the world's crime.

26. Speaking of the privatization of the public sphere, particularly of public services, Jorge Balán maintains that "Latin American cities that provide limited and inefficient public services with an obvious bias favoring the middle classes—not necessarily the upper-income groups, who have always resorted to the private sector for health, education, and security—are also attempting to balance the budget in the face of a fiscal crises . . . Subsidized public services, even if essential, are reduced or privatized" (3). It can be argued that this turn to privatization and gradual diminishing of public services is affecting the traditional constituency of said services, namely the middle classes as well as the low-income populace.

27. For urban studies scholar Adrián Gorelik the sociospatial segmentation of the city is reflected in its cultural discourse. The city becomes a patchwork of decadent, ruinous parts that are juxtaposed to shining enclaves of wealth and avant-garde technology. Gorelik affirms that "[e]ssa é a modernização atual, pós-expansiva, cuja mescla de tempos replica a leitura cultural da cidade como ruína da modernidade" ([t]he chronological mixture of contemporary modernization, replicates the reading of the city as a ruin of modernity; 77). *Subúrbio*'s emphasis on ruins, decaying spaces, and bodies relates to the wreckage of modernity and of modernization as well as to the consequences of said failure of modernity for the metropolitan population.

28. Zygmunt Bauman associates the manufacture of waste with the production of modernity. According to him, "The production of 'human waste,' or more correctly, wasted humans (the 'excessive' and 'redundant,' that is the population of those who either could not or were not wished to be recognized or allowed to stay), is an inseparable accompaniment of modernity. It is an inescapable side-effect of *order-building* (each order casts some parts of the extant population as 'out of place', 'unfit' or 'undesirable') and of *economic progress* (that cannot proceed without degrading and devaluing the previously effective modes of 'making a living' and therefore cannot but deprive their practitioners of their livelihood)" (*Wasted* 5, emphasis in the original). The hierarchical construct of modernity is thus ensconced on its wasteful foundation.

29. "metal workers' homes, cut in half by the avenue, like caries that pitilessly take over a dirty mouth. Toilets, rooms, living rooms and kitchens exposed to the curb had an apocalyptic air about them."

30. In their essay on globalization, neoliberalism, and socioeconomic underdevelopment, Jorge Nef and Wilder Robles summarize what they call the "neoliberal package" (37) in six main policies aimed to augment profitability: 1) reestablishment of the rule of the market; 2) reduction of taxes; 3) reduction of public investments; 4) deregularization of the private sector; 5) privatization of public enterprises; 6) "*the elimination of the collectivist concept of the 'public good.'* This is to be replaced with a view of the common good emphasizing 'individual responsibility'" (38; emphasis in the original).

31. "[j]ust the home."

32. An example of such an investment is the *Unidades Pacificadoras de Polícia* (UPPs; Pacifying Police Units), funded by the Secretaria Estadual de Segurança Pública do Rio de Janeiro (State Secretariat for Public Security of Rio de Janeiro).

33. "a boy who had many deaths imprinted on his face, like a thin mustache."

34. In its 2011 report, Human Rights Watch (HRW) found that between 2009 and 2011, the National Council of Justice had ordered the release of some 25,000 prisoners being held arbitrarily and noted that 44 percent of prisoners were pretrial detainees. Moreover, the report points out that there are more than 40,000 intentional homicides annually in the country. In the first six months of 2010, Rio de Janeiro's police force was responsible for 505 of these deaths. In addition to these staggering numbers, the HRW also signaled widespread reports of police operating within extralegal militias and death squads that carry out extortion, killings, and other violent crimes.

35. In 2005, 53 percent of the most violent areas were in hands of the Comando Vermelho (Red Command), while in 2008 this percentage had fallen to 38.8 percent, according to statistics released in 2009 by sociologist Alba Zaluar and the Núcleo de Pesquisa da Violência da Universidade do Estado do Rio de Janeiro (Nupev-Uerj) (Center for Research on Violence at the State University of Rio de Janeiro).

36. In his discussion of the plague in literature and myth, philosopher René Girard explains that death, often the death of a scapegoat, is frequently represented as a form of cleansing, allowing the community to recongregate and heal itself after the sacrifice. In *Subúrbio*, the demise of the old man represents a similar effort to eradicate a malaise from the social body. Nonetheless, death, in this context is an unfruitful placebo for an incurable disease. The leprosy of the social corpus stems from the rotting of a larger (both national and global) socioeconomic structure. The old man's perversion of family and of desire is but a symptom (even if a mortal one) of the pest.

37. "[t]he father beat the mother because of his nerves . . . he fought with everyone . . . often the boy cried and the girl would also be beaten because the boy had to be quiet. . . . The girl would even pinch him, but then her little brother would cry more . . . If everybody had a room

of their own, the problem would be solved. . . . But the family had no money to move."
38. "the curves of her little arms, her little legs, the small waist, and the little buttocks."
39. I would like to thank my colleague, Rebecca Atencio, for her careful reading of Chapter 2 and for her invaluable comments and suggestions.
40. "—cow-cow-cow."
41. "whore-whore, a whore's daughter."

CHAPTER 3

1. A life narrative told by an often disempowered subject to a mediator.
2. "a blitz, the police searches everyone, groping their privates, their breasts, their buttocks, asking questions and restricting movement."
3. "Law" in this context means both the judicial set of rules that—in theory at least—govern social relations within the nation-state, and the dominant symbolic order that dictates the prevalent episteme.
4. Recently, the nongovernmental organization Justiça Global issued a report stating that the police force in Rio de Janeiro criminalizes poverty. In an interview with *BBC Brasil*, the organization's director, Camilla Ribeiro, stated that the same logic that criminalizes poverty postulates the logic of annihilation as an efficient form of social control (Corrêa).
5. For Agamben, the "state of nature" is coterminous with the "state of exception" and does not signify a state prior to the founding of the city. He maintains that "the state of nature is not a real epoch chronologically prior to the foundation of the City but a principle internal to the City, which appears at the moment the City is considered *tanquam dissolute*, 'as if it were dissolved'" (in this sense, therefore, the state of nature, is something like a state of exception) (*Homo Sacer* 105).
6. Among recent critical texts are Teresa P. R. Caldeira, *City of Walls: Crime, Segregation and Citizenship in São Paulo* (2000); Carlos Alberto Messeder Pereira (ed.), *Linguagens da violência* (Languages of violence, 2000); Andrelino Campos, *Do quilombo à favela. A produção do "espaço criminalizado" no Rio de Janeiro* (From *quilombo* to favela, 2004); Alba Zaluar and Marcos Alvito (eds.), *Um século de favela* (A century of favela, 2006); and Regina Dalcastagnè, *Ver e imaginar o outro: Alteridade, desigualdade, violência na literatura brasileira contemporánea* (To see and imagine the other: Alterity, inequality, violence in contemporary Brazilian literature, 2008), to cite but a few. Beyond Ferréz's literary texts, the genre of *literatura marginal* has experienced a boom. Among these texts are several that portray prison systems, such as Luís Alberto Mendes's *Memórias de um sobrevivente* (Memories of a survivor, 2001), Guilherme S. Rodrigues's *Código de Cela, o mistério das prisões* (The cell's code, the mystery of the prisons, 2001), Jocenir's *Diário de um detento* (Diary of a prisoner, 2001), Humberto Rodrigues's *Vidas do Carandiru—Histórias*

Reais (Lifes of Carandiru—Real Stories, 2002), André du Rap's *Sobrevivente André du Rap, do Massacre do Carandiru* (Survivor André du Rap, from the Carandiru massacre, 2002), and Luís Alberto Mendes's *Às Cegas* (Blinded, 2005). Narratives centered on marginalized characters include Ademiro Alves's (Sacolinha) *Graduado em marginalidade* (Graduate in marginality, 2005).

7. Beyond having published two acclaimed novels—*Capão Pecado* (Sinful woodlands, 2000, 2005) and *Manual prático do ódio* (Practical handbook of hatred, 2003)—Ferréz also came out with the short story collection *Ninguém é inocente em São Paulo* (Nobody is innocent in São Paulo, 2006). Furthermore, he also has a book of concrete poetry, *Fortaleza da desilusão* (Fortress of disillusion, 1997); a children's book, *Amanhecer Esmeralda* (Emerald dawn, 2005); and finally, a comic book, *Inimigos não levam flores* (Enemies don't take flowers, 2006).

8. Boaventura de Sousa Santos defines resistance to the globalizing process (that he divides in "globalizing localisms" and "localized globalisms") in terms of transforming unequal exchanges into exchanges where authority is shared and of a struggle against exclusion and subalternity. ("Os processos da globalização" 73). Resistance against globalization either assumes *cosmopolitismo* (a cosmopolitan format) or broaches what Sousa Santos calls *patrimônio comum da humanidade* (humanity's common patrimony). Both forms of resistance are enmeshed with the variegated manners of socioeconomic and epistemic violence and inequality that arise in the globalized frame of reference. Regarding the platforms of resistance against (neoliberal) globalization, see also Hardt and Negri.

9. Ação Educativa is an organization established in 1994 to promote education and youth rights, with an attention to social justice, participatory democracy, and sustainable development in Brazil.

10. In the back cover of *Cronista de um tempo ruim* (Chronicler of a bad time, 2009), the first volume available by Selo do Povo, Ferréz explains that the rationale for this publishing endeavor is that of a stamp, a "[s]elo feito para livros de bolso, livros estes escritos por e para mãos operárias, rebeldes, marginais, periféricas. Que possa alcançar o público despossuído de recurso que geralmente vê o livro como um item raro e elitista" (seal made for paperbacks, books that were written by and for working hands, rebellious, marginal, peripheral. That will be able to reach the disenfranchised reading public that in general sees the book as an exceptional and elitist item).

11. *Cidade de Deus, Carandiru* (2003, directed by Hector Babenco); *Tropa de elite* (Elite troop, 2007, directed by José Padilha).

12. This is the rationale underlying Padilha's *Tropa de elite* and that also shines through in the documentary *Notícias de uma guerra particular* (News of a private war, 1999, directed by Kátia Lund and João Moreira Salles).

13. However, directors such as Fernando Meirelles do purport to have a social transformation in mind when creating films such as *City of God*. For a comprehensive discussion of this topic, see the essays in Else Vieira's anthology *"City of God" in Several Voices: Brazilian Social Cinema as Action* (2005).

14. In the anthology's initial text, Ferréz proclaims *literatura marginal*'s outsider status and its autonomy, asserting that this genre is opposed to hegemonic "opinion" (*Literatura marginal* 9).

15. I use the term "contrapuntal reading" in the sense that Edward Said defined it in *Culture and Imperialism* (1993).

16. For a discussion of Ferréz's fiction in the context of the testimonial genre, specifically his novel *Manual prático do ódio*, see Rebecca Atencio's insightful article "Dangerous Minds: Brazil's 'Escritura da exclusão' and Testimonio" (2006).

17. As remarked by Ferréz, marginal literature is a "literatura feita à margem dos núcleos centrais do saber e da grande cultura nacional, isto é, de grande poder aquisitivo" (literature created at the margins of the central nuclei of knowledge and of national culture, this is to say, of socioeconomic power; *Literatura marginal* 12). As such, it—at least in theory— also stands "outside" the institutionalized critical apparatus that lends artistic validity to literary production. Nonetheless, it can be argued Ferréz has become part not only of mainstream literature (his stories appear in many short story collections and his first novel was republished by the influential Editora Objetiva (which also published *Manual prático do ódio*), but also of mainstream literary criticism. In most studies dealing with contemporary Brazilian literature, Ferréz's textual production is either mentioned or analyzed in detail.

18. For Ferréz, the main objective of marginal literature is "fazer o povo ler" (to make the people read; *Literatura marginal* 13).

19. Lúcia Sá affirms that the cultural production emerging from Capão Redondo both expresses the violent reality of the locality and affirms a pride of place (134).

20. "never get involved with a brother's girlfriend, otherwise you will be capped."

21. Benito Martinez Rodriguez coins the expression "mutirão da palavra" (community initiatives dealing with the written and spoken word) to characterize the communitarian underpinnings of the book. *Mutirão* (joint effort) is normally used in the context of home building or infrastructural projects specific to a certain community. Rodriguez's article references the multiple contributions from community members inserted throughout the novel's first edition.

22. "Dear 'system,' you might not read, but its OK, at least you have seen the cover page."

23. The boy featured on the front cover is not anonymous, however. On the back cover we learn that the photo is that of the author himself. This

detail emphasizes the novel's "realism" and its intimate connection to the community for which Ferréz is a both a spokesperson and another inhabitant.

24. According to the online version of *O Globo*, youth violence is on the rise in Brazil, affecting especially black males. *O Globo* maintains that in 1980 about 30 young people were murdered, and in 2007, this number was 50.1. Of those murdered in 2007, 90 percent were black men. The article states that in 2002, 46 percent more blacks than whites were murdered. In 2007 this percentage grew to 108 percent (Weber).

25. We see a portion of the inside of the bar, where two figures stand around a pool table.

26. In April of 2010, 45 people died in the low-income community of Morro do Bumba, in Niterói, when the residents' homes collapsed due to intense rains. The neighborhood had been erected on a former waste dumping site.

27. Mike Davis observes that "in the Third World, by contrast, slums that lack potable water and latrines are unlikely to be defended by expensive public works or covered by disaster insurance. Researchers emphasize that foreign debt and subsequent 'structural adjustment' drive sinister 'trade offs between production, competition and efficiency, and adverse environmental consequences in terms of potentially disaster-vulnerable settlements.' 'Fragility' is simply a synonym for systematic government neglect of environmental safety, often in the face of foreign financial pressures" (125).

28. In the text's second edition, Realismo Frontal has become Negredo.

29. "Realismo Frontal has the immense pleasure of participating in this important literary work that engages society in general."

30. "Welcome to the end of the world."

31. The poem has been omitted from the Objetiva version of *Capão Pecado*. In addition, the preface that prefigures the story, mimicking a fable, has been inserted at the end of the novel in the second edition, thus becoming a summary of sorts instead of a foreshadowing.

32. The dedication is omitted in the second printing.

33. "All the characters in this book exist or have existed, but *Manual prático do ódio* is fictional. The author never killed anybody for money, but he understands what this means—from the murderer's point of view."

34. *Cinema da Retomada* refers to the renaissance of Brazilian cinema since the 1990s that occurred partly in response to tax incentives such as the Lei do audiovisual (Lei Federal 8685/93) (Federal Audiovisual Law/ Law 8685/93) that was passed in 1993. The law allowed businesses to deduct 100 percent of their investment from their taxes.

35. Literary narratives of crime and social transgression have enjoyed popularity in Brazil for some years now. The most prominent examples of writers that focus on various modalities of criminality are perhaps Rubem Fonseca, also quite popular in Argentina, Peru, and Mexico; and his

"disciple," Patricia Melo. Beyond this, increasingly, documentary narratives about figures with ties to the criminal underworld are enjoying prominence. Besides some of the texts mentioned earlier in this chapter (Lins, Varela, M. V. Bill, and Celso Athayde), one can mention books such as Caco Barcellos's *Abusado. O dono do morro Dona Marta* (Abused: The boss of the *morro* Dona Marta, 2004), which relates the story of Marcinho VP, a drug lord from the *carioca* favela of Dona Marta. In addition, one can also mention Antônio Carlos Prado's *Cela forte mulher* (Prison-cell women, 2003) that deals with the experiences of women prisoners in female penitentiaries.

36. In his article "Toward Uncivil Society: Causes and Consequences of Violence in Rio de Janeiro," sociologist Robert Gay maintains that 60 percent of the Brazilian workforce is in the informal sector, which means that "informal sector workers in Brazil not only generally receive low wages but also that they lack the legal protections, guarantees, and potential benefits associated with a signed work card, or *carteira assinada*. More important, it also means that they have been largely unaffected by recent increases in social spending, which have been absorbed by programs such as pensions and social security that benefit primary workers in the formal sector" (204).

37. According to a 2003 document by the Instituto Brasileiro de Geografia (IBGE), a quarter of the Brazilian workforce is employed in the informal sector. In 2003, the informal economy generated R$ 17.6 billion. Among those working in the informal sector, 69 percent were self-employed, 10 percent were in the informal workforce, and 5 percent were not salaried. These 2003 numbers are similar to those of 1997. Of the nonsalaried workers, 64 percent were male and 64 percent were female (Instituto Brasileiro de Geografia).

38. "Recently, the Lula administration has attempted to offset this through the implementation of social programs such as the *Bolsa Família*, established in 2003. The program aims at counteracting intergenerational poverty by providing impoverished families with a monthly stipend per child attending school. Furthermore, children receive one to two meals a day on the days they attend school. *Bolsa Família* has had a significant impact in the reduction of hunger and, according to some sources (including the World Bank and the United Nations Development Program [qtd. in Soares, Ribas and Osório]), in diminishing the social gap in Brazil. Nonetheless, inequality persists—in 2008, 22 percent of the populace was living below the poverty line.

39. According to data from the Brazilian Institute of Geography and Statistics (PNAD/IBGE) the population of Brazil in 2004 was just over 182 million. Of this total, 137.7 million were 15 years old or older and 34 million were in the 15 to 29 age bracket. Of the same total population, 14.7 million were classified as illiterate (with less than one year of schooling) and a further 16 million had less than four years of schooling and were considered

to be functionally illiterate. This represents a functional illiteracy rate of 24.1 percent. If we consider those over 15 who had not concluded primary education (nine years in Brazil), we have a further 37 million. Thus, over 68 million Brazilians over 15 years of age have not concluded primary education, which represents almost 50 percent of the total population of those over 15 years old. In the 15 to 29 age bracket, 12 million young people have not concluded primary education and almost 2 million are illiterate (qtd. in Ireland).

40. Citing a study by renowned Brazilian scholar Alba Zaluar from the 1980s, Angelina Peralva observes that perceptions of work directly affect social interactions. In the last three decades, poor youths have not experienced work as mode of life. Rather, these young people have seen it as a means to access consumption. Moreover, Peralva indicates that young people no longer take familial priorities into account and that their patterns of consumption have become increasingly individualized (31).

41. Paulo's story resembles that of Rael and Paula. He is orphaned at an early age and is raised by his grandmother. We learn that his father dies and that his mother ran away with her boss leaving the infant Paulo behind (*Manual* 77).

42. Sérgio Adorno maintains that the involvement of favela youth with crime, especially the drug trade is "not a reaction to a world of social injustices and moral degradation, or to the shrinking opportunities offered by the formal job market. On the contrary, it is a response to that which is offered by consumer society and the possibilities of affirming a masculine identity associated with honor and virility in an era characterized by the restriction and reduction of the options of personal choice" (112). The profit from drug trafficking and other modes of contravention allows peripheral youth to partake in consumer society and to affirm a prescribed social identity vis-à-vis their own community and hegemonic society.

43. "Burgos was caught in the act, but the police report was not written. The policeman, resorting to all their academic training, took him to Guaraci and threw him into the river after shooting him in the head." BO refers to Boletim de Ocorrência (Police Report).

44. Paulo Sérgio Pinheiro describes the police force in many Latin American countries as "border guards" (*guardias fronterizos*) in that they uphold the separation between the affluent and the poor segments of the population. Pinheiro postulates that, in this framework, police violence is not penalized as it is visited primarily upon the impoverished social and individual bodies (19). In this context, it can be argued that the dilapidation of citizenship occurs at both the social and civic levels. Social rights are negated in that the poor population cannot count on the protection of the authorities. Civil rights are denied in that they must also contend with the abuse of said authorities.

45. Three of the most (in)famous instances are as follows: In 1993, 21 people were killed in the *carioca* favela of Vigário Geral. The suspects were

part of a death squad composed of police officers that carried out the massacre in retaliation for the deaths of four police officers. Also in 1993, eight homeless youths were killed in front of the Candelária Church in downtown Rio de Janeiro. In 2000, Sandro Rosa do Nascimento, one of the survivors of the massacre, was suffocated en route to a police station after he was detained for sequestering a bus in Rio de Janeiro. These three incidents have been widely publicized, appearing in films such as Jeff Zimbalist and Matt Mochary's *Favela Rising* (2005) that takes as its point of departure the killings in Vigário Geral. The Candelária massacre and Sandro Rosa do Nascimento's story are broached in José Padilha's docudrama *Ônibus 174* (Bus 174, 2002) and in the feature film *Última Parada 174*.

46. "A bar on top of the hill was loudly broadcasting rap lyrics. The songs irritated the 'pigs' that invaded *seu* Tinho Doido's establishment. Before being silenced due to a gunshot [wound], the sound system bellowed its last verse: I don't trust the police, race of motherfuckers."

47. Agamben postulates that, "[l]ike the concepts of sex and sexuality, the concept of the 'body' is always already caught in a deployment of power. The 'body' is always already a biopolitical body and bare life, and nothing in it or the economy of its pleasure seems to allow us to find solid ground on which to oppose the demands of sovereign power" (*Homo sacer* 187).

48. On May 4th, 2010, Paulo Vanucchi, minister of human rights, affirmed that the lack of prosecution of human rights violations during the military regime feeds into continued abuses in the present. Vanucchi explains that this cycle results from the impunity enjoyed by those who committed crimes during the dictatorship ("Tortura de hoje").

49. "A masked servant of the state, commonly called 'pig,' considers whether the boy shall live or die, even though the answer for 34 other boys was a 'no.' . . . He loads the gun. He is respected by the very same oppressed people that he judges and condemns, he thinks about the things that they have been telling him for years, that it's their fault, the fault of this inferior race, the race that robs, kidnaps, the race that kills, that does not follow God's laws, the race that must be exterminated."

50. Two recent examples of police violence against poor young residents include *motoboys*: On April 9th, 2010, the military police tortured and killed the *motoboy* Luis Eduardo Pinheiro de Souza. On May 8th, 2010, the military police beat and killed another *motoboy*, Gerson Lima de Miranda ("'Falta de Comando'"). *Motoboys* are usually poor young male residents of the *periferia* and are often seen with suspicion by the middle and upper social echelons as well as by the authorities because some *motoboys* engage in drive-by robberies.

51. The socioartistic endeavors championed by activists such as Ferréz and Racionais MCs fit the mold of insurgent citizenship, which has, according to Holston, fundamentally changed the "conception of Brazilian society" that "assumed Brazil's masses to be silent and mostly

ignorant citizens who were incapable to making competent decisions on their own and who needed to be brought into modernity by an enlightened elite and their plans for development. In the insurgent formulation, the residents of the periphery imagine that their interests derive from their own experience, not from state plans, that they are informed and competent to make decisions about them, and that their own organizations articulate them" (*Insurgent* 248). As indicated in Chapter 3 of this book, both Ferréz's two novels and his other productions posit the primacy of "insiderness" to both articulate the reality of the *periferia* and to generate viable options of empowerment through art and community engagement. State powers are not only absent from this equation, but are represented to be forces of subjugation, the sovereign powers that establish and maintain *homo sacer*.

CHAPTER 4

1. With "divided city" I am alluding to Rio's characterization as the *cidade partida* (broken city). The description was coined by journalist Zuenir Ventura to describe Rio's pattern of sociogeographic segregation and the tensions that have risen from these divisions.
2. *Carioca* refers to the inhabitants of the city of Rio de Janeiro.
3. Quilombos are communities of runaway slaves. Vaz uses the term to refer to a safe space for people who are socially, economically, and culturally disenfranchised.
4. "Ciranda," which appears in the second volume of *Inferno provisório*, O *livro das impossibilidades*, focuses on characters that live in a place called Beco do Zé Pinto. This is to say that "Ciranda" takes place in a *cortiço* (tenement), the precursor to the modern favela—what Paulo Lins calls the *neofavela*.
5. In 2010 the documentary *Favela on Blast* (directed by Leandro HBL and Wesley Pentz) was released. The documentary deals with the Brazilian funk phenomenon.
6. *Morro* (hill) has become a synonym of favela in Brazilian Portuguese. The word refers to the hillside areas in which many of Rio de Janeiro's low-income communities are located.
7. For a detailed discussion of Viva Rio's emergence, development, mission, and impact, see George Yúdice's *The Expediency of Culture* (2003).
8. *Nego* is a popular abbreviation for the word *negro* (black man).
9. "Who denies me work, bro / Will not have another chance to deny / The black man is a hard worker / Everyone knows, no one can deny. / Who denies me salary, bro / Will not have another chance to deny it / My sweat has a price, Sir / Sir still does not want to pay."
10. Petrobras sponsors various social projects centered on citizenship and culture (Petrobras "Promovendo a cidadania") as well as cultural initiatives, including national films, theater and musical productions, museums, etc.

11. The volumes published in *Tramas urbanas* include DJ T. R.'s *Acorda hip-hop!* (Wake up hip-hop!, 2007), Pires's *Cidade ocupada* (Occupied city, 2007), Vaz's *Cooperifa* (2008), Lenz's *Daspu—A moda sem vergonha* (Daspu—Shameless fashion, 2008), Buzo's *A Favela toma conta* (The favela takes over, 2007), Salles's *Poesia revoltada* (Revolted poetry, 2007), Araújo and Salles's *História e memória de Vigário Geral* (History and memory of Vigário Geral), Lemos and Castro's *Tecnobrega* (2008), and Raffa's *Trajetória de um guerreiro* (A warrior's trajectory, 2009).

12. When Davida launched Daspu in 2005, Daslu threatened with a lawsuit, claiming that the "namesake" was a "deboche, visando denegrir a imagem da loja" ([it was] a joke, aiming at denigrating the store's image] (Moraes). When the dispute became known through the media, Daslu dropped the lawsuit.

13. Davida created Daspu when Brazil declined a donation of US $40 million in anti-AIDS funding from the United States due to a provision that would require recipient countries to sign an antiprostitution pledge.

14. "more than the Internet the periphery is the big novelty of the 21st century."

15. Describing peripheral culture as "novelty" also disregards the rich cultural tradition(s) of this space. It locates recent manifestations in a historical vacuum that allows for its packaging as a "new" commodity.

16. Beyond theater, Faustini is also involved in several other cultural activities. He has directed several critically acclaimed theater pieces (*Eles não usam Black Tie* [They do not wear black tie, 2000], *A luta secreta de Maria da Encarnação* [Maria Encarnação's secret struggle, 2001], *A hora da estrela* [The hour of the star, 2006], *A comédia do coração* [The heart's comedy, 2006], and *O inimigo do povo* [The enemy of the people, 2007]). Beyond his participation in Reperiferia, Faustini has taught acting at the Casa das Artes Laranjeiras (Art House Laranjeiras) (CAL, 2000), where he founded the Cia de Teatro Brasileiro (Brazilian Theater Company). He produced several commended projects with this company, including the *Comédias Cariocas de Costumes* (Carioca comedy of costumes). Faustini has also directed several documentaries, including *Chão de estrelas* (Floor of stars, 2002) and *Carnaval, bexiga, funk e sombrinha* (Carnival, *bexiga*, funk and umbrella, 2006), which received honorable mention in the eleventh Mostra do Filme Etnográfico (Ethnographic Film Expo). Finally, Faustini was one of the organizers of the seminar Das Utopias ao Mercado (From utopias to the market), which included several distinguished participants such as Maria Rita Kehl. And from 2008–2010 he was the secretary of culture and tourism for the municipality of Nova Iguaçu.

17. AfroReggae started out in the favela of Vigário Geral and currently is established in Cantagalo, Nova Iguaçu, Parada de Lucas, and Complexo do Alemão. Its mission also has commonalities to that of Reperiferia.

18. Soares's description of the book's content goes on for a paragraph. His juxtaposition of various genres (novel, Bildungsroman, urban ethnography, social history of Rio's suburbs) and literary references (Laurence Sterne, Wander Antunes, James Joyce, Baudelaire, etc.) capture the text's eclectic style and content. Soares concedes that the book is ultimately "unclassifiable." I will not attempt to categorize *Guia afetivo da periferia*. Rather, as delineated in the chapter, my concern is to identify what textual strategies Faustini employs to figuratively reclaim the city and, within this itinerary, the position of citizens in the urban landscape. This chapter will not dwell on Faustini's other cultural engagements, but instead will focus solely on his narrative. As in the preceding chapters, the goal of this chapter is to examine how narrative—whether fictional, semifictional, or nonfictional—is a forum of citizenship.

19. Rio de Janeiro's Zona Sul comprises an area between the Maciço da Tijuca and the Bahia de Guanabara. Beachfront neighborhoods are São Conrado, Vidigal, Leblon, Ipanema, Copacabana, Leme, and Arpoador, which are located on the Atlantic coast. Botafogo, Flamengo, Urca, and Glória are situated on the Bahia de Guanabara. Interior neighborhoods are Lagoa, Jardim Botânico, Gávea, Laranjeiras, Cosme Velho, Catete, and Humaitá. Most of the vicinities are well-established and have middle- to upper-middle-class residents, although there are variations in income between the neighborhoods as well as within them.

20. "I walk through the entire downtown. I like to cross those stilts and feel the wind hit-ting me in the face. It is as good as asking for a *guaraná Convenção* and a hot dog in Santa Cruz's Curral Falso square."

21. Paulo Coelho is a best-selling Brazilian author of mystical-inspired fiction. His novel *The Alchemist* (1987) has become one of the best-selling books in history, with more than 65 million copies sold. Coelho is widely translated into various languages and his books are example of literature as a mass cultural phenomenon.

22. Vans offer an alternative and more comfortable mode of transportation than buses. Usually owned by private companies, the vans are costlier than public transport but offer certain amenities, such as fewer passengers and air conditioning, that buses lack. Vans are also faster than city buses.

23. Ipanema has become internationally known through the Bossa Nova song "The Girl from Ipanema." Since then, this upper-middle class neighborhood has been synonymous with bohemian-chic culture. The area boasts expensive restaurants, bars, theaters, art galleries, and cafés. Ipanema's beach, especially around Posto 10, is known to congregate the carioca hip youth.

24. Some images that go beyond Rio's city limits are "Brasília" (107), "Praia na Ilha do Governador" (Beach on Ilha do Governador; 113), "Eu e minha tia em Paquetá" (Me and my aunt in Paquetá; 161), and "Eu e minha irmã em Mauá e Porto das Caxias" (Me and my sister in Mauá and

Porto das Caxias; 164–65). As with the other images included in the text, these photographs also depict significant moments in the narrator's life. Most of the snapshots relate to family outings.

25. Rebecca Atencio observes that in this respect, Brazilian marginal literature, though having certain similarities with the Spanish-American testimonial genre, differs from the Spanish language *testimonio* in that the identification is implicit rather than explicit (Atencio personal communication).

26. "Sitting on the curb, waiting for the van, watching the angry sea that swallowed Escobar—this is the Ipanema I knew for many years."

27. Nonetheless, Machado de Assis's character Escobar, who the protagonist of *Dom Casmurro* suspects is having an affair with his wife, drowns in Flamengo, not in Ipanema. The question is whether this literary mistake is intentional, which would suggest another form of connecting Rio's various neighborhoods—in this instance through the Atlantic ocean, an omnipresent element in the city's social and cultural life.

28. "What happens in the minds of people who transverse the city in the wee hours of the morning? Does the city invade the space of their thoughts? How does one build one's roads?"

29. The Cesarão is Latin America's largest subsidized housing complex. Built in the 1970s and inaugurated in 1981, the Cesarão, officially named Conjunto Residencial Octacílio Câmara, now houses approximately 80,000 people.

30. Though Faustini's text is decidedly more autobiographical than either Ruffato's or Bonassi's, their books also draw on autobiographical information. Ruffato's characters evoke his own childhood and youth in Cataguases. Thus, for example, the working class women who work as laundresses in several narratives of *Inferno provisório* remit to the author's own mother, who washed clothes for others. The same applies to Ferréz's novels that contain characters reminiscent of the author himself (see, for example, the "nerdy" Paulo in *Manual prático do ódio*). All the fictional texts discussed in this book draw from lived experience, which reinforces the idea of literature as an expression of insurgent citizenship.

31. "[t]he possibility of pavement on our street was secondary only to my mother's happiness when the sink got a backsplash of yellow tiles."

32. "the sunshine that came through the swivel window, reflecting on the drops of water on the yellow tiles."

33. "She went from rich and eccentric aunt to the first of my grandmother's daughters who tried to break the [social] cycle to which this family was circumscribed."

34. Since its beginnings, the Cesarão, like many other subsidized housing projects, has expanded in a somewhat haphazard manner. Homeowners have added to the original structure in order to either have more space available as families grew or to use the additional space as a source of income by renting the added space.

35. "Surfing in the river, *favelado?*"
36. "there, at the Candelária Church, a street kid had ripped a Champion watch from my pulse . . . I remember that seeing the murder scene, I made an effort not to feel avenged. Vengeance was a word I learned in the soap operas."
37. "you are a street vendor and arrange red and yellow lines of *Serenata de Amor* chocolates on the blue tarp spread on the sidewalk, imitating the display window of the boutique behind you."
38. The surrounding favelas are Favela Francisco de Castro, Favela do Morro da Coroa, Favela Baronesa, and Favela Ocidental Fallet.
39. "In Paciência, my friend and I were once stopped by the police. Only one of them was slapped in the face. He was black. I was invisible. It was as if I was not there."
40. "With the All Star I would cross the city and participate in demonstrations. With the Redley I would stroll in the Praça do Curral Falso, in Santa Cruz. With a Commander, I went to punk shows in at the Praça da Bandeira."

Epilogue

1. From the state of Minas Gerais.
2. Thus, for example, the program will build cisterns in rural areas of the drought-plagued Northeast to help farmers.
3. The expressway will connect Barra da Tijuca to Santa Cruz, Campo Grande, and Guaratiba e Recreio dos Bandeirantes and will serve as a route for the Bus Rapid Transit, one of the transportation projects planned for the World Cup.
4. In the *New York Times* article, the author, Michael Kimmelman, describes how in Kiberia (Nairobi, Kenya) local residents use garbage as fuel for community stoves. Kimmelman observes that "[t]raditional wood and charcoal fires cause rampant respiratory disease [there]. Refuse fills the streets. So a Nairobian architects designed a community cooker, fueled by refuse residents collect in return for time using the ovens."

WORKS CITED

Adler Pereira, Victor Hugo. "Documentos da pobreza, desigualdade ou exclusão social." *Estudos de literatura brasileira contempôranea* 30 (2007): 11–26.

Adorno, Sérgio. "Youth Crime in São Paulo: Myths, Images and Facts." *Citizens of Fear: Urban Violence in Latin America.* Ed. Susana Rotker. New Brunswick: Rutgers UP, 2002. 102–16.

Adorno, Sérgio, Eliana B. T. Bordini, and Renato Sérgio de Lima. "O adolescente e as mudanças na criminalidade urbana." *São Paulo em Perspectiva* 13.4 (1999). Web. 26 April 2010. 62–64.

AfroReggae, Grupo Cultural. "Missão e Visão." Grupo AfroReggae. Web. 1 June 2011.

Agamben, Giorgio. *Homo Sacer: Sovereign Power and Bare Life.* Trans. Daniel Heller-Roazen. Stanford: Stanford UP, 1995.

———. *State of Exception.* Trans. Kevin Attel. Chicago: U of Chicago P, 2005.

Akkari, A. J. "Desigualdades educativas estruturais no Brasil: Entre estado, privatização e descentralização." *Educação and sociedade* 22.74 (2001): 163–89. Web. 5 Nov. 2010.

Almeida, Célia, et al. "Health Sector Reform in Brazil: A Case Study of Inequality." *International Journal of Health Services* 30.1 (2000): 129–62.

Alves, Ademiro [Sacolinha]. *Graduado em marginalidade.* São Paulo: Scortecci, 2005.

Amnesty International. *Amnesty International Annual Report 2011—Brazil.* Amnesty International, 2011. Web. 15 June 2011.

Appadurai, Arjun. *Modernity at Large: Cultural Dimensions of Globalization.* Minneapolis: U of Minnesota P, 1996.

Appadurai, Arjun, and James Holston. "Introduction: Cities and Citizenship." *Cities and Citizenship.* Ed. James Holston. Durham: Duke UP, 1999. 1–20.

Araujo, Maria P. N, and Écio Salles. *História e memória de Vigário Geral.* Rio de Janeiro, RJ: Aeroplano Editora e Consultoria, 2008.

Archdiocese of São Paulo (Brazil) and Joan Dassin. *Torture in Brazil: A Shocking Report on the Pervasive Use of Torture by Brazilian Military Governments, 1964–1979.* Austin: U of Texas P, 1998. Ilas Special Publication.

Arendt, Hannah. "The Rights of Man: What Are They?" *Modern Review* 3.1 (1949): 24–37.

Arias, Enrique Desmond. "Conclusion: Understanding Violent Pluralism." *Violent Democracies in Latin America*. Ed. Daniel M. Goldstein and Enrique Desmond Arias. Durham: Duke UP, 2010. 242–64.

Arias, Enrique Desmond, and Daniel M. Goldstein. *Violent Democracies in Latin America*. Durham: Duke UP, 2010.

———. "Violent Pluralism: Understanding the New Democracies of Latin America." *Violent Democracies in Latin America*. Ed. Daniel M. Goldstein and Enrique Desmond Arias. Durham: Duke UP, 2010. 1–34.

Armony, Ariel C. "Fields of Citizenship." *Citizenship in Latin America*. Ed. Joseph S. Tulchin and Meg Ruthenburg. Boulder: Lynne Rienner, 2007. 95–110.

Atencio, Rebecca J. "Dangerous Minds: Brazil's 'Escritura da Exclusão' and Testimonio." *Hispania* 89.2 (2006): 278–88.

———. Letter to the author. 20 July 2993. MS.

Augé, Marc. *Non-Places: Introduction to an Anthropology of Supermodernity*. New York: Verso, 1995.

Avelar, Idelber. *The Letter of Violence Essays on Narrative, Ethics and Politics*. New York: Palgrave Macmillan, 2004.

———. *The Untimely Present*. Durham: Duke UP, 1999.

Avelar, Idelber, and Cristopher Dunn. "Introduction." *Brazilian Popular Music and Citizenship*. Ed. Idelber Avelar and Cristopher Dunn. Durham: Duke UP, 2011. 1–27.

Azevedo, Aluísio. *O cortiço*. São Paulo: Martins, 1968.

Babenco, Hector, dir. *Carandiru*. Visual Material. Brasil: Columbia Tristar Home Entertainment, 2003. Film.

Balán, Jorge. "Introduction." *Citizens of Fear: Urban Violence in Latin America*. Ed. Susana Rotker. New Brunswick: Rutgers UP, 2002. 1–6.

Banck, Geert A. "Mass Consumption and Urban Contest in Brazil: Some Reflections on Lifestyle and Class." *Bulletin of Latin American Research* 13.1 (1994): 45–60.

Barcellos, Caco. *Abusado: O dono do Morro Dona Marta*. Rio de Janeiro: Record, 2003.

Barrionuevo, Alexei. "Educational Gaps Limit Brazil's Reach." *New York Times* 9 April 2010, online ed., sec. Americas. Web. 10 Sept. 2010.

Baudrillard, Jean. *The Consumer Society: Myths and Structures*. 1970. Trans. George Ritzer. Los Angeles: Sage Publications, 2007.

———. *Simulacra and Simulation*. 1994. Trans. Sheila Faria Glaser. Ann Arbor: U of Michigan P, 1994.

Bauman, Zygmunt. *Community: Seeking Safety in an Insecure World*. Cambridge: Polity, 2001.

———. *Consuming Life*. Cambridge: Polity, 2007.

———. *Liquid Modernity*. Cambridge: Polity, 2000.

———. *Liquid Times: Living in an Age of Uncertainty*. Cambridge: Polity, 2007.

———. *Postmodernity and Its Discontents*. New York: New York UP, 1997.

———. *Society under Siege*. Cambridge: Polity, 2008.

———. *Wasted Lives: Modernity and its Outcasts*. Cambridge: Polity, 2004.

Bentes, Ivana. "Sertões e favelas no cinema brasileiro contemporâneo: Estética e cosmética da fome." *Alceu* 8.15 (2007): 242–55.

Biron, Rebecca. *Murder and Masculinity: Violent Fictions of Twentieth-Century Latin America*. Nashville: Vanderbilt UP, 2000.

Bittencourt, Luis. "Crime and Violence: Challenges to Democracy in Brazil." *Citizenship in Latin America*. Ed. Joseph S. Tulchin and Meg Ruthenburg. Boulder: Lynne Rienner, 2007. 171–86.

Bonassi, Fernando. *Entre a vida e a morte. Casos de polícia*. São Paulo: FTD, 2004.

———. *O céu e o fundo do mar: Novela*. São Paulo: Geração, 1999.

———. *O menino que se trancou na geladeira*. Rio de Janeiro: Objetiva, 2004.

———. *100 histórias colhidas na rua*. São Paulo: Página Aberta, 1996.

———. *(Pânico—horror and morte). O amor em chamas*. São Paulo: Estação Liberdade, 1989.

———. *Prova contrária*. Rio de Janeiro: Objetiva, 2003.

———. *Subúrbio*. São Paulo: Scritta, 1994.

Bonassi, Fernando, and João Wainer. *Diário da guerra de São Paulo*. São Paulo: Publifolha, 2007.

"Boom brasileiro opõe classes médias tradicional e emergente, diz 'FT.'" *British Broadcasting Corporation Brasil* 21 July 2011, online ed., sec. Economia. Web. 21 July 2011.

Bourdieu, Pierre. *Distinction: A Social Critique of the Judgement of Taste*. 1979. Trans. Richard Nice. Cambridge: Harvard UP, 1984.

Braga, Samantha. "Diligências num caleidoscópio, com Luiz Ruffato." *Protocolos críticos*. Ed. Adelaide Cahlman de Miranda et al. São Paulo: Iluminuras; Itaú Cultural, 2009. 119–32.

Brown, Wendy. *Edgework: Critical Essays on Knowledge and Politics*. Princeton: Princeton UP, 2005.

Buarque de Hollanda, Heloísa. *Impressões de viagem*. 2nd ed. São Paulo: Brasiliense, 1981.

———. "Introdução." *Guia afetivo da periferia*. Marcus Vinícius Faustini. Coleção Tramas Urbanas. Rio de Janeiro: Aeroplano, 2009. 7.

Butler, Judith. *Bodies That Matter: On the Discursive Limits of Sex*. New York: Routledge, 1993.

Buzo, Alessandro. *Favela toma conta*. Coleção Tramas Urbanas. Rio de Janeiro: Aeroplano, 2008.

Caldeira, Teresa P. R. *City of Walls: Crime, Segregation, and Citizenship in São Paulo*. Berkeley: U of California P, 2000.

———. "Crime and Individual Rights: Reframing the Question of Violence in Latin America." *Constructing Democracy: Human Rights, Citizenship, and Society in Latin America*. Ed. Elizabeth Jelin and Eric Hershberg. Boulder: Westview, 1996. 197–214.

———. "Fortified Enclaves: The New Urban Segregation." *Cities and Citizenship*. Ed. James Holston. Durham: Duke UP, 1999. 114–38.

Canclini, Néstor García. *Consumers and Citizens: Globalization and Multicultural Conflicts*. 1995. Trans. Lidia Lozano. Minneapolis: U of Minnesota P, 2001.

———. "Quién habla y en qué lugar: Sujetos simulados e interculturalidad." *Estudos de literatura brasileira contemporânea* 22 (2003): 15–38.

Canzian, Fernando. "Total de pobres deve cair à metade no Brasil até 2014." *Folha de São Paulo* 13 June 2010, online ed., sec. Mercado. Web. 13 June 2010.

Cárdia, Nancy. "The Impact of Exposure to Violence in São Paulo: Accepting Violence or Continuing Horror?" *Citizens of Fear: Urban Violence in Latin America*. Ed. Susana Rotker. New Brunswick: Rutgers UP, 2002. 152–86.

Carneiro, Flávio. *No país do presente*. Rio de Janeiro: Rocco, 2005.

Carvalho, José Murilo de. *Cidadania no Brasil: O longo caminho*. Rio de Janeiro: Civilização Brasileira, 2001.

Casulo. *Dos olhos pra fora mora a liberdade*. São Paulo: self-published, 2010.

Centre on Housing Rights and Evictions. "Brazil: World Cup and Olympics Put Housing Rights at Risk." *Centre on Housing Rights and Evictions*, 5 March 2010. Web. 30 Aug. 2011.

Certeau, Michel de. *The Practice of Everyday Life*. Berkeley: U of California P, 1984.

Colon, Leandro. "Brasil tem 3° pior índice de desigualdade no mundo." *Estadão.com.br*. Agência Estado, 20 July 2010. Web. 20 July 2010.

Cony, Carlos Heitor. *O caso Lou: Assim é se lhe parece*. Rio de Janeiro: Civilização Brasileira, 1975.

Corrêa, Alessandra. "Ong acusa polícia do Rio de criminalizar a pobreza." *British Broadcasting Corporation Brasil* 27 Oct. 2009, online ed. Web. 27 Oct. 2009.

Correio Braziliense. "Programa Brasil sem miséria é lançado nesta quinta-feira em Brasília."

Cosson, Rildo. *Romance-reportagem: O gênero*. Brasília: Editora UnB, 2001.

Dagnino, Evelina. "Citizenship in Latin America: An Introduction." *Latin American Perspectives* 20.2 (2003): 3–17.

———. "Confluência perversa, deslocamentos de sentido, crise discursiva." *La cultura en las crises latinoamericanas*. Ed. Alejandro Grimson. Buenos Aires: CLACSO, 2004. 195–216.

Dalcastagnè, Regina. "A cidade e seus restos." Brazilian Studies Association Conference. Brasília, 23 July 2010. Lecture.

———, ed. "Vozes na sombra: Representação e legitimidade na narrativa contemporânea." *Ver e imaginar o outro: Alteridade, desigualdade, violência na literatura brasileira contemporânea.* Ed. Regina Dalcastagnè. São Paulo: Horizonte, 2008. 78–107.

DaMatta, Roberto. *A casa e a rua.* Rio de Janeiro: Guanabara, 1987.

Daspu. "Quem somos." *Putique—a loja da DASPU.* Daspu, n.d. Web. 17 April 2011.

Davis, Diane. "The Political and Economic Origins of Violence and Insecurity in Contemporary Latin America: Past Trajectories and Future Prospects." *Violent Democracies in Latin America.* Ed. Daniel M. Goldstein and Enrique Desmond Arias. Durham: Duke UP, 2010. 35–64.

Davis, Mike. *Planet of Slums.* New York: Verso, 2006.

Davis, Mike, and Daniel Bertrand Monk. "Introduction." *Evil Paradises: Dreamworlds of Neoliberalism.* Ed. Mike Davis and Bertrand Monk. New York: New P, 2007. ix–xvi.

Dealtry, Giovanna. "O romance relâmpago de Luiz Ruffato: Um projeto literário-político em tempos pós-utópicos." *Alguma prosa: ensaios sobre literatura brasileira contemporânea.* Ed. Masé Lemos, Giovanna Dealtry, and Stefania Chiarelli. Rio de Janeiro: 7 Letras, 2007. 169–78.

Debord, Guy. *The Society of the Spectacle.* New York: Zone, 1983.

"Desenvolvimento Traz Novos Desafios a Direitos Humanos No Brasil, Diz Anistia." *British Broadcasting Corporation Brasil* 12 May 2011, online ed. Web. 12 May 2011.

Dias, Ângela Maria. "Cenas da crueldade: Ficção e experiência urbana." *Ver e imaginar o outro: Alteridade, desigualdade, violência na literatura brasileira contemporânea.* Ed. Regina Dalcastagnè. São Paulo: Horizonte, 2008. 30–40.

DJ TR. *Acorda hip-hop!: Despertando um movimento em tranformação.* Coleção Tramas Urbanas. Rio de Janeiro: Aeroplano, 2007.

Dostoevsky, Fyodor. *Notes from the Underground.* Fairfield: 1stworld, 2009.

Douglas, Mary. *Purity and Danger: An Analysis of the Concepts of Pollution and Taboo.* London: Routledge, 1966.

Durkheim, Emile. *Suicide: A Study in Sociology.* Glencoe: Free, 1951.

Ellsworth, Brian. "Brazilian Infrastructure Lags Behind the Boom." *Reuters.* Thomson Reuters, 24 Nov. 2010. Web. 3 Dec. 2010.

Eslava, Fernando Villarraga. "Literatura marginal: O assalto ao poder da escrita." *Estudos de literatura brasileira contemporânea* 24 (2004): 35–52.

Falcão, Márcio, and Ana Flor. "Dilma sanciona projeto de assistência social." *IHU Online,* 6 July 2011. Web. 7 July 2011.

Falcão: Meninos do tráfico. Dir. M. V. Bill. Som Livre, 2006. Film.

"'Falta de comando.' Secretário afasta comandantes de PMs acusados de matar motoboy em SP." *O Globo Online* 11 May 2010, sec. Bom Dia São Paulo. Web. 11 May 2010.

Faustini, Marcus Vinicius. *Guia afetivo da periferia.* Coleção Tramas Urbanas. Rio de Janeiro: Aeroplano, 2009.

Fausto Neto, Ana Maria, and Consuelo Quiroga. "Juventude urbana pobre: Manifestações públicas e leituras sociais." *Linguagens da violência.* Ed. Carlos Alberto Messeder Pereira et al. Rio de Janeiro: Rocco, 2000. 221–35.

Ferréz. *Amanhecer Esmeralda.* Rio de Janeiro: Objetiva, 2005.

———. *Capão Pecado.* São Paulo: Labortexto Editorial, 2000.

———. *Cronista de um tempo ruim.* São Paulo: Selo, 2009.

———. "Demorou 10 anos, mas vencemos!!!." *Ferréz.* São Paulo, 2010.

———. "Depois eu que sou louco." *Ferréz.* São Paulo, 2010.

———. *Determinação.*São Paulo: Tratore, 2003.

———. *Deus foi almoçar.* São Paulo: Planeta, 2012.

———. *Fortaleza da desilusão.* São Paulo: Self-Published, 1997.

———. *Inimigos não levam flores.* São Paulo: Pixel, 2006.

———, ed. *Literatura marginal. Talentos da escrita periférica.* Rio de Janeiro: Agir, 2005.

———. *Manual prático do ódio.* Rio de Janeiro: Objetiva, 2003.

———. *Ninguém é inocente em São Paulo.* Rio de Janeiro: Objetiva, 2006.

Foucault, Michel. *Discipline and Punish: The Birth of the Prison.* Trans. Alan Sheridan. New York: Pantheon, 1977.

———. *The History of Sexuality: An Introduction.* Trans. Robert Hurley. New York: Random House, 1990.

———. *Madness and Civilization: A History of Insanity in the Age of Reason.* 1961. Trans. Richard Howard. New York: Vintage, 1988.

Franco, Jean. *The Decline and Fall of the Lettered City: Latin America in the Cold War.* Cambridge: Harvard UP, 2002.

———. "Fear and Loathing in the *Polis:* The Dark Side of Modernization." *Manchester Spanish and Portuguese Studies* 13 (2002): 1–19.

Freire, Marcelino. *Angu de sangue.* São Paulo: Ateliê, 2000.

———. *Balé, ralé.* São Paulo: Ateliê, 2003.

———. *Contos negreiros.* Rio de Janeiro: Record, 2005.

Freitas, Lorena. "A instituição do fracasso. A educação da ralé." *A ralé brasileira. Quem é e como vive.* Ed. Jessé Souza. Belo Horizonte: UFMG, 2009. 281–304.

Fundação Oswaldo Cruz and Federação de Órgãos para Assistência Social e Educacional. "População da periferia de São Paulo sofre com o descompromisso de políticas públicas e administração voltada para a exclusão." *Mapa da injustiça ambiental e saúde no Brasil.* Fundação Oswaldo Cruz. 5 May 2010. Web. 5 May 2010.

Galvão, Patrícia. *Parque Industrial.* São Paulo: Alternativa, 1933.

Gay, Robert. "Toward Uncivil Society: Causes and Consequences of Violence in Rio de Janeiro." *Violent Democracies in Latin America.* Ed. Daniel M. Goldstein and Enrique Desmond Arias. Durham: Duke UP, 2010. 201–25.

Girard, René. "The Plague in Literature and Myth." *"To Double Business Bound": Essays on Literature, Mimesis, and Anthropology.* Baltimore: Johns Hopkins UP, 1978. 833–50.

Giroux, Henry A. "Beyond the Biopolitics of Disposability: Rethinking New Gilded Age." *Social Identities* 14.5 (2008): 587–620.

Goirand, Camille. "Citizenship and Poverty in Brazil." *Latin American Perspectives* 30.2 (2003): 18–40.

Gordon, Linda. "Social Control and the Powers of the Weak (*Heroes of Their Own Lives*)." *On Violence: A Reader.* Ed. Bruce B. Lawrence and Aisha Karim. Durham: Duke UP, 2007. 226–54.

Gorelik, Adrián. "O moderno em debate: Cidade, modernidade, modernização." *Narrativas da modernidade.* Ed. Wander Melo Miranda and Silviano Santiago. Belo Horizonte: Wander Melo Miranda, 1999. 33–54.

Guedes, Fabiana. "Pelos becos e vielas da periferia." *Le Monde Diplomatique Brasil* Feb. 2009, sec. Literatura: 36–37.

Habermas, Jürgen. *The Theory of Communicative Action.* Trans. Thomas McCarthy. Boston: Beacon, 1984–87.

Hardt, Michael, and Antonio Negri. *Multitude: War and Democracy in the Age of Empire.* New York: Penguin, 2004.

Harrison, Marguerite Itamar. "'São Paulo Lightning': Flashes of a City in Luiz Ruffato's *Eles eram muitos cavalos.*" *Luso-Brazilian Review* 42.2 (2005): 150–64.

Hannerz, Ulf. "Thinking about Culture in a Global Ecumene." *Culture in the Communication Age.* Ed. James Lull. London: Routledge, 2001. 54–71.

Harvey, David. *A Brief History of Neoliberalism.* Oxford: Oxford UP, 2005.

———. *The Limits to Capital.* New York: Verso, 2006.

Hautzinger, Sarah. "'Here the Cock Does Not Crow, for He Is Not the Lord of the Land': Machismo, Insecurity and Male Violence in Brazil." *Cultural Shaping of Violence. Victimization, Escalation, Response.* Ed. Myrdene Anderson. West Lafayette: Purdue UP, 2004. 49–57.

Heater, Derek. *A Brief History of Citizenship.* New York: New York UP, 2004.

Hegel, Georg Wilhelm Friedrich, and Samuel Walters Dyde. *Hegel's Philosophy of Right.* London: Bell, 1896.

Heilborn, Maria Luisa. "Violência e mulher." *Cidadania e violência.* Ed. Guilherme Velho and Marcos Alvito. Rio de Janeiro: UFRJ and FGV, 1996. 89–98.

Holston, James. "Citizenship in Disjunctive Democracies." *Citizenship in Latin America.* Ed. Joseph S. Tulchin and Meg Ruthenburg. Boulder: Lynne Rienner, 2007. 75–94.

———. *Insurgent Citizenship: Disjunctions of Democracy and Modernity in Brazil.* New Jersey: Princeton UP, 2008.

———. "Spaces of Insurgent Citizenship." *Cities and Citizenship.* Ed. James Holston. Durham: Duke UP, 1999. 155–76.

Holston, James, and Teresa P. R. Caldeira. "Democracy, Law, and Violence: Disjunctions of Brazilian Citizenship." *Fault Lines of Democracy in Post-Transition Latin America.* Ed. Felipe Agüero and Jeffrey Stark. Miami: North South Center, 1998. 263–98.

Horkheimer, Max, and Theodor W. Adorno. *Dialectic of Enlightenment*. New York: Continuum, 1988.

Ianni, Octavio. *A sociedade global*. 1992. Rio de Janeiro: Civilização Brasileira, 2005.

"Infraestrutura precária atrapalha 'futuro brilhante' do Brasil, diz 'Ft.' *Folha Online* 6 May 2010. Web. 6 May 2010.

Instituto Brasileiro de Geografia. "Economia informal urbana—2003. Brasil tem mais de 10 milhões de empresas na informalidade." 2005. *IBGE*, 5 May 2010. Web. 7 May 2010.

Ireland, Timothy D. *Brazil: Non-Formal Education*. Paris: UNESCO, 2007. *UNESCO*. Web. 5 July 2009.

Isin, Engin F., and Greg Marc Nielsen. *Acts of Citizenship*. New York: Zed, 2008.

Isin, Engin F., and Patricia K. Wood. *Citizenship and Identity*. Thousand Oaks: Sage, 1999. Politics and Culture.

Iwasso, Simone. "Cresce a diferença entre escola pública e privada do país." *Veja Online* 10 Aug. 2010. Web. 10 Aug. 2010.

Jameson, Fredric. *Postmodernism, or, the Cultural Logic of Late Capitalism*. Durham: Duke UP, 1991.

Jelin, Elizabeth. "Women, Gender, and Human Rights." *Constructing Democracy: Human Rights, Citizenship, and Society in Latin America*. Ed. Elizabeth Jelin and Eric Hershberg. Boulder: Westview, 1996. 177–96.

Jinkings, Daniella. "Anistia Internacional denuncia despejos forçados e falta de serviços básicos nas comunidades pobres do país." *Agência Brasil* 12 May 2011. Web. 28 Aug. 2011.

Kennedy, Randall. *Nigger: The Strange Career of a Troublesome Word*. New York: Pantheon, 2002.

Kimmelman, Michael. "Rescued by Design." *New York Times* 23 Oct. 2011, online ed., sec. Architecture. Web. 23 Oct. 2011.

Klein, Naomi. *The Shock Doctrine: The Rise of Disaster Capitalism*. New York: Metropolitan, 2007.

Koonings, Kees. "Shadows of Violence and Political Transition in Brazil: From Military Rule to Democratic Governance." *Societies of Fear: The Legacy of Civil War, Violence and Terror in Latin America*. Ed. Kees Koonings and Dirk Krujit. New York: Zed, 1999. 197–234.

Kowarik, Lúcio. *Escritos urbanos*. São Paulo: Editora 34, 2000.

Kristeva, Julia. *The Powers of Horror: An Essay on Abjection*. Trans. Leon S. Roudiez. New York: Columbia UP, 1982.

Lajolo, Marisa. "Trajeto de leitura de um romance em trânsito: *Mamma, son tanto felice*, de Luiz Ruffato." *Ficção brasileira no século XXI*. Ed. Helena Bonito C. Pereira. São Paulo: Mackenzie, 2009. 97–108.

Landman, Todd. "Violence, Democracy, and Human Rights in Latin America." *Violent Democracies in Latin America*. Ed. Daniel M. Goldstein and Enrique Desmond Arias. Durham: Duke UP, 2010. 226–41.

Langer, André. Interview by Instituto Humanitas Unisinos Online. "O trabalho visto a partir dos jovens pobres. Entrevista especial com André Langer." *IHU Online*, n.d. Web. 12 Jan. 2010.

Lemos, Ronaldo, and Oona Castro. *Tecnobrega: O Pará reinventando o negócio da música*. Coleção Tramas Urbanas. Rio de Janeiro: Aeroplano, 2009.

Lenz, Flavio. *Daspu: A moda sem vergonha*. Coleção Tramas Urbanas. Rio de Janeiro: Aeroplano, 2008.

Les Amants Du Pont-Neuf. Dir. Leos Carax. Miramax Home Entertainment, 1999. Film.

Lins, Paulo. *Cidade de Deus: Romance*. São Paulo: Companhia das Letras, 1997.

Locke, John, and J. W. Gough. *The Second Treatise of Civil Government and a Letter Concerning Toleration*. Oxford: Blackwell, 1946.

Louzeiro, José. *Lúcio Flávio, o passageiro da agonia*. 8th ed. Rio de Janeiro: Record, 1983.

Lowe, Elizabeth. *The City in Brazilian Literature*. Rutherford: Fairleigh Dickinson UP, 1982.

Lula. *See* Silva, Luiz Ignácio Lula da

Luna, Lara. "'Fazer viver e deixar morrer'. A má-fé da saúde pública no Brasil." *A ralé brasileira. Quem é e como vive*. Ed. Jessé Souze. Belo Horizonte: UFMG, 2009. 305–28.

Lund, Kátia et al. *Notícias de uma guerra particular*. Brazil: VideoFilmes, 1999.

Machado de, Assis. *Dom Casmurro*. Rio de Janeiro: Instituto Nacional do Livro, 1969.

Maciel, Carlos Alberto Batista. "O habitus precário e as danças da subcidadania." *A invisibildade da desigualdade brasileira*. Ed. Jessé Souza. Belo Horizonte: UFMG, 2006. 239–58.

Maciel, Fabrício, and André Grillo. "O trabalho que (in)dignifica o homem." *A ralé brasileira. Quem é e como vive*. Ed. Jessé Souza. Belo Horizonte: UFMG, 2009. 241–80.

Marshall, T. H. *Citizenship and Social Class, and Other Essays*. Cambridge: Cambridge UP, 1950.

Martín-Barbero, Jesús. "The City: Between Fear and the Media." *Citizens of Fear: Urban Violence in Latin America*. Ed. Susana Rotker and Katherine Goldman. New Brunswick: Rutgers UP, 2002. 25–36.

Martin, Del. "Battered Wives." *On Violence: A Reader*. Ed. Bruce Lawrence and Aisha Karim. Durham: Duke UP, 2007. 255–61.

Martinez Rodriguez, Benito. "O ódio dedicado: algumas notas sobre a produção de Ferréz." *Estudos de literatura brasileira contemporânea* 24 (2004): 53–68.

Marx, Karl. *Early Writings*. Trans. T. B. Bottomore. New York: McGraw, 1964.

Marx, Karl, and Friedrich Engels. *The Communist Manifesto*. 1848. Trans. Samuel Moore. London: Penguin, 1967.

Marx, Karl, et al. *Capital: A Critical Analysis of Capitalist Production.* New York: Modern Library, 1936.

Máximo, Luciano. "Acesso ao ensino médio atinge 'esgotamento.'" *Jornal da Ciência* 17 June 2010, online ed., sec. 6. Web. 17 June 2010.

Meirelles, Fernando, and Kátia Lund. *Cidade de Deus.* Rio de Janeiro: O2 Filmes, 2003.

Melgaço, Lucas de Melo. "A cidade e a negação do outro." *Com ciência. Revista eletrônica de jornalismo científico* 118 (2010). Web. 10 May 2010.

Melo, Liana, Letícia Lins, and Ana Paula Carvalho. "4,3 milhões ainda no trabalho infantil." *O Globo Online* 8 Sept. 2010. Web. 8 Sept. 2010.

Méndez, Juan E. "Problemas de la violencia ilegal: Una introducción." *La (in)efectividad de la ley y la exclusión en América Latina.* Ed. Guillermo O'Donnell, Paul Chevigny, and Juan E. Méndez. Buenos Aires: Paidós, 2002. 31–36.

Messeder Pereira, Carlos Alberto "O *Brasil do sertão* e a mídia televisiva." *Linguagens da violência.* Ed. Carlos Alberto Messeder Pereira et. al. Rio de Janeiro: Rocco, 2000. 113–43.

Milani, Feizi M. "Adolescência e violência: Mais uma forma de exclusão." *Educar em revista* 15 (1999). Web. 26 April 2010.

Monteiro, Tânia. "Bolsa Familia é única renda de 88% dos beneficiários." *O estado de São Paulo* 27 May 2011, online ed., sec. Política. Web. 28 May 2011.

Moraes, Rebeca de. "Grife Daspu lança 'Putique' na internet." *Folha de São Paulo* 9 May 2009, online ed, sec. Tec. Web. 10 May 2009.

Morais, Lecio, and Alfredo Saad-Filho. "Lula and the Continuity of Neoliberalism in Brazil: Strategic Choice, Economic Imperative or Political Schizophrenia?" *Historical Materialism* 13.1 (2005): 3–32.

Morin, Edgar. *The Cinema or the Imaginary Man.* Minneapolis: U of Minnesota P, 2005.

Murari, Luciana. *Natureza e cultura no Brasil (1870–1922).* São Paulo: Alameda, 2009.

Nance, Kimberly A. *Can Literature Promote Justice?: Trauma Narrative and Social Action in Latin American Testimonio.* Nashville: Vanderbilt University Press, 2006.

Nef, Jorge, and Wilder Robles. "Globalization, Neoliberalism, and the State of Underdevelopment in the New Periphery." *Critical Perspectives on Globalization and Neoliberalism in the Developing Countries.* Ed. Richard L. Harris and Melinda Seid. International Studies in Sociology and Social Anthropology. Boston: Brill, 2000. 183.

O'Dougherty, Maureen. *Consumption Intensified: The Politics of Middle-Class Daily Life in Brazil.* Durham: Duke UP, 2002.

Oliveira, Nelson de, ed. *Cenas da favela: As melhores histórias da periferia brasileira.* Rio de Janeiro: Geração, 2007.

Oliver, Dawn, and Derek Benjamin Heater. *The Foundations of Citizenship.* New York: Harvester Wheatsheaf, 1994.

Padilha, José Dir. *Ônibus 174.* New York: Hart Sharp. 2002. Film.

Paoli, Maria Celia, and Vera da Silva Telles. "Social Rights: Conflicts and Negotiations in Contemporary Brazil." *Cultures of Politics, Politics of Cultures: Re-Visioning Latin American Social Movements.* Ed. Sonia E. Alvarez, Evelina Dagnino, and Arturo Escobar. Boulder: Westview P, 1998.

Pedrazzini, Yves. *A violência das cidades.* Petrópolis: Vozes, 2006.

Peixoto, Fabrícia. "Brasil tem democracia forte, mas incompleta, afirmam analistas." *British Broadcasting Corporation Brasil* 6 May 2010, online ed., sec. Primeira Página. Web. 6 May 2010.

Pellegrini, Tânia. *Despropósitos. Estudos de ficção brasileira contemporânea.* São Paulo: Annablume, FAPESP, 2008.

——. "No fio da navalha: literatura e violência no Brasil hoje." *Estudos de literatura brasileira contemporânea* 24 (2004): 15–34.

Penna, João Camillo. "Estado de exceção: Um novo paradigma da política?" *Estudos de literatura brasileira contemporânea* 29 (2007): 179–204.

——. "Sujeitos da pena." *Juventudes, subjetivações e violências.* Ed. Helena Bocayuva and Silvia Alexim Nunes. Rio de Janeiro: Contracapa, 2009. 101–28.

Peralva, Angelina. *Violência e democracia. O paradoxo brasileiro.* São Paulo: Paz e Terra, 2000.

Pereira da Silva, Ângela Maria. "A cultura da violência contra a mulher. Entrevista especial com Ângela Maria Pereira Da Silva.", 18 April 2009. *IHU Online.* Web. 23 Feb. 2011.

Petrobras. "Literatura produção: Coleção Tramas Urbanas." *Projetos Patrocinados.* Petrobras, n.d. Web. 4 June 2011.

——. "Promovendo a cidadania." Rio de Janeiro. *Meio Ambiente e Sociedade.* n.d. Web. 4 June 2011.

Phillips, Tom. "Rio de Janeiro Favelas to Get Facelift as Brazil Invests Billions in Redesign." *Guardian* 5 Dec. 2010, sec. World. Web. 9 Jan. 2011.

——. "Rio World Cup Demolitions Leave Favela Families Trapped in Ghost Town." *Guardian* 26 Apr 2011, sec. World. Web. 5 May 2011.

Pinheiro, Paulo Sérgio. "Introducción: la efectividad de la ley y los desfavorecidos en América Latina." *La (in)efectividad de la ley y la exclusión en América Latina.* Ed. Guillermo O'Donnell, Paul Chevigny, and Juan E. Méndez. Buenos Aires: Paidós, 2002. 15–31.

Pires, Ericson. *Cidade ocupada.* Coleção Tramas Urbanas. Rio de Janeiro: Aeroplano, 2007.

Prado, Antonio Carlos. *Cela forte mulher.* São Paulo: Labortexto, 2003.

Proust, Marcel. *Remembrance of Things Past.* New York: Random House, 1924.

Raffa, D. J. *Trajetória de um guerreiro: História do Dj Raffa.* Coleção Tramas Urbanas. Rio de Janeiro: Aeroplano, 2007.

Rama, Angel. *La ciudad letrada.* Hanover: Ediciones del Norte, 1984.

Rathbone, John Paul. "Much Still to Do for the President Elect." *Financial Times* 15 Nov. 2010, Special Report: 1–6. Web. 15 Nov. 2010.

Rathbone, John Paul, Jonathan Wheatley, and Richard Lapper. "Brazil: Special Report." *Financial Times* 3 Feb. 2010, Special Report. Web. 3 Feb. 2010.

Redação Revista Fórum. "Pesquisa revela que 90% dos jovens sofrem ou praticam violência nos relacionamentos." *Revista Forum Online.* 4 March 2010. Web. 10 Feb. 2011

Reis, Eliza P. "Modernization, Citizenship, and Stratification: Historical Processes and Recent Changes in Brazil." *Daedalus* 129.2 (2000): 171–94.

Reiter, Bernd. *Negotiating Democracy in Brazil: The Politics of Exclusion.* Boulder: First Forum, 2009.

Reperiferia. "Apresentação." *Reperiferia.* Rio de Janeiro, n.d. Web. 3 June 2011.

Resende, Beatriz. *Contemporâneos. Expressões da literatura brasileira contemporânea.* Rio de Janeiro: Casa da Palavra, 2008.

Richard, Nelly et al. *Cultural Residues: Chile in Transition.* Minneapolis: U of Minnesota P, 2004.

Rifkin, Jeremy. *The Age of Access: The New Culture of Hypercapitalism, Where All of Life Is a Paid-for Experience.* New York: Tarcher/Putnam, 2000.

Rollemberg Mollo, Maria de Lourdes, and Alfredo Saad-Filho. "Neoliberal Economic Policies in Brazil (1994–2005): Cardoso, Lula and the Need for a Democratic Alternative." *New Political Economy* 11.1 (2006): 1–26.

Rotker, Susana. "Cities Written by Violence: An Introduction." *Citizens of Fear: Urban Violence in Latin America.* Ed. Susana Rotker. New Brunswick: Rutgers UP, 2002. 7–22.

Rousseau, Jean-Jacques. *The Social Contract and, the First and Second Discourses.* New Haven: Yale UP, 2002.

Ruffato, Luiz. "Até aqui, tudo bem! (Como e por que sou romancista—Versão 21)." *Espécies de espaço: territorialidades, literatura, mídia.* Ed. Izabel Margato and Renato Cordeiro Gomes. Belo Horizonte: UFMG, 2008. 317–24.

———. *Domingos sem Deus.* Rio de Janeiro: Record, 2012.

———. *Eles eram muitos cavalos.* São Paulo: Boitempo, 2001.

———. *Estive em Lisboa e lembrei de você.* São Paulo: Companhia das Letras, 2009. Amores Expressos.

———. *Histórias de remorsos e rancores.* São Paulo: Boitempo, 1998.

———. *Mamma, son tanto felice.* Rio de Janeiro: Record, 2005.

———. *O livro das impossibilidades.* Rio de Janeiro: Record, 2008.

———. *O mundo inimigo.* Rio de Janeiro: Record, 2005.

———. *(os sobreviventes) Contos.* São Paulo: Boitempo, 2000.

———. *Vista parcial da noite.* Rio de Janeiro: Record, 2006.

Ruffato, Luiz. Interview by Eliane Brum. "A igreja do livro transformador. O escritor Luiz Ruffato conta como foi salvo pela literatura. Entrevista com Luiz Ruffato." *Época* 31 Jan. 2011. Web. 24 Feb. 2011.

Ruffato, Luiz. Interview by Heloísa Buarque de Hollanda and Ana Ligia Matos. "Literatura com um projeto." *Revista Z* 4.1 (2006). Web. 11 Feb. 2010

Sá, Lúcia. *Life in the Megalopolis: Mexico City and São Paulo*. New York: Routledge, 2007.

Said, Edward W. *Culture and Imperialism*. New York: Knopf, 1993.

Salles, Ecio. *Poesia revoltada*. Coleção Tramas Urbanas. Rio de Janeiro: Aeroplano, 2007.

Sanglard, Jorge. "Vista parcial da noite." 12 November 2012 *Portal cronotópios. A vivíssima literatura contemporânea brasileira*. Web. 8 June 2010.

Santos, Márcio Renato dos. "Polifonia proletária. Com o projeto Inferno Provisório, Luiz Ruffato insere a história brasileira dos últimos 50 anos na malha literária." *Rascunho. O jornal de literatura do Brasil*. 2010. Web. 13 June 2010.

Santos, Wanderley Guilherme dos. *Cidadania e justiça: A política social na ordem brasileira*. 2nd. ed. Rio de Janeiro: Campus, 1987.

Sassen, Saskia. *Cities in a World Economy*. 2nd ed. Thousand Oaks: Pine Forge, 2000.

Satori, Giovanni. *Homo Videns: la sociedad teledirigida*. Trans. Ana Soler Díaz. Madrid: Taurus, 1999.

Schøllhammer, Karl Erik. "Breve mapeamento das relações entre violência e cultura no Brasil." *Estudos de literatura brasileira contemporânea* 29 (2007): 27–56.

———. *Ficção brasileira contemporânea*. Rio de Janeiro: Civilização Brasileira, 2009.

Schwab, Klaus. *The Global Competitiveness Report 2010–2011*. Geneva: World Economic Forum: Centre for Global Competitiveness and Performance, 2010. Web. 1 July 2010.

Schwarz, Roberto. *Ao vencedor as batatas: Forma literária e processo social nos inícios do romance brasileiro*. São Paulo: Livraria Duas Cidades, 1977.

Secretaria Municipal de Habitação. "Conheça o programa." *Secretaria Municipal de Habitação*. Web. 10 May 2011.

Silva, Armando. *Imaginarios urbanos: Bogotá y São Paulo, cultura y comunicación urbana en América Latina*. Bogotá: Tercer Mundo, 1992.

———, ed. *Urban Imaginaries from Latin America*. Kassel: Documenta, 2003.

Silva, Cristina Maria da. "A fúria de um inferno provisório: Narrando alteridades na literatura contemporânea." *XI Congresso Internacional da ABRALIC. Tessituras, Interações, Convergências*. 2008.

Silva, Luiz Ignácio Lula da. "Carta Ao Povo Brasileiro." 22 June 2002. Address.

Silva, Maurício. "A narrativa mininalista de Fernando Bonassi." *Revista estudos de literatura brasileira contemporânea* 28 (2006): 47–58.

———. "Histórias de rua ou sexo & violência. O realismo suburbano de Fernando Bonassi." *XI Congresso Internacional da ABRALIC. Tessituras, Interações, Convergências*. 2008.

Soares, Fábio Vera, Rafael Ribas, and Rafael Guerreiro Osório. "Evaluating the Impact of Brazil's Bolsa Família: Cash Transfer Programs in Comparative Perspective." *Latin American Research Review* 45.2 (2010): 173–90.

Soares, Luiz Eduardo. "Prefácio." *Guia afetivo da periferia*. Marcus Vinicius Faustini. Coleção Tramas Urbanas. Rio de Janeiro: Aeroplano, 2009.

———. "Uma interpretação do Brasil para contextualizar a violência." *Linguagens da violência*. Ed. Carlos Alberto Messeder Pereira et al. Rio de Janeiro: Rocco, 2000. 23–46.

Soares, Luiz Eduardo, André Batista, and Rodrigo Pimentel. *Elite da tropa*. Rio de Janeiro: Objetiva, 2005.

Sousa Santos, Boaventura de. "Os processos da globalização." *Globalização: Fatalidade ou utopia?* Ed. Boaventura de Sousa Santos. Porto: Afrontamento, 2001. 31–111.

———. "Toward a Multicultural Conception of Human Rights." *Moral Imperialism: A Critical Anthology*. Ed. Berta Esperanza Hernández-Truyol. New York: New York UP, 2002. 39–60.

Souza, Jessé. "A construção do mito da 'brasilidade.'" *A ralé brasileira. Quem é e como vive*. Ed. Jessé Souza. Belo Horizonte: UFMG, 2009. 29–40.

———. Interview by Uirá Machado. "É um erro falar que existe nova classe média, diz sociólogo." *Folha de São Paulo* 14 Feb. 2011, online ed. Web. 14 Feb. 2011.

———. *Os batalhadores brasileiros. Nova classe média ou nova classe trabalhadora?* Belo Horizonte: UFMG, 2010.

Souza Martins, José de. *A sociedade vista do abismo*. Petrópolis: Vozes, 2002.

"SP tem 1% dos homicídios do mundo, diz ONU." *O Globo Online* 10 Jan. 2007, sec. Plantão. Web. 4 Aug. 2009.

Stepan, Alfred. "The New Professionalism of Internal Warfare and Military Role Expansion." *Authoritarian Brazil*. Ed. Alfred Stepan. New Haven: Yale UP, 1973.

Tavares, Flávia. "A cada 2 minutos, 5 mulheres espancadas." *O estado de São Paulo* 21 Feb. 2011, online ed. Web. 21 Feb. 2011

Telles, Maria Celia Paoli and Vera da Silva. "Social Rights: Conflicts and Negotiations in Contemporary Brazil." *Cultures of Politics, Politics of Cultures: Re-Visioning Latin American Social Movements*. Ed. Evelina Dagnino, Sonia E. Alvarez, and Arturo Escobar. Boulder: Westview, 1998. 64–92.

Tobar Acosta, María del Pilar. "Ecos da migração—a questão da representação do migrante em romances da literatura brasileira contemporânea." *Revista Água Viva* 1.1 (2010). 1–21.

Trento, Angelo. "Miséria e esperanças: A emigração italiana para o Brasil: 1887–1902." *Trabalhadores no Brasil. Imigração e industrialização*. Ed. José Luiz del Roio. São Paulo: Ícone e EDUSP, 1990. 15–42.

Tropa de elite. Dir. José Padilha. Weinstein Company Home Entertainment, 2008. Film.

Última parada 174. Dir. Bruno Barreto. LC Barreto Productions. 2008. Film.

United Nations. "Understanding the Problem (From the United Nations Resource Manual Strategies for Confronting Domestic Violence)." *Women and Violence.* Ed. Miranda Davies. New Jersey: Zed, 1994. 1–9.

Valente, Luiz Fernando. "Brazilian Literature and Citizenship: From Euclides da Cunha to Marcos Dias." *Luso-Brazilian Review* 38.2 (2001): 11–27.

Varella, Drauzio. *Estação Carandiru.* São Paulo: Companhia das Letras, 1999.

Vaz, Sérgio, ed. *Cooperifa: Antropofagia periférica.* Coleção Tramas Urbanas. Rio de Janeiro: Aeroplano, 2008.

———. "Interview by Claudiney Ferreira." *A literatura na periferia.* São Paulo: Itaú Cultural, 2010. Web. 17 March 2011.

———, ed. *O rastilho da pólvora: uma antologia poética do Sarau Da Cooperifa de 43 artistas anônimos da periferia.* São Paulo: Itaú Cultural, 2004.

Ventura, Zuenir. *Cidade partida.* São Paulo: Companhia das Letras, 1994.

Villaverde, João. "Queda da desigualdade de renda no país coloca mais 31, 9 milhões no mercado." *Amigos do president Lula.* 31 August 2010. Web. 5 July 2011.

Viva Rio. "About Viva Rio." Rio de Janeiro. n.d. Web. 1 June 2011.

Wacquant, Loïc. "The Penalisation of Poverty and the Rise of Neo-Liberalism." *European Journal on Criminal Policy and Research* 9.4 (2001): 401–12.

———. *Urban Outcasts: A Comparative Sociology of Advanced Marginality.* Cambridge: Polity, 2008.

Wandscheer, Lisiane. "Tortura de hoje não pode se alimentar das torturas do passado." *Jornal de Brasília Online.* 4 May 2010. Web. 3 July 2010.

Weber, Demétrio. "Mapa da violência: Em dez anos, país registra 512,2 mil assassinatos." *O Globo Online* 30 Mar. 2010, sec. País: Estatísticas. Web. 5 May 2010.

Williams, Raymond. *The Country and the City.* New York: Oxford UP, 1973.

World Bank. "Bolsa Família: Changing the Lives of Millions in Brazil." *World Bank,* n.d. Web. 10 April 2010.

Yashar, Deborah J. "Citizenship Regimes, the State, and Ethnic Cleavages." *Citizenship in Latin America.* Ed. Joseph S. Tulchin and Meg Ruthenburg. Boulder: Lynne Rienner, 2007. 59–74.

Young, Iris Marion. *Inclusion and Democracy: Oxford Political Theory.* New York: Oxford UP, 2000.

———. "Together in Difference: Transforming the Logic of Group Political Conflict." *The Rights of Minority Cultures.* Ed. Will Kymlicka. Oxford: Oxford UP, 1995: 155–76.

Yúdice, George. *The Expendiency of Culture: Uses of Culture in the Global Era.* Durham: Duke UP, 2003.

Zaluar, Alba. "Democratização inacabada: fracasso da segurança pública." *Estudos avançados* 21.61 (2007). Web. 26 April 2010.

———. "Teleguiados e chefes: juventude e crime." *Religião e sociedade* 15 (1990): 54–67.

Zibordi, Marcos. "Literatura marginal em revista." *Estudos de literatura brasileira contemporânea* 24 (2004): 69–88.

Zimbalist, Jeff, and Matt Mochary. "The Film." *Favela Rising.* n.d. Web. 5 May 2011.

Zimbalist, Jeff, and Matt Mochary, dir. *Favela Rising.* Santa Monica: Genius Entertainment, 2005. Film.

Žižek, Slavoj. *Violence: Six Sideways Reflections.* New York: Picador, 2008. Big Ideas/Small Books.

INDEX

208n54, 209n66, 211n17, 219n44,221n10, 223n18
acts of, 160, 172
Aristotelian, 4
civic-republican, 4
civil, 11, 41, 43, 46, 73, 75, 103, 123, 133, 152, 164, 195
cultural, 6, 14, 173, 191
differentiated, 3–4, 6–7, 9–21, 23–26, 29, 31, 42, 45–46, 49–53, 68, 70, 73–74, 76–79, 81, 84, 88, 90, 96, 100–104, 112, 115, 117, 121–22, 126–27, 131, 133–36, 143, 149, 152, 154, 156, 160–62, 164–65, 185, 200n14, 201n6
disjunctive, 16, 19, 124, 196–97
formal, 4, 40, 76, 161
hegemonic, 12
insurgent, 2–3, 11–20, 24–25, 45, 48, 51–52, 57, 69–70, 74, 115, 128, 160–62, 164, 170, 191, 197, 220n51, 224n30, 201n6
liberal, 179
political, 7, 9, 19, 73, 125, 131, 152
social, 6, 11, 16, 34, 43, 45, 48, 52, 55, 57–58, 61–64, 68, 70, 73–76, 79, 103, 133, 155, 164, 173, 179, 195
substantive, 4, 7, 40, 76, 133, 161, 170
symbolic, 17
universal, 4
urban, 200n14
civilly disjunctive democracies, 9, 123
Collor, F., 9, 87, 211n21
Comando Vermelho, 213n34
communitarian, 4, 10, 16, 19, 21, 44, 74–75, 81, 99, 102–3, 106, 109, 116, 127, 136, 150, 157,

158, 167, 173, 185, 190, 196–97, 216n21
community, 4–5, 12, 14, 17, 19–21, 36–37, 43, 46, 48, 55–56, 63, 67, 74, 76, 81, 88, 97, 99–100, 102, 116, 121–25, 127–28, 131, 133–36, 141–42, 147, 150, 153, 155, 157–58, 162, 164, 167–68, 171–72, 175, 179, 183, 188, 194–96, 213n35, 216n21, 217n23, 217n26, 219n42, 221n51, 225n4
Conceito Moral, 142
concentration camp, 154
consumer, 6, 10, 66, 69, 90, 147, 200n14
citizens, 25, 110
consumerism, 109
culture, 137
goods, 28, 75, 150
market, 148, 205n27
society, 123, 219n42
consumption, 20, 34, 61, 65, 69–70, 79, 89, 98, 107, 109–10, 113, 119–20, 123, 126, 144, 147, 149–51, 157, 170, 186–87, 196, 208n51, 219n40
contrapuntal, 132, 216n15
Cony, C. H., 85
Cooperifa, Sarau da, 121
cortiço, 26, 112–13, 221n4
Cosmética da fome (Cosmetics of hunger), 166
Cosson, R., 85–86
Costa e Silva, A., 207n49
counterhegemonic, 12, 129, 134
crisis/crises, 3, 12–16, 15, 19, 32, 37, 44, 46, 51–53, 162, 79, 84, 87, 99–100, 102–3, 115, 126–28, 130, 133, 135, 147–50, 163, 179, 199n3, 209n66

Dagnino, E., 6, 12, 91–92, 109
Dalcastagnè, R., 58, 132, 214n6

Wacquant, L., 148–49, 154
Washington Consensus, 76
Williams, R., 18
working class, 6, 11, 15–17,
      19, 23–28, 31–34, 44–47,
      50, 55, 57, 64–70, 74–79,
      100–101, 103, 108–9, 113,
      117, 122, 133, 149, 172,
      178–79, 181–83, 201n4,
      203n13, 204n24, 205n26,
      224n30
World Bank, 9, 218n38

Yashar, D., 4
Young, I. M., 7
Yúdice, G., 6, 12, 91, 161, 167,
      185, 189, 221n7

Zaluar, A., 150–51, 213n34, 214n6,
      219n40
Zibordi, M., 174–75, 188
Zimbalist, J., and Mochary, M.,
      220n45
Žižek, S., 51
zoe, 54–55, 125, 137, 151, 155–56

Printed in the United States of America